HANDBOOK FOR BOOMERS

Successful Strategies for the
Middle Years of Life

FRANKLIN ROSS JONES

iUniverse, Inc.
New York   Bloomington

Handbook for Boomers
Successful Strategies for the Middle Years of Life

The information, ideas, and suggestions in this book are not intended as a substitute for professional medical advice. Before following any suggestions contained in this book, you should consult your personal physician. Neither the author nor the publisher shall be liable or responsible for any loss or damage allegedly arising as a consequence of your use or application of any information or suggestions in this book.

iUniverse books may be ordered through booksellers or by contacting:

iUniverse
1663 Liberty Drive
Bloomington, IN 47403
www.iuniverse.com
1-800-Authors (1-800-288-4677)

Because of the dynamic nature of the Internet, any Web addresses or links contained in this book may have changed since publication and may no longer be valid. The views expressed in this work are solely those of the author and do not necessarily reflect the views of the publisher, and the publisher hereby disclaims any responsibility for them.

ISBN: 978-1-4502-4850-1 (sc)
ISBN: 978-1-4502-4851-8 (ebook)
ISBN: 978-1-4502-4852-5 (dj)

Printed in the United States of America

iUniverse rev. date: 9/14/2010

For Mary Julia Whaley, an extraordinary person and assiduous worker.

Contents

Acknowledgements

The wide variety of subject matter dealt with in *Handbook for Boomers* required considerable sources of information. The author, though a career human development specialist whose work and experience have touched every major area written about here, could never have completed this work alone. Many sources must be recognized for their invaluable aid in bringing this volume to fruition.

First, I must thank my assiduous assistant and aide Betty Levin. Specialists in many fields contributed by reading chapters, making criticisms, corrections, and suggestions. They are as follows. Attorney Albert Teich J.D., Dr. Raymond Morgan - Reading Specialist, Dr. Peter Stewart PhD - Historian and Researcher, Dr. Stuart Helms M.D., Raymond Friedman - Tax Expert, Julia Whaley - Retired College Chemistry Professor, Ezra S. Elkayam, M.D., P.A. - Neurology, Panos Vasiloudes M.D. - Dermatology, Elizabeth Mason, M.D. - Researcher and Endocrinologist, Jessica Silva - Pharmacist, Clarence Jones - Personal Assistant, Barbara Jones, Susan Richardson - Public Health Expert, Mary Ann Martin - Researcher, and Andrew Jones - Computer Specialist.

Many agencies and institutions also assisted greatly in providing data, ideas and information. Foremost is the National Institutes of Health in Bethesda, MD. Also important were the U.S. Department of Health and Human Services, U.S Department of Labor, U.S. Bureau of Census, Social Welfare Commission of Virginia, Harvard Medical School Publications, Mayo Hospital and Clinic, U.S. Chamber of Commerce, National Park Service, Medicare and Medicaid Services, the YMCA of America, Duke University, and Old Dominion University. It takes a village to start with but many more to finish!

Preface

The *Handbook for Boomers* is the culmination of several aspects related to my career. These include teaching and research on the psychology of human development resulting in numerous articles and studies, along with three editions of a human development textbook and several other books on the subject. In addition, I had several years of radio programs dealing with the problems and issues of middle age persons. Many listeners of those programs encouraged me to combine the talks into a book. The idea for this book came from my radio audience.

The Boomer group encompasses those individuals born in the United States between 1946 and 1964. This represents seventy-seven million people living today! This volume's salient features are those which the Boomers are likely to need at some time in their lives. It is designed to help Boomers who may not have the time, wherewithal, or who don't know where to go for help in resolving problems and issues of important life affairs. This work begins with a discussion of the current status of the Boomer group -- their cultural circumstance, longevity prospect, societal expectation and developmental tasks. Continuing, the universal problem of stress is laid out with a thorough analysis and therapy offered. Followed by a chapter on major aspects of health featuring diagnosis, treatment and follow-up of major and minor illnesses. Health care regimen is reviewed here. The next chapter covers caring for parents which is a major concern for many. Next, you'll find a chapter on recreation and leisure, then one on second careers and getting a job. For the Boomers, remarriage is in the offing for nearly half of them. So, the next chapter deals with love, sex, and marriage, followed by one on divorce and its aftermath. The last chapter speaks of the good life and provides strategies to make it all worthwhile by pointing the way to a brighter future.

The opinions and ideas found in this volume are those of the author. It is intended to provide helpful information and material dealing with those topics presented here. Before any serious decision is made by the reader, advice from one's own broker, physician, psychologist, psychiatrist, or relevant consultant should be sought. The responsibility, loss, risks, liability, personal or otherwise is disclaimed by the writer and publisher. This volume is presented as a guide, but definitive decisions by an individual should be made with an appropriate specialist.

CHAPTER ONE

THE BOOMER YEARS

"The Way We Are"

The Boomers, often characterized as an infant group—"baby boomers", have long since cast aside that name for in their growing maturity they have obtained a significant place in America. The "Greatest Generation" which preceded them made their reputation for two principal reasons, their ability to overcome the depression and to bring about a victorious end to World War II.

The boomers are a phenomena in their own right for they have already changed life as we know it in recent decades. By definition Boomers are those born between 1946 and 1964, seventy some million. As Tim Smart of *U.S. News and World Report* expressed it, "they have changed everything from music to marriage to mutual funds." "This healthy, wealthy and wise band of zoomers," he calls them, "are charging toward retirement with some 50,000 turning 50 each day." He says they have transformed the suburbs, brought about the "soccer moms" with it and played a commanding role in school and community affairs.

In the middle 1990's 14 million were 50 plus, of those 90% had graduated from high school, 25% from college, 73% had some form of investment, 75% owned their own home and according to an AARP report the top 25% had average salaries of 100,000 dollars. However, the lowest group of people was disproportionately composed mostly

1

of women who made only $10,000,. Things are changing. In 2007 all of the second wave boomers born between 1956 and 1964 using the earlier figures are doing better than the earlier group. These glowing praises for the Boomers may be somewhat overstated when you consider that less than fifty percent of adult women are not married. Those not married included never married, widowed, single living with someone, or divorced. For many two jobs are necessary, child care problems for some exist and having little time for personal interests and leisure.

To continue, retirement experts say the "Boomers" are independent, youthful with prospects of a long life and well off! Their bank accounts fattened by two wage earners in many families. Their bodies strengthened by years of exercise, their minds stimulated by a college and sometimes post graduate education are generally far better equipped for retirement than their parents were. However Boomers need little advice in most areas of life generally—work about money, family, health matters, caring for children or community cooperation and patriotism. On the other hand, they may not know the broad frame work psychic/social that impinges itself upon all of us. It is the blue print of what determines the character and way our lives play out. Some will need specific advice on certain issues, which this book will provide in plain, understandable ways.

Most of us have learned from childhood through youth that we will possess an identity—not just a nickname when we become future adults. We are asked what do you want to be when you grow up? Do you want to do what your Daddy does? Or go to College? Get married, mainly for girls? Or go to work like your Mom? When we are adolescents our identity is focused on our bodies and the role we should take fantasizing about our place, be like a friend? a teacher? An athlete? T.V. Star? or a Movie Star, all the while we complete our schooling. For many adolescents indecision will continue past twenty and maybe to the mid-twenties before a steady work life begins. This doesn't mean they will be failures necessarily, some will achieve an identity and become productive. A positive identity for an adult means one has useful work, is a positive role model, is a caring family person and responsive to the needs of others. The identity is well formed, strong, the role is secure and safe from ordinary difficulties that burdens others.

A crisis time for identity for some comes in the middlescent years (middle age generally from 40 to 60's). A crisis of identity is compounded by the necessity of serving a middle man function of relating to two generations—one's parents and one's children—and at the same time forwarding one's own personal fulfillment. This is sometimes called the generation squeeze. Sinclair Lewis expressed this when he wrote in *Babbitt*, "I'm sick of it" He rages............

Having to carry these generations: Whole damn bunch lean on me. Pay half of mother's income, listen to Henry T., to Myre's worrying, be polite to Mart, and get called an old grouch for trying to help the children. All of them depend on me and picking on me and not a damn one of 'em grateful! No relief, and no credit, and no help from anybody. And to keep it up for—good lord, how long?

Generally Boomers won't be faced with this much responsibility and many will be prepared for it. However, for some, those in their middle years, the claims of time and energy are unrelenting, and although men and women reach the peak of their influence upon society and economic status at this time, it is true that at the same time society makes its maximum demands upon them.

The Boomers who become adults first face the social tasks—part of the blue print—as selecting a mate, finding a job, managing a home or apartment, carrying out civic responsibility and finding a suitable social group. Those Boomers in the middle age group have certain expectancies that are different. Some of the following would not apply to those who do not have children or are single. The tasks for others suggests these standards...

- Establish a standard of living
- Help adolescent youth become responsible persons and independent
- Relate to one's mate as a person
- Accept and adjust to the physical changes of aging

- Develop leisure activities
- Adjust to aging parents

If one is out of tune with these then some difficulty is likely to occur that will require adjustment. There was a time when development was viewed as being complete when one reached twenty-one. Adult life, however, does not plateau at an early age. Any individual's life goes through dimensions of time: (1) "life time"—one's age: human development theorists think physical development in general is complete first (on average by 25) mental development (by 30) and emotional maturity by 60; (2) "social time"—how age is graded, its status, etc., and the expectations society has for us (like the social tasks mentioned earlier); and (3) "historical time"—those political and economical circumstances into which one is born which dynamically affect the life that is lived. Many middle-aged persons born in the 1920's and 1930's who were radically affected by the depression lived lives handicapped by lack of economic resources for college educations, travel, special training, clothes, food and medical care.

A significant element of the Boomers is the place women are taking—their cohort of the first wave of the group who were born from 1946 to 1956 now in their fifties and early sixties is astounding. Witness what has taken place in politics, where you have a woman as the Speaker of the House of Representatives. Congress has scores of women, the Senate and governorships more than ever. To top it all a woman in a close run for the presidency of the United States! The traditional role of women has been radically changed with many foregoing marriage until later in life or do not plan on it. The yesteryear of raising a family first then having a career has been reversed, for thousands who plan a career first. Hundreds of CEO's of large companies are women. Fifty years ago few women were school superintendents, now there are hundreds in mid-size to major cities. Women dominate real estate agencies, many areas of banking and even barber shops.

To continue, more women attend college than men, more graduate and Title XI has given equal rights to women in college sports with men helping to lead to the development of team sports for women like softball, basketball, etc. Many women are now presidents of prestigious universities and colleges. The seats of mayorships are occupied by women in large and small cities across the nation. They are also evidenced in the military from privates to generals. They are heavily involved in church ministry, medicine and even into being chefs and are managing countless types of businesses. Although their salaries do not match those of men, improvement is coming. One early outstanding example is that in the 2007 summer the famed English Tennis Tournament Wimbledon paid participants, women and men, equal amounts for the first time in their illustrious history.

In today's world many Boomers will have adjustments to make like one that comes to mind for women at thirty-five or even earlier, we find that over half are not married. This means they are perhaps living with someone outside of marriage, widowed, living alone, or never married, some living with someone but not married. This approach by couples is growing, popularized by young people and spread to middle class adults who are in their middle years. Of course, living together without matrimony has always been around particularly among the poor and poverty stricken populations.

Whatever the situation many women having divorced will need help in looking after children after school hours if they are forced to work when they formerly didn't, become conversant about insurance policies, health policies, home care, car and like protection. Also they will perhaps need to know something about investments and many other things not thought of immediately which they may not have been aware of like home repairs, schooling, recreation, how to organize their time, handle stress and other things. Many men will need this information for women in their former lives have been the knowledgeable source for solutions of many of these problems. This handbook is designed to assist you with these difficulties in a straightforward manner, short, concise and is organized to easily locate and relieve your anxiety.

Finally another word about Boomers is sex differences when they reach middle age, in that, women develop active mastery styles particularly in the larger world—in work and in community—whereas men mainly develop passive mastery styles becoming more nurturance while women often become more aggressive, some become leaders, start college degrees, get a job for the first time, start a business, get a divorce, or get interested in politics, the church or education. Men often begin a hobby, or start a new career, try mentoring, become more caring, change jobs, give the family more attention or become more interested in community affairs.

Boomers, generally need little assistance in most of the areas we have examined though some may need an idea or help on a subject as caring for parents, or retirement, even second careers—we have it here in this book for you. Also some other issues that follow.

What are the experiences other thousands have had with love, marriage the second time around and divorce? How do you solve the problems the thousands have in the balancing act between the younger and older generation? Self-fulfillment and leisure time during the middlescent years are increasingly urgent issues. So what do you need to know about the prospects of a second career at forty-five? What about physical and mental health? Finally, what are the necessary ingredients of the "good life"? The chapters in this book are arranged to aid you in answering these and other questions and solving some of life's most stressing problems. This information will certainly help you answer your questions!

CHAPTER TWO

STRESS AND TENSION

"Am I Normal?"

Stress is any condition that makes you change. It may be external or internal. External stress comes from the environment. There are two kinds—physical and psychological. If our physical needs are not satisfied such as hunger, warmth or sex this becomes stressful. Psychological stress involves adjustment which is a burden often overwhelming. Most people can handle this stress where the need for change comes slowly. The demand for immediate change often creates stress.

Internal stress is often called psychological stress. It is less visible. We are often unaware or partly aware of what is bothering us when we feel anxious or insecure. When we have guilt feelings or feelings of being worthless, humiliated, and are insecure, it gives us a constant fear of failure in life. Unconscious conflicts often involve contradictions such as love and hate of the same individual or object (the school or a crooked curving road). Many conflicts are carried over from childhood but still persist. The child is constantly reminded of his physical and mental limitations for instance. Everyone brings a perceived notion about stress to each situation and it will differ from that from others for example the need to make a public presentation may overwhelm some people for others no problem with a little adjustment.

7

Even other people become sources of stress. Sartre, the French philosopher-writer, has one of the characters in a play to reflect—"hell is other people." Stress coming from interpersonal relations may be imposed deliberately or accidentally; it may also be felt consciously or unconsciously. The boy who goads his little brother to tears because he is resentful and envious may know he is tormenting his brother but not aware of his reasons for doing so. An over-protective mother may hide from herself the reasons for babying a child, but may deny that she is a source of stress and frustration to him. Every child growing up is faced with frustration, criticism, demands, and aggression. This is part of testing the nature of the world or "reality testing." All parents put some demands on their children. The controls placed upon children by their parents serve to counter some of aggressive and sexual impulses. It aids in channeling behavior into acceptable outlets and to become responsible citizens. If the stress for the child is so that he can overcome it without much difficulty, the child's ego will be strengthened, his self-concept enhanced and he will be able to meet future stress with greater confidence. If stress is more than a child can bear and adjustment cannot be made, the ego will be overwhelmed and less able to cope with later stress. For the Boomer results of stress found under four categories are listed below.

PHYSICAL	EMOTIONAL	MENTAL	BEHAVIORAL
sex problems	unhappy	deciding what to do	life has no meaning
sweaty hands	curses more	tasks are difficult	poor work habits
heart beats rapid	lonely	inattentive	burn out
indigestion	sadness	can't concentrate	change in close relationships

Physical stress that is powerful in its effect can harm long term health by contributing to emotional or physical illnesses ranging from heart problems to the lowly headache! It may irritate problems that a person is already at risk of having. Stress may cause cortisol to suppress the immunity system making possible the risk of bacterial infections as tuberculosis and group A streptococcal disease as stress appears. Flu and colds also may accompany stress.

Withstanding Stress

How well an individual withstands stress depends upon a number of factors—their physical and mental health, their environment, their perception of a stressful situation and the number of acute stresses suffered over a given period of time. Drs. Holmes and Rahe (University of Washington Medical School) both psychiatrists a few years ago found that though people (Sample: 5,000 persons from Japan, Canada, Europe and the United States) are different there is agreement on the relative importance of stress events. On this chart below, the people who had scores of 300 or over in a year experienced significant health problems. Life events are ranked according to their stress value in the chart below. The top value of the Life Change Units (LCU) is given 100. Holmes and Rahe believe that small hassles can often mean as much as major events. Here's his list of hassles and uplifts which they sampled getting information from a number of men and women 48-52 for these lists. Holmes and Rahe found the daily uplifts do little to compensate for the hassles.

Some of the items are listed below with their Life Changing Values (LCU)

Death of a spouse	100	Son or Daughter leaving home	29
Divorce	73	Trouble with in-laws	29
Marital Separation	63	Wife begins or stops work	26
Jail term	63	Trouble with the boss	23
Close family death	63	Change in husband's work	26
Marriage	53	Change in residence	20
Fired from job	47	Change in school	20
Pregnancy	45	Change in sleep habits	16
New family member	39	Vacation	13

Large stock loss	30	Christmas	12
Minor violation of the law			11

Stress is often related to outside factors like one's work, their family, their environment, the community, or unlikely events. Sometimes internal reasons create stress as too high expectation for oneself, bad health, poor attitudes, or erratic behavior and worry. If you can recognize the signs of stress you can know the basic of your symptoms and provide a start toward managing your stress.

Interpersonal Problems

There are many elements involved in relations between persons that one cannot control, which need to be understood. There are also events which you cannot change so therefore need to be accepted. Some of these situations are as follows:

Family Problems:
Each person in a family brings a different situation with other members of the family. This is so because they represent different ages, gender, intelligence, personality and sociality and other indefinable factors. If one child has trouble in school this effects the entire family or if a youth takes to drugs this creates a problem for the group, or if there is divorce or loss of work by the father all find this is stressful!

Community Organizations:
Where there is lack of harmony among people who belong to organizations in churches, social clubs, city or town councils, civic organizations between members that become serious can become stressful such as in the case of their involvement in decisions relating to tax issues, road building, school construction to be made and people have their egos and virtually their lives tied to certain outcomes. This can create the ultimate in pressure and nerve wrenching. These issues go beyond the leaders.

Marital Difficulties:

Marriage is entered into early mainly in the twenties and although the couple is aware of the various aspect that are involved in a union, the major motivation seems to be characterized by the expression "I love you so much I could eat you up." All too soon this unrealistic view—a mate that's perfect is human—like most they have weaknesses and, of course, usually there are strengths, too. But along the way changing take place, children arrive, new jobs and places to live, personal needs and sex and help demands of our parents all make for the need for the ultimate in communication between a wife and her husband, inevitable differences and conflicts will arise that demands compromise. Sometimes the need for outside help, someone to talk over the problems which is desirable.

The fact about stress that should be remembered is that everyone needs some stress in life or the good helps one be happy and joyful such as first love's thrill, or first noted achievement, school or work success or the body used in a triumphant manner like learning to swim, etc., in short this stress is positive, called eustress. Negative stress if heavy and constant requires attention to allay disastrous results.

Handling Stress

There are two major components involved in controlling stress (1) the method used by the body for controlling intense stress and (2) the method in which the individual recognizes and copes with stress. When stress is severe enough the pituitary gland located at the base of the brain releases hormones setting in motion a "fight or flight" response. This hormone, adrenocorticotropic, is secreted in the face of danger in large amounts. This hormone causes the adrenal glands to make and release additional hormones. The hormones adrenaline, epinephrine, and cortisol quickly causes the blood pressure to increase, muscle becomes tightened and the brain becomes alert. In short the body is ready to fight or run away. Muscles are taut, heart is beating fast, eyes dilate and the body perspires all systems ready for action! More oxygen in the blood further prepares the body for defense real or imagined. If intense stress becomes a pattern then the future prospect are serious with various diseases in the offing.

The second aspect in managing stress relates to how the person responds to every day stress, for instance do they recognize the nature of stress. There are four categories of stress we earlier recognized. Examples of the four types are enlarged to include these.

PHYSICAL	EMOTIONAL	MENTAL	BEHAVIORAL
headache	over anxious	forgetful	drinks heavily
easily tired	anger	pushes people	smoking more
poor appetite	difficulty listening	worry a lot	slap dash
sleeps poorly	easily upset	fuzzy thinking	not neat
constipated	on edge	no humor sense	unhappy
overeating			

Stress between a married couple are due to lack of communication, management of children, housekeeping, sexual relations, personal habits, humorless, or a variety of things. It is important to note that stress in interpersonal relations is not always one-sided. In marriage conflicts, often each party puts the other partner under stress. A cycle is set up which one of the parties fails to meet the needs of the other. Frustration and tension develop creating an additional barrier preventing the needs of either partner from being met. Though the presence of people causes stress, so does absence from them. Separation from supporting friends and loved-ones often upsets us. The sudden loss of love can be traumatic and where dependence is so great, even death can occur. This is seen in cases of elderly couples where shortly after the death of a mate, the remaining partner dies.

Job Problems:

There are many aspects of our work life that are likely to cause us some difficulty at some point in our lives. The irritation at work can come from other workers, our bosses, the work place, the routine which sets up competition which becomes stressful and an environment which is less than friendly but suggestive of the old song "sixteen tons and what do you get another day older and deeper in debt."

Some problems occur because some workers wish to control people and change things in the workroom. Ultimately some workers will have to leave when stress becomes so great as in a recent case where the author knew of a chemist who left his career position due to an obnoxious boss. The boss who was not a degreed chemist continually ordered unnecessary tests. The chemist resigned and fortunately a few years later became the head of a laboratory. Many workers cannot do this, their only hope is to try, through communication, to understand the things they can't change and accept those things they had little control over. If stress is too great, look for another place to work. Dr. Robert Sutton, Sanford University, says you can do something (Bob Sutton Blog) to keep from falling prey.

- Resist a jerk from the beginning
- Push back if you can
- Keep a record of nasty behavior
- Limit the amount of contact if you can
- Try to maintain emotional detachment
- Recognize when it is time to leave

For further information, contact the following website: www. Bob Sutton Typepad.com.

There is help for you when the burden is too great. You are up against a wall and are at wits end there are sources of help. To seek is not a sign of weakness or cowardliness but good sense for it takes intelligence to realize you need counsel and direction from the outside. Professional counseling is available for marriage, business, mental health and other circumstances, these professionals unless associates with an organization you are affiliated with will charge you for their service. Your minister may be a person with whom you can talk to about your problems, or a psychologist that some companies have available for their employees. For serious mental problems there are psychiatrists who your doctor could recommend you see. Your physician would be a person to discuss stress with for he or she could identify the difference between stress and mainly medical problem.

Your Part in Controlling Stress

Recognizing that stress is a common everyday occurrence that we must live with is important. One significant symptom of stress is anger, which can increase and extend the wrenching feeling that occurs and sometimes effect severely the body itself. When anger occurs one needs to back off, take time to think, give the brain time to catch up with your emotions. Forget about outrage against a person or thing, throw your feelings into activity—go for a walk, curse to the wind, practice relaxation, take a swim, play tennis, watch a movie, cut the grass, garden, listen to music you like, talk to a friend or a lover, practice positive talk to yourself. In this talk you rule out the negative events and try to calmly begin to see the logical and rational aspects that relate to your situation. Some everyday suggestions for improving day by day stress is seen below.

1. Balance work with play. It is a must to schedule time for fun and recreation. Remember that a good hobby can be relaxing. Of course, work can be a cure for emotional situations that are hard to bear such as the death of a loved one, a divorce, or losing out in love.
2. Loaf a little. Some people feel guilt when they're not constantly working, but the change of pace that comes from doing nothing but sitting and talking can bring renewed zest to life.
3. Get enough rest and sleep. To be at our best we need generally to have between 7 to 8 hours of sleep per night. Accumulative sleep losses contribute to nervousness and illness. If possible, take a nap or at least lie down sometime during the day. This slows down the pace. A nap will filter out much anger and stress!
4. Work off tensions. When angry or upset we can blow off steam or work off our feelings with physical exercise. Jump into some activity like gardening, playing tennis, taking a long walk, swimming or playing some sport. This not only helps relieve anger but makes it easier to face and handle irritating problems more calmly. Regular exercise is therapeutic in its own right.

5. Talk out troubles. Those things that appear to be serious problems generating high degrees of strain can be discussed with clergymen or your physician. If warranted the physician will refer you to a guidance clinic or family service agency.

6. Learn to accept what you cannot change. Many of us get upset over things we cannot control. We ask ourselves when people cannot be made to suit our ideals, "Isn't everybody that way—even me?" And in the long run, what difference does it really make if we cannot change a certain situation at least in most cases.

7. Get away from it all. The act created by simply leaving a situation which has us in a quandary may be important. Go to a movie, visit a friend or take a few days off. These distractions help one to cope and allow us a chance to catch our breath and to regain the composure we need to face everyday problems. This may give us a new perspective to face a nagging problem.

8. Avoid self-medication. Do not use drugs or tranquilizers without consultation with your physician. Remember anything that reduces tension (drugs, alcohol, eating) becomes habit forming. Many physicians feel prescribing Valium, Ativan, Restoril, Klonopin and Stivan (they are a group under the name Benzodiazepines) is of less evil than the potential tragedy of "nervous breakdown," heart attack, loss of loved one, divorce, loss of a job or catastrophic illness. Rarely do physicians have or take the time to develop a program for getting someone off a drug. CNS depressants such as Xanax, Valium and Ativan are the most commonly used for sleeping and relaxation. Restarol, Sonota, Rozerem and Lunesta are most often prescribed. They are less addictive and when used properly provide better rest. Newer drugs like Effexor and Paxil CR cover general anxiety. Drugs can reduce blood pressure and heart rate directly. They do not eliminate the actual stress, which caused the increase in heart rate or blood pressure, anxiety, or tension. Unless

the stress is identified and corrected, however, the drugs that block the normal response to stress can cause more problems than they expect to relieve.

9. Have regular visits to a physician. One's physical condition affects a person's outlook on life. The body that is fit can take stress, disappointments, and handle tensions more easily. A clean bill of health will also provide you extra peace of mind.

10. Eat less. Americans are over-fed, over-weight, and under-exercised. All of this relates to stress. Emphasize foods that you like that are good for you!

11. Take one thing at a time. It may seem impossible but make yourself, particularly when you feel the pressures of too much to do. Remember, of all the people in the world, you are the most important! So take charge of your life! Everyone needs help, love, understanding and support in developing and maintaining a wellness life pattern. You should therefore have at least two persons you can count on for companionship and support when you need them. Beyond this one should set goals and priorities. Plan your work. Tension and anxiety really build up when work seems endless. Make a list of things to do and do them one at a time. Their completion will give you confidence. Finally, don't drift along with troublesome and stressful situations. If a marriage is bad, rehabilitate it or resolve it. Eliminate those friends who are really not your friends (where the exchange of attention and energy is unequal) and settle those matters that are bothersome to you, besides they give you needless worry. It's your life and you can manage it.

12. Organize your time.

Organizing Your Time and Priorities

1. How you spend your time - Present Time Allotments

Activity:	Example: (24 hours)	My List:
Sleeping	8 hours	?
At work, on the job	9 hours	?
Work you take home	½ hour	?
Shopping	½ hour	?
With friends	1 hour	?
Alone pursuing a hobby	1 hour	?
Reading, watching TV	2 hours	?
Chores at home	½ hour	?
With the family	1 hour	?
Miscellaneous activities	½ hour	?
Other _____		

2. List the important people in each activity

List the most important people in your life. List according to time you invest.

Do they invest the same amount in you?

3. List your ideal allotment of time.

4. What might you actually do to change the time spent on the various activities to make them more ideal for you?

5. List the priorities in your life. Make the changes that relate to improve your activities to meet your goals and ease the stress of getting there. What in your ideal list of activities is out of line with reality?

6. List the changes that will help make life better for you. Consider:
    *   More exercise
    *   Taking a day off
    *   Some time to be alone
    *   Share time with others
    *   Try not to blame others, check your part
    *   Be honest about your motivation for working so hard.
    *   Is there some other area of life you want to avoid like marriage, children or parents?

Help With Daily Stress By Learning How To Relax

There are various techniques for learning to learn relaxation. One like napping doesn't have to be learned but served to relax in that it slows the body down and along with it usually the mind also particularly if sleep is involved. One prominent method, recommended by Professor Herbert Benson of the Harvard Medical School, suggests you focus on an image; a pleasant one, a prayer, or just your breathing in a quiet place that's comfortable. Close your eyes, assume a passive attitude, and relax your body. Breathe slowly and as you exhale, go over the image you focused on repeating it even if other thoughts interfere. Continue doing this for twelve to twenty minutes. Try to practice this several times a day.

You will find that once you have learned this procedure you will be able to use it whenever you are faced with making a talk or other events stressful to you. The mental focusing method—on a phrase, payer or breathing will move your mind from daily stresses and worries. A passive view toward distracting thoughts means less worrying about how well you're doing with cleaning the house or making an inventory of the stock but gives you an easy way to get your mind back where you were when your thoughts went astray.

Other possibilities for relaxation are:
1. Muscle relaxation—sit in a comfortable chair and close your eyes. Scan your body beginning with your toes and come up the body. Tighten your muscles in one part of

   your body and hold it for five or six seconds, then relax
   them and move to the next group of muscles.

2. Breathing relaxation—Lie down or sit in an easy chair
   with your feet apart and hand on your stomach. Breathe
   slowly counting to four or five allowing the stomach to
   rise about one inch. You should feel the movement in
   your head and don't move your head or shoulders. Repeat
   the exhaling counting to four or so. The air is flowing out
   so are the tensions. Repeat this six to ten times.

3. Visualization—Lie quietly thinking about a pleasant
   scene, talk to yourself about how good you feel, how
   calm it is and how relaxed you are! Your heart is beating
   regularly and you are cool. Breathe slowly and deeply
   imaging you're in a place of beauty and quietness. After
   six to ten minutes get up slowly. Repeating this over will
   make it possible to find relaxation quickly and sure in the
   future.

Burnout—A Special Problem With Stress

It happens to many people—of all types—ordinary working
people to executives to engineers, teachers, physicians, lawyers or even
housewives. It happens when people place stress upon themselves and
affects those living or working in a stressful environment. Burnout
occurs frequently where the work is extraordinarily repetitive.
Burnout is often associated with high achievement and for people
on the path toward it and burnout reveals itself in ragged edges by
the way they bristle at criticism, have little patience, are habitual
smokers, heavy coffee drinkers, heavy alcohol consumers, use
uppers or downers and require constant stimulation and excitement
to provide euphoric moments.

Burnout describes a person who is fatigued and/or frustrated who
are pursuing some goal or pattern of life or relationship that has failed
to provide expected rewards. When one's expected level of success
is miles away and its achievement resulting in frantic persistent and
accelerated attempts to succeed, then trouble (burnout) is on its way.
Friction is building with its inevitable drain of energy, vitality and
ability to function. Said in another way, burnout means to deplete

oneself, to exhaust one's physical and mental resources, to wear oneself out by excessively striving to reach some unrealistic goal imposed by one's self or by the values of society.

Herbert Freudenberger, a noted psychologist and author (who coined the term "burnout"), suggested the following questions as clues to whether or not a person is on the road to burnout. An affirmative reply to most of the questions forecast a coming problem.

- Are you working more now and enjoying it less whether it relates to marriage, your job, friendship or love?
- Do you find it more difficult to confide in others?
- Must you force yourself as a rule to do routine things?
- Are you listless, bored, constantly seeking excitement?
- Would you rather be somewhere else doing something else with somebody else?
- Have you lost the joy of sex?
- Do you think more than you used to within?
- Do you need a tranquilizer to face the day? Need an upper?
- Are you resigned about your future?
- Is your need for a particular crutch increasing, like smoking, drugs, eating, nail biting?

The Two States of Burnout

The first state of burnout is the feeling state—the time in which tiredness, detachment, cynicism and touchiness take over. At this point the reserve energy, resources and ability to function is working. The second states involves non-feeling—this is the time in which the person denies any thing is wrong in her life or his—friends may think they'll get through them.

According to Freudenberger the state of feeling burnout is noted by constant tiredness. One is controlled by what they think they should do whether at home, work, in friendships or love—according to the environment. When one has failed to or refused to keep in touch with their inter feelings. One needs to think about their life, get away from the crowd and consider three things. (1) What situations gives you energy or drains you? (2) Are you involved in them or detached? and (3) Are you enthusiastic about them or cynical? Put down the answer to these questions for your answers will help you get in touch with yourself!

The non-feeling state of burnout involves real danger—the denial that anything is wrong—for this follows the first stage exhaustion. If denial is seeping into your life, you can tell by the number of times you have said "I don't care" or "that's not me." These denials are denials of failure, the denial of fear, the denial of age and perhaps death. The denial of failure is widespread in our society. There is little room for failure, and not much room for mediocrity when the taxes are due money to pay for the good life and good education for our children. Many set unrealistic goals for themselves—success however is a personal matter—some deem success is making $35,000 a year while others feel themselves a failure making $85,000 a year! With others it is a status concern, of holding a certain position, it may be civic or social—to be a member of a certain club or group—for those who have not made their dream some compensation is necessary. For some this means over-compensation—splurge by financial misspending or bolstering one's ego with extramarital affairs—for some reevaluation of their goals, abilities and their basic interests.

The Denial of Fear

Have you remembered your parents telling you, "the doggie won't bite," "the water isn't deep," or "you won't fall"? The normal fears we have are defense mechanisms designed by nature to make us careful, conservative in order to protect our bodies and lives. Many of our parents have, at least among the boys, sent us back to fight the bully who just beat us up. Be brave, you can do it, otherwise you're a sissy. Many persons have spent their lives trying to prove they're no sissy, they are good girls or that they are brave—no failure, no fear—damn the torpedoes full speed ahead!

The Denial of Age

Oh, to be thirty again. But there are thirty-year-old people who deny they are that old. Everywhere you look the emphasis is on youth. Sixty and seventy year olds are getting face lifts. Tummy tucking is fashionable! Forty and fifty year old men are turning back

21

the clock with affairs of the libido, some are making a last surge to compete with the younger, more ambitious persons are moving up the ladder by working harder at their jobs. Fifty-year-old women trying to get into the job market will experience some difficulty. The overly made-up youthfully dressed matron invites unflattering comparisons in a room with pretty young women. And in denial of fear we often damage ourselves by pointing out or deficiencies and playing down our strengths. We exhaust our systems by placing the extra burden of fear upon them.

Denial of death is the most intense form of denial. From earlier times—childhood up we are subliminally aware of death. As we grow older we worry about death in another sense—will there be time to get all those things done that I would like to do? But those who enter life vigorously are ruled by the life force, others by death wish. Most people are in the center of life's movements but some are haunted by the pervading aura of fatality. This coloration of life keeps them, at least to some degree or more, detached, ruthless and essentially disengaged. Some middle age persons when told to slow down, change their pace, take a vacation, react in denial, "there's nothing wrong with me." That's what the sixty-five year old woman with a broken collarbone said when her daughter asked her not to go on a canoeing trip. She went anyway disdaining (think I'm not up to it) the warning and ended up with a concussion and nearly drowning when the canoe turned over.

There are three things we believe that are essential to turning back burnout.

1. Understanding the problems and your connection to them.
2. Getting sensitive to yourself—your inner self and feelings.
3. Developing a plan—assess your situation, locate the false cures—then carry out the plans you have made. Go back to the sheet on Organizing Your Time and Priorities and work through it if you did not do it. Note section five which concerns "Burnouts" and reveals how one lives.

In summary, look at your friendships and judge what you give to them. If things are not going too well try to figure out why and the ways you may be contributing. Don't blame others. See first how much blame should rest with you. Do you distance yourself from other people? Are you stingy about sharing yourself? Do you listen to others and sympathize with their problems? Maybe their faults should be judged less harshly and is your forgiveness more easily offered.

Now your work, is it about to devour you? Can you do a good job without being so intense? Could you take a day off? Delegate some responsibility to others? Over commitment may keep a fellow worker from an opportunity. What are the real reasons for working so hard? Is it some other area of life you want to avoid. Marriage perhaps? home, responsibility or problems with parents? These goals are undertaken for the wrong reasons so face up to yourself while you look at your life! If you're uncomfortable don't wiggle out of seeing the truth for it will save you grief and help you in the long run!

Perhaps the best way to make your body and through it your mind relax is to get into some activity. Burnout continued will eventually make the person a neurotic, neurasthenic, psychosomatic—colds that linger, backaches, headaches and finally an emotional cripple. The best activity we believe is physical—swimming, jogging, tennis, dancing, riding a bicycle, walking, working-out, yard work, hiking and the like. Vigorous exercise will give you more energy, help you metabolize your food, help reduce and firm up your body. You should do this regularly three to four times a week. Meet someone new, new people are great for putting a new face on things. Set aside some time for yourself to be alone and think about yourself, learn to relax. Check the suggestions given earlier on how to relax. The old Ink Spot lyrics popularized by Perry Como come to mind—

"Alone from night to night you'll find me, too weak to break the bonds that bind me. I can't escape for it's too late now, I'm just a prisoner of love."

You can break these bonds of stress and escape—with a program and will!

GOOD LUCK!

Mental Health and Personality Problems

To be normal is also to be human, which brings with it frailty of some type. Hence most normal adults are touched by fears and conflicts—so no one is 100% normal. However, the following list provides a number of important characteristics of normal behavior.

1. Has realistic attitudes. The healthy adult faces facts pleasant and unpleasant. He enjoys driving a car but knows the hazards involved so he keeps his car in good condition and avoids driving in severe weather and recklessly.
2. Is independent. The mentally well person forms and acts on reasoned advice. He or she will seek opinions and once they have facts they are capable of making a decision and accepting the consequences.
3. Has affection for others. This person takes pleasure in being loving and kind to others—spouses, children, relatives, friends—and is sympathetic to less fortunate people. He doesn't need a lot of people with whom to be intimate as less mature persons would nor the need to be the center of attention.
4. Has reasonable dependence on others. The mature person can receive love as well as give it. Feels the need to relate to and share with others.
5. Can make long-range choices. The normal person can usually forgo short-range gratification for the sake of long-range goals, that is turn aside more immediate pleasure for future gains.
6. Reacts moderately. Most normal persons get angry and use hateful language and thoughts to express it. But normal persons do not do this for long. Although badly treated, a normal person doesn't develop a lasting hatred with someone or institution over it.
7. Is comfortable with himself. An adult so labeled has a relaxed conscience and is not constantly reminded of his failures. He or she recognizes that they sometimes fail at what they try to do or that they don't always do things

as well as they would like to but they can still relax and enjoy leisure.

8. Adjust well to work. Most normal persons are satisfied with their work and change their jobs only for good reasons. They recognize the day to day grind and unpleasant tasks are part of the job but nonetheless take a positive view of it and persist.

9. Accept roles of women and men. The healthy person treats the opposite sex with dignity and as an equal. They accept their sex roles and those of a different race with as equals. Good sexual adjustment is part of the normal person's life. The mature person has the ability to sustain a single relationship with a sexual partner, to enjoy sex and companionship.

10. Continues to be creative and to learn. The normal person has the ability to keep learning. One element of our times is change. The tell-tale clue of the mature person is an acceptance of change—our environment, our friends, our jobs, our physical bodies—and all with a minimum of trouble.

Among the normal there are various types of people—some are extroverts and some introverts. Sr. Karen Horney, noted therapist, suggests there are three basic types (1) those who move toward others, (2) those who move against others, and (3) those who move away from people. These might be teachers, professional football players, shoemakers, dentists, writers or cab drivers. Unhappily they might be robbers, playboys or a street sleeper.

The maladjusted person is one who has a personality problem that is term neurotic. This person usually lives with threats and anxiety, which may interfere with normal functioning in daily living. However in most cases particularly if they have a job they can maintain their life without hospitalization for that provides a structure which makes a buffer protecting them from the bizarre and volatile change. Some general aspects of the slightly disturbed persons are:

1. They have many fears, worries, tensions, emotional discomforts generally exaggerated, these are continual and not realistic. The maladjusted person anticipates getting a disease and panics at the thought of it. Find ways to combat this fear by pairing it with a ritual, like saying over and over "you can't get me" or "you didn't get me." The neurotic always emphasizes the negative.
2. They display exaggerated sensitivity. These types of neurotic cannot tolerate any criticism. The disturbed maladjusted might quit their job over slight criticism. Even normal people don't like to be berated for work performance but they can take it but these people are also sensitive to letting control of their children go even as they become adolescents—fearful of danger!
3. They express feelings of being crazy. Excessive worry, fear and depression sometimes gives a person the feeling they are crazy. They don't know why they feel the way they do. They may think that the fact that they wonder may be evidence that they are crazy.

The problem with people with personality difficulties is rooted in the unconscious. The unconscious mind is like a storage room that houses all of our experiences and thoughts of the past. Part is released to the present by the mind gradually and briefly because of the human tendency to forget what is unpleasant and hateful. The neurotic behaves in strange and unusual ways because of guilt or inferiority feeling. He can no more look into his unconscious than you can look into a mirror to see how you look with your eyes closed. The healthy self is seldom in conflict with his unconscious mind and usual desires. The neurotic on the other hand is constantly forced to surrender to his unconscious. You might say he is controlled by this closet of past thoughts. Some minor personality problems are these common ones:

1. Anxiety reaction—This type of person is in a constant state of anxiousness expecting doom to descend any moment often some unnamed happening. They experience

episodes of mild panic and show physical indications through sweating, dizziness, palpitations, diarrhea, breathing problems or pain the heart or chest. This is often associated with losing a friend or loved one.

2. Phobias—There are two types involved here, common and specific one. A common one is claustrophobia, fear of closed places or the opposite is agoraphobia, fear of open spaces. Potamophobia is fear of running water, fear of things half-forgotten related to water—an over turned boat or even a car wreck or cave-in.

3. Hypochondria—This individual thinks he has some illness. She monitors her body constantly noting any and everything that seems somewhat different—heart beat, fatigue, perspiration. These people rarely have a basis for their complaints. Many unmarried persons have this problem and it has been found when they marry they get over their phobia. Others getting busy helps!

4. Depression—It is normal when one has lost their job, just been divorced, loses a spouse or parent in death. This is a normal reaction in experiencing grief and setbacks. Most people suffer the "blues" or lack of interest in their surroundings sometimes. They suffer from not being able to get ahead or think they're getting little out of life. They wake up to find there are more bills, than fun, more work than hours to fill it.

The Seriously Mentally Disturbed

The answer to the question: Am I crazy? This is a misconception, for even a psychosis is a relative matter that may at least in part cause the problem. Remarkable cures for psychosis can be brought about by removing such a person from a restrictive environment, eliminating or reducing stressful situations, or by improving a person's physical health. We all may wonder as to the degree of sanity we possess at a given time. It is normal for people to feel that they are "as crazy as a loon"—the bird that is. The problem is that most people do not obtain help for milder forms of maladjustments even though they should. If individuals exhibit some of the following problems, then help should be sought. These problems are not matters for the do-it-yourself therapy. You should not muddle through with them; you should get expert help. In any event, check these suggestions by noted therapist Dr. Benjamin Miller:

- Is the person's behavior suitable for the occasion? Does he pout or complain on every kind of occasion where frustration is faced in everyday situations? Inappropriate reaction to day to day happenings may be a signal that trouble is coming.
- Major changes in traits or behavior? Does a person who has been an introvert suddenly begin to be very vocal, a careful housewife overnight becomes a poor one, the well-dressed person becomes careless and sloppy? Change from long-established patterns of behavior may provide a clue to abnormal behavior.
- Is there a reason for the behavior? In response to why you do this or think that, normal people usually have an acceptable reason. The disturbed may not have a reason but may act on things they have imagined. If continued, this may be a sure hallmark of illness.
- Does one have control of his actions? Sometimes we have urges that are crazy or are seized with an absurd idea to do something. Normal persons resist giving in to these but the mentally ill do not. They see no reason to control themselves and they may even think they can do the impossible.
- Has one's emotional strength been lost? Many of us have at times been temporarily overwhelmed with shock or grief and periods of crisis which may be connected with our jobs or love affairs but we bounce back and regain our composure. The mentally ill go into depression for long periods of time and indeed may not come out of it without some help.
- Is one's behavior destructive? Long term, chronic destructive behavior in an adult or child is an attribute of mental sickness. If a child continually damages property,

mistreats animals (pets) or himself and others, the call for help is clear. Adults who do the same things are also suspect and if they beat up on their children, spouses and others, immediate assistance is needed!

Personality disorders like alcoholism, sex deviations and drug addiction may be the symptoms of problems that can be relieved by therapy. Therapy for any symptoms such as those mentioned above can usually be treated on an outpatient basis. Modern medicines and treatment can effect miracles in many cases mental as well as physical, so one should seek aid with mental problems. The seriously disturbed (those with psychoses) usually are classified as either functional organic. The organic refers to those with brain damage, tumors, senility, poisons, etc. The functional psychoses are seen as (1) schizophrenia, (2) paranoia and (3) manic-depressive. Most physicians will recommend counseling centers for alcoholism, drugs, etc., or stress management programs where individual effort is not enough to bring wellness. New yellow pages provide action indexes for emergency help.

An interesting study was reported by P. Rosenhan in *Science* a few years ago. In the experiment eight normal well-established individuals with no previous history of personality problems got themselves admitted to different mental hospitals reporting that they had had auditory hallucinations. No other symptoms were reported and in all other respects they behaved normally. All except one were admitted to the hospitals and diagnosed as schizophrenic. The other "patient" received a diagnosis of manic-depressive psychosis. The original labeling colored all the subsequent reviews and nothing about their behavior was entered into the reports on them. We should not take this to mean mental illness is a joke. But it does suggest we should hesitate to label people as "sick," considering the difficulty of diagnosis through troubled behavior may be obvious and needs care.

In conclusion, you can evaluate for yourself and others by understanding the causes of stress and depression. The first step is recognizing the problem exists. You help yourself by talking it over with someone you trust thereby keeping things in perspective—keep stress in bounds before it causes trouble and know where to go for help. Help from professionals keep minor problems from becoming serious ones. Stress is widely found among people everywhere. This chapter should help find some answers for you. Good luck!

CHAPTER THREE

HEALTH PROBLEMS

"So You Want to Live to Ninety"

More people live to be 90 than ever before. But it is not automatic, since the life expectancy is 77-78 years taking men and women together. How can one achieve that goal? Choosing ones parents and grandparents would help. The cause of variation in people is their genetic make-up, their environment, their previous medical history, their nutritional habits, mental health status and life styles. Our bodies mature between 25 and 30 years. Signs for flush of aging appear in humans and plants and other animals as soon as full maturity is achieved. Scientists do not know all the answers but they do know some. For instance, we know adding vitamins to the diet (not promiscuously) can reduce the free-radical damage. Free radicals are highly reactive destroying cells in our body. These radicals are generated as a natural part of our metabolism. They are also increased by exposure to x-ray, tobacco smoke, sunlight, ozone and auto fumes. These free radicals damage the DNA (which provides the pattern for cell reproduction) that lead to disease. Besides this information, smaller amounts of food—essential components and quantities—tend to increase the years of living. It has long been recognized that if one has grandparents and parents that live to be eighty or more years old then it is more likely to convey an advantage to you for a longer than average length of life. Statistics from the

U.S. Department of Health and Human Services (2004) tell us that a person living to 65 can except a considerable number of years to follow, in fact females at 65 on average can reach 85 before their demise. Males can expect 17 more years – living to 82 years. So to hope to reach the goal of 90 you must first reach of the goal of 65, that's obvious. There are other related kinships that bare on the trail to reaching 90. The early death of sisters and brothers or even other kinsmen figure in on the projection of longevity, if they were in their 40's or 50's when they died of a heart attack, cancer, or some other malady it reduces the likelihood of extra years.

Living to 65 is taken for granted by most people. Particularly early in adult life when there is a tendency to burn the candle at both ends and "damn the torpedoes, full speed ahead" where we over eat or under exercise! In the last decade according to U.S. Department of Health and Human Services (2004) the nation has found itself with 66% of adults over weight. The rate of diabetes has dramatically increased, many are obese. And other major diseases noted and projected. Eat, drink and be merry is America's theme song and although sensible people and organizations are working to turn the tide, head way is making slow progress. Today there is a major concern which involves the health of the individual. This is the economy and the loss of millions of jobs which effects the nature of health care. Many have to make the choice between check up and check out – clothing, supermarket, gas station, or medicine. Charities are having a difficult time helping the needy. Money to sustain the necessities to maintain a healthy life may be lacking because of income. Hard times create a climate of more suicides, more divorces, and mental problems which inveigh against long life.

Those who are married have advantages that single, divorced, or widowed and couples though wedded are living alone. Couples provide reciprocal care through attention to the needs of the other, protection, sharing stress, and succor. All add to a more secure life and added years of life. The personality of each spouse tend to balance the other and provide a more even pathway for the family life.

If you are educated and your parents are educated at the college level particularly as graduates this conveys a considerable advantage to living a longer life! Living to be 65 is a big step, still if your goal is 90 years you have a way to go. Education is one of those areas which help close the 8 years gap for men and 5 year gap for women. Why is this so? For several reasons the educated parents are more likely to have employment to live sufficient to provide you with good nutritious food, medical care, opportunity to experience a variety of situations and go to events and get an education, to travel, and to be associated with a broader culture than ordinary. Your education at the college level provides you with horizons which afford opportunity to give you the chance to pursue what interests you or fits your ability. Having an education enables you to understand many important written articles, forms, books, documents, IRS material, science stories, local and world events, which are largely lost by those less educated. Your knowledge often secures you from making grave mistakes, simply by being a superior reader. One understands motives of the behavior of people, trends, and can reason with the college education, that most likely would never be accomplished outside schooling at a higher level.

Of course there are other significant things one must consider; brain power and genetics both bear on the future of good health. If one is of higher intelligence even if born of poor parents or ordinary intelligent parents this is a boon. But it doesn't happen often. Studies of long life by anthropologists in recent years have taken them to third world countries in rural areas where people who are generally poor. They live simple lives, eat little, and live in close knit families, but investigators discovered many who are 90 to 100 years old. Nutrition scientists believe that less food if balanced is an essential aid to extending life. Some studies done in post World War 2 show a dramatic drop in major diseases such as heart problems. This was due it was thought to relate to less food and Spartan lives to make a living and improved metabolism and reduced fat intake.

Birth order has been found to impact on the intelligence, principally on the young age of the mother (over 20) assumed to be healthier and has more energy to be expended on caring for the infant. However one must not discount the experience the mother has offering after bearing a child or children and still is only 30 – that is worth consideration. But the first born some research shows has more intelligence (judged by IQ) that gives them advantages in getting an education, a job, in general living and subsequently the life span. The first born gets more attention from the parents than the siblings that follow. If the parents have many children it is thought that many times the oldest children actually look after and have a considerable hand in raising the youngest children.

The ongoing life is an important element in life expectancy. The heavy inveterate smoker, drinker, and those on drugs are all at risk. If they have been a smoker beginning at 20 they will at 50 likely have a problem of some type if not cancer, leading to it, or emphysema, pneumonia, tuberculosis, or lung problems, if they are a heavy drinker at 20 until 50 the forecast is calamitous. Undoubtedly stress is involved and in fact a known killer as is participants in all major diseases. Drug users are culpable in shorting the life journey too! When under stress the body gives off excess cortisol ("stress hormone") which is harmful to the body and if constant creates life shortening problems. Beyond the use of these crutches urban life is fraught with hazards which cut the span of life short. The things which will help extend life are simple but important.

- Exercise regularly
- Sleep 7 to 8 hours every day, retiring and rising at the same time
- Regular doctor appointments twice a year
- Avoid medicine at your own recognizance
- Eat a balanced diet, limit calories and sweets, emphasize fruits and vegetables
- Limit fats, saturated and trans fats and poly unsaturated fats
- Take regular vacations and in between times go on outings
- Be a good neighbor and generous
- Have time for your family, give them first priority
- Have a hobby
- Work hard, play hard
- Keep cholesterol in control, eat little sodium
- Connect with spirituality. The Annals of Epidemiology (2008) report studies linking health and spirituality and prayer and

meditation to an improved immune system and fewer episodes of chronic inflammation. All contribute to life's extension.

Heredity and Environmental Factors

The influence of heredity, and environment on the aging process are so intertwined that it is impossible for scientists to say with certainty where one begins and the other ends. Functional stress will affect each individual differently during the late thirties and into the 40's and 50's since no two humans exactly duplicate each other heredity, environment or experience.

Many long-lived people come from mountainous regions like those reported from these republics of Georgia where many are reported to live beyond 100. The oxygen-poor and pollution-free environment would be a tonic to their cardiovascular systems. Blood vessels that feed the heart widen and become more efficient. Another factor may be their isolation—that they are separated from the pressures and worries of civilization. The most important factor, however, is thought to be their life-styles, which focus on vigorous, physically demanding work. A caution suggested by research into these claims note that many of these people overstate their age due to the great veneration given to old people.

Everyone is familiar with early childhood diseases such as chicken pox, measles and mumps, but what types of physical strain should one be alert to in middle life? Certain ailments and stress factors do occur more often this time of life to millions of Americans. What are they? What are the symptoms and causes? How can they be prevented and what effect do they have on our bodies' systems and longevity?

Physical age represents the functional condition of one's body and its symptoms indicators. There may be a marked variation between one's chronological age and one's physiological age. Chronological age becomes a progressively poorer indication or measure of the body's capacities as one grows older as the effects of environment play a larger role.

AARP reports (2008) four world locations (this one from Costa Rica) where people live the longest. The reasons (1) strong sense of purpose, (2) drink hard water (high calcium content), (3) focus on family, (4) eat light dinners, (5) keep social networks, (6) keep hard at work, (7) get some sun, (8) embrace a common history.

Inherited factors undoubtedly play some role for the long-lived. Part of this may be due to special groups inbreeding, thereby reducing the amount of dilution of genes from outsiders. However, geneticists believe inter-breeding is better than inbreeding for racial health. The food that all these long-lived people eat is a common link also. Wasting food is unthinkable, as they never eat more than their bodies require; they strictly avoid excess fats and animal protein and intake ample vitamins, minerals and fiber in their foods. Fortified maize and beans are their fundamental core diet.

Another element enters the picture that is being focused on by psychologists is steadiness. Reported in the *Journal of Psychological Science* (June/July 2007) research by Brent Roberts of Illinois University on conscientiousness and health show traits making up conscientiousness such as orderliness, industry, reliability, conventionality, etc., can increase over the life span. This is true even though they occupied a lesser role earlier in one's life and the increase in these factors will be directly related to improvement in health and longevity. Daniel Mroczek of Purdue University in the *Journal of Psychological Science* says being neurotic more than average it not of itself a prediction of early death. But if these people (men be studied) get more and more fretful the downward spiral increases their risk of dying of cancer and heart disease.

The purpose of this chapter is to provide information on major and minor health problems and preventive medicine. Everyone may eventually face some of the circumstances noted in the following pages or if not you personally, then a friend or relative might.

MAJOR HEALTH PROBLEMS

LIFE CHANGES AND DISEASES THAT MOST OFTEN OCCUR DURING THE MIDDLE YEARS OF BOOMER LIFE AND THEIR PROGNOSIS

Some knowledge of the physical changes and difficulties that become prominent by the late 30's and into the 40's and 50's are presented here. Knowledge of these problems will help us in the future by knowing the general circumstances of these situations. The categories discussed are: Heart and circulation, cancers, bone, diabetes, weight problems and associated lesser problems and preventive medicine.

Heart (Circulatory Problem)

Diseases affecting the heart and circulatory systems are the major cause of death in this country. Heart disease caused 652,486 deaths in 2006 (NY Times Almanac, 2010). Presently, 50 million have high blood pressure or hypertension and under control only one-third of them! It is during the middle years that many of these diseases appear. Four major types which affect adults over 40 are (1) coronary heart disease, (2) high blood pressure—hypertension, (3) hemorrhage or blood clotting in the heart, and (4) heart failure. Heart failure—this results when the heart muscle begins to weaken and the pump (heart) does not work efficiently. The result is the accumulation of fluid in the body leading to swollen legs, weight gain and shortness of breath (accumulation of fluid in the lungs). The most common cause, however, is many years of inadequately controlled hypertension. This can develop as a complication of a coronary thrombosis, drug induced heart disease (alcoholism) or simple wearing out of the heart muscle. Most cases can be controlled by the proper use of medicines.

Coronary heart disease involves two principal kinds—disease of the coronary arteries (Arteriosclerosis) or "hardening of the arteries," and coronary thrombosis. In the first of these diseases, the arteries are hardened affecting the blood supply to the heart by narrowing the tubes and creating an unsmooth lining in the artery. This has the effect of tending to allow settlement of blood in the grooves and the forming of clots. The smaller the artery the more pressure required to pump blood to the body. A major symptom here is pain over the heart, sometimes brief; (as in angina) other evidence of trouble is dizziness, nausea, fatigue and irregular heartbeat. Failure of the heart to receive enough oxygen creates the pain. Drugs may be prescribed by the physician such as nitroglycerin to bring relief to pain and increase the flow of blood through the arteries. Early diagnosis is important in heart problems; the treatment usually includes rest, diet, medication and possibly surgery which is increasingly commonplace in certain situations—by-pass, valve replacement and heart transplant.

In coronary thrombosis, a blood clot forms within a coronary artery cutting off the entire supply of blood to a section of the heart. This block (occlusion) may cause injury or destroy part of the heart muscle. The heart attack that occurs causes severe and prolonged pain. Hospitalization is essential to affect therapy, providing oxygen, good nursing, anti-blood clotting medicines and a controlled environment. In reality, thrombosis is often superimposed on coronary plaques and most patients have a combination of both.

Angioplasties

Angioplasty is a procedure used with a heart attack victim to unblock a constricted or clogged artery. A thin tube tipped by a plastic balloon is inserted into the blocked artery and then inflated to force open the blockage and restore blood flow. Over a million persons in the U.S. suffer heart attack could be aided by use of angioplasties procedure. Most heart attacks are treated by drugs primarily.

Most heart attacks are treated only with clot-busting drugs, which can be given anywhere. Most hospitals cannot do quick artery-clearing angioplasties, and doctors are reluctant to postpone treatment while patients are moved to hospitals that can. A Danish study published in Summer 2003 New England Journal of Medicine concludes that a transfer to an angioplasty center cuts the risk of death and major complications by about 40 percent. Comparing 1,129 patients with major heart attacks, 14 percent either died or suffered another heart attack or disabling stroke when treated with drugs alone during the month-long study. Only 8 percent died when transferred to another hospital for angioplasty. Nearly all were transferred within two hours.

The question of transfers potentially affects hundreds of thousands of patients. In the United States, heart attacks kill about 460,000 yearly, according to the National Institutes of Health. Institute of Heart, Blood and Lung, Bethesda, MD, 2008.

The attacks occur when clogged and clotted arteries crimp the stream of blood to heart muscle. Several factors have limited angioplasties, though. They require sophisticated surgical backup in case something goes wrong. Clot dissolving drugs like TPA can be given by emergency room doctors. Several studies have suggested that the benefits of angioplasties might outweigh delays for hospital transfer. The Danish study helps settle the question, some doctors said. In the nationalized Danish health system the researchers took special precautions that ordinary hospitals might not take. Potential transfers were whisked past emergency rooms straight to a cardiac care team.

Hypertension or high blood pressure affects some 50 million Americans, including more than one-third of the adult population 50 and over. Worldwide a billion people have hypertension. Nearly half of the people with hypertension are undetected and of those who have been diagnosed, half of these remain untreated. The effect of high blood pressure is seen on the heart, brain, and kidneys. However, it is usual to have no symptoms at all. The symptoms may include headaches now and then, fatigue, insomnia, dizziness and excessive flushing.

Generally high blood pressure creates symptoms only after it has produced disease in some organ like the heart or kidney. Four categories are recognizable; essential hypertension, secondary hypertension, malignant hypertension and borderline hypertension. In the essential hypertension (1st stage), the most common (about 85%) the blood pressure is over 150/95, the 150 represents the systolic (the pumping pressure) inside the blood vessels and 95 represents the diastolic (the relaxed or resting) pressure between heartbeats. The tension with this type may be that the heart is pumping too much blood or that the arteries are too small to handle adequate supplies of blood. Secondary hypertension (stage two) is attributed to specific organic causes such as hardening of the arteries, kidney disease or blockage to kidney blood flow. Malignant hypertension is a situation where blood pressure sometimes jumps as high as 200/115 or higher very rapidly and damages body organs within hours or days. This type is less frequently seen. In borderline hypertension, the blood pressure intermittently rises above the normal levels for each given age group or sex—primary and secondary problems usually in these people in time. Incidentally, the word malignant does not refer to a "growth" or tumor but the severity of the pressure problem. African-

Americans and men generally over 40 and men and women with a family history of high blood pressure, emotional behavior and obesity, etc., problems run greater risks of having high blood pressure than others.

New standards for blood pressure puts 45 million Americans whose blood pressure is 120-139 millimeters of mercury—the systolic—the top number in a reading (pressure in the arteries when the heart is contracting) or 80-89 diastolic (the bottom number is the pressure when the heart is at rest between beats) at risk. The new guidelines provided by the National Heart, Lung and Blood Institute (2004) are the Federal Standards for blood pressure. These standards are given on the web site of the Journal of the American Medical Association (www.jama.com). The blood pressure categories are as follows.

Federal guidelines say certain blood pressure levels, once thought normal, are now considered to be actually high enough to signal "prehypertension."

Pressure Normal	Pre-hypertension	Stage one hypertension	Stage two hyper-tension
Systolic Less than 120	120-139	140-159	More than 160
Diastolic Less than 80 Treatment (Otherwise Healthy) None	80-89 None	90-99 Diuretics for most, possibly other drugs	More than 100 Two-drug combo, usually one is a diuretic
With other None diseases*	Medically treat Diseases	Multiple medications	Multiple medications

*Previous heart attack, diabetes, kidney disease or certain other diseases
SOURCE: National Heart, Lung and Blood Institute, 2004**AP/VP**

People with readings in this range (139 over 89 called high normal) do not have high blood pressure and do not need to take medication. But the new guidelines advise doctors that such people are likely to develop high blood pressure, and should be advised to try to lower their pressure by losing excess weight, exercising more, quitting smoking, cutting back on salt, having no more than one or two alcoholic drinks a day, and eating more fruits, vegetables and low-fat dairy products. The risk of heart disease and stroke starts to rise at readings as low as 115/75, and doubles for each increase of 20/10 millimeters of mercury.

People whose reading is normal at age 55 have a 90% chance of eventually developing high blood pressure though fortunately diet and exercise can change those prospects. The National Health Institute is suggesting 30 minutes of exercise 4 or 5 times a week (split in two sessions if necessary of walking or aerobics, also weight lifting, tennis, jogging, swimming, etc.). Some authorities suggest 30-45 minutes of vigorous exercise seven days per week. More for weight loss. Remember hypertension has no symptoms until the pressure has damaged the arteries and cause them to stiffen which increases the pressure more. You can begin a program of exercise even at sixty, if done gradually with walking as the best approach. Don't be discouraged.

Risk	Lowering Risk
High blood pressure disregarded	Check blood pressure regularly once a year or more suggested by the doctor. Physical exam each year for adult. Diastolic blood pressure should be reduced.
Atrial fibrillation— erratic heartbeat may result in small clots that might go to the brain.	Warfarin or aspirin can greatly decrease the risk of stroke.
Atherosclerosis and high cholesterol levels	Cholesterol level should be in line with new guidelines, eat low fat foods & diet, exercise regularly—take such medicine as Lipacor for rapid reduction.

Stroke risk is high after several months of a TIA	The precursor of the TIA, its signs and help can be given by your doctor.
People with heart problems should not smoke making proneness to clotting greater.	Give up smoking and take aspirin or anticoagulate.
Diabetes increases risk of cardiovascular disease and stroke	Taking insulin or other medicine. Tailor diet through an M.D. preferably an Endocrinologist.
Obesity even 25% overweight increases risk of serious problems.	Exercise and diet as suggested by a doctor.
A mechanical heart valve requiring thin blood by Warfarin, etc.	Physicians or a lab will assist you with regular checkups and levels of medicine.
Check vitamins and minerals particularly Vitamin E level in the diet	Take Vitamin E and other minerals to help avoid strokes.

National Institutes of Health, Institute of Heart, Blood and Lung, Bethesda, MD, 2007

The following information comes from the American Institute for Cancer Research, the National Institutes of Health (where the author was on protocol for fifteen years), and the Harvard Medical School:

Stroke is common in middle age. The cause of this sickness is blockage in a brain artery or hemorrhage of a brain artery by rupture causing bleeding in surrounding brain tissue. A clot sometimes happens suddenly that may involve days of being dizzy, stumbling around, clumsy movement or the mouth ultimately being drawn to one side or difficulty talking. If the hemorrhage is large, often death occurs quickly. Sometimes a surgeon can remove the clot that causes the stroke. The damage to the brain usually causes the body or some parts to be paralyzed. Stroke occurs when normal circulation of the blood through the brain is cut off. Deprived of oxygen, brain cells die and fail to exercise control over parts of the body they normally direct. Damage of this type to one side of the brain usually results in the loss of control of muscles, etc., on the opposite side of the body. Usually rehabilitation methods can re-teach a person to use affected muscles, limbs and speech apparatus again. In some instances the effect of the stroke clears up without leaving apparent damage.

Small strokes or TIA's (Transient Ischemic Attack) occurs when the blood is cut-off in a small vessel (capillary) in the brain resulting in numbness in the hands, legs, face, lips or garbled speech which usually lasts a brief period of possibly an hour or so. It leaves no mark or little effect. These attacks may be the precursor of a large and more devastating one. To counter this, Coumadin (Warfarin) is often prescribed mainly to those with atrial fibrillation, Trental and Topamax for others and heart patients to thin the blood securing smooth passage through the blood vessels. In many, attention is also given to cholesterol levels, sugar control, diet in general and exercise.

Physicians will check to see if other conditions can mimic the TIA migraine such as low blood sugar, low blood pressure, brain tumor, irregular heart rhythm and labyrinthitis (viral infection of the inner ear). Risk factors of having strokes may reduce their chances by knowing what they are and reducing them.

Intravenous use of the thrombolytic drugs to break up clots if given within three hours of having a transient ischemic stroke (TIA). The risk of dying following an attack in the period of following up to six months but lower your risks of dying or of being dependently impaired over the next six months. Most physicians recommend the drug be used to prevent long-term risks. Stroke rehabilitation specialists can assist the impaired victim adjust and recapture movement of hand, speech, walking, etc. Most of these stroke patients are moved to short term nursing homes then hopefully home care where independence can be established and family can help with the importance of exercise and care.

Cholesterol

Cholesterol is a fat important to the healthy body supplying some hormones, cell membranes, and needed tissues. A high level of cholesterol is a risk for coronary artery disease leading to heart attack. There are two kinds. It is produced by the liver in our bodies and is found in foods that come from animals like fish, meats, and dairy products. Foods from plants like fruit, vegetables, nuts, and grains do not have cholesterol.

Triglycerides are another type of fat that is found in the blood and circulates in the blood as a source of energy. High levels of triglyceride are connected to coronary artery disease and maybe pancreas problems.

Several types of blood fats exist

1. Low Density Lipoprotein (LDL) – The major cholesterol carrier in the blood vessels LDL moves cholesterol to areas all over the body, piles up in the arteries leading up to your heart and brain.
2. High Density Lipoprotein (HDL) – HDL is cholesterol that cleans up and helps lower the LDL cholesterol in your blood. It is therefore called the "Good cholesterol." High levels of HDL mean less risk of atherosclerosis. HDL level rises with weight loss and exercise, though in the latter case, it must be a large amount of physical activity.
3. Triglycerides – Another kind of blood fat is called by the name hypertriglyceridemia. This condition tends to lead the development of atherosclerosis it is not as sure as those LDL, cholesterol and total cholesterol combined.

Risk factors are diet, age – increase after fifty, weight, gender (men at a younger age, women after 50), genetics (some predisposed to high levels), disease (diabetics, health problems, stress, and life styles). Medicines that lower cholesterol are Mevacor, Zocor, Lipitor, Cresta, Pravochol, Trica, Lopid, and Wellchol.

	Desirable Level	Borderline	Undesirable Level
Total Cholesterol	Below 200	200 - 240	Above 240
HDL Cholesterol	Above 45	35 - 45	Below 35
LDL Cholesterol	Below 130	130 - 160	Above 160
Total to HDL Ratio	Below 4.5	4.5 - 5.5	Above 5.5
LDL to HDL Ratio	Below 3.0	3.0 - 5.0	Above 5.0

National Institute Of Heart, Blood and Lung, NIH, Bethesda, MD 2005

You should test cholesterol every three to five years, if you have high cholesterol levels more often.

Reducing Your Cholesterol

The first is to eat a low-fat, low-cholesterol diet. Your total fat consumption—saturated, polyunsaturated and monounsaturated should be less than 30 percent of your daily intake of calories. Keep your cholesterol intake to fewer than 300 milligrams per day. Saturated fats contained in butter, whole milk, hydrogenated oils, chocolate, shortening, etc. should be one third of your total fat consumption. Reduce your total fat and cholesterol intake, limit your consumption of meats such as beef, pork, liver and tongue (always trim away excess fat). In addition, avoid cheese, fried foods, nuts and cream, and try to curb your intake of eggs to no more than four per week. Try to eat meatless meals several times a week, use skim milk and include fish in your diet. Eat a variety of vegetables, pasta, grains and fruit. Check the label of the foods you buy, and restrict your choices to foods containing 3 grams of fat or less per serving. If you are overweight reduce by regular exercise, walking, swimming, aerobics, health spa exercise machines.

Carrier molecules (HDL and LDL) are made of protein and are called apoproteins. They are necessary because cholesterol and other fats (lipids) can't dissolve in water which also means they can't dissolve in blood. These apoproteins are joined with cholesterol and form a compound called lipoproteins. The density of these lipoproteins is determined by the amount of protein in the molecule. "Bad" cholesterol is the low-density lipoprotein (LDL), the major cholesterol carrier in the blood. High levels of these LDLs are associated with atherosclerosis. "Good" cholesterol is the high-density lipoprotein (HDL); a greater level of HDL—this is like a drain cleaner you pour in the sink—is thought to provide some protection against artery blockage.

To summarize what can help prevent heart disease follows closely to the factors that cut the risk of having a stroke.

- No smoking
- Reduce high blood pressure
- Reduce high stress
- Exercise – vigorously and regularly
- Cut your weight drastically if obese (20% or greater overweight). Diet.
- Reduce high cholesterol
- Be watchful for signs of problems such as family history and genetics.
- Cut excess alcohol consumptions to one or two drinks.

CANCER

Cancer (Neoplasms)

The second leading cause of death in the United States is cancer. 565,650 people died of cancer in 2009 (NY Times Almanac, 2010) Cancer is among the causes of death of those 65 and older, but among 45 to 64 years it is the number one killer. It is estimated that one of every four persons will get some form of cancer. It is not contagious even its terminal form. However, the AIDS virus (Autoimmune

Deficiency Syndrome) which can cause a form of cancer is highly contagious through blood and semen contact. A final cure has remained elusive, but much is known and new drugs that help slow its effect or cure are improving the fight against AIDS.

Nonetheless millions of Americans have survived cancer. The incidence of cancer is high among the middlescent. Cancer is a malignant tumor—a shapeless mass of cells which keeps on growing without order. Cancer is a disease of the cells (cytology) rather than organs, which are frequently its target. Normally the nature adult body reproduces only those cells that are needed for repair of injured tissue. In cancer, there is an irregular multiplication of cells in one or more parts of the body. A lump or mass of tissue called a tumor may be benign (harmless) or malignant. A benign tumor may need to be removed because of its size or that it is potential to become malignant in the future. Cancer is greatly feared because it gives little advance warning; the warning signals emphasized by the American Cancer Association are easily confused with minor or other problems, leaving one in a quandary and fearful but more importantly its causes and cures are unknown. The types of cancer are divided into two groups: sarcomas—those which usually affect the bones and muscles, and carcinomas—make up the largest group involving the breast, stomach, lungs, womb, skin, and tongue.

Hodgkin's Disease (usually found in the young) is classified as a cancer as is Leukemia, a form of cancer where immature white blood corpuscles multiply in overwhelming numbers. These cells are produced in the bone marrow. They are longer lived than the normal white blood cells and accumulate in the marrow and various organs until they prevent enough cells to function.

The following data was given by the American Cancer Society from their Bulletin Publication Staff 2009. The most common forms of cancer in middle-aged women is breast cancer; however, the leading cause of cancer deaths in women is lung cancer due to smoking. An estimated one in nine life time risk that women will develop breast cancer. Breast and uterine cancer can be cured if discovered early, which proves the need for vigilance in testing and examination. But the outlook for lung and throat cancer is lethal in most instances with the five-year survival rate being only 10%

or less. Besides this, smokers generally are more likely to have all kinds of neoplasms—esophagus, bladder, kidney, stomach, prostate, and pancreas (as well as heart disease and emphysema). In women, smoking causes menopause to occur earlier, it also predisposes them to osteoporosis, heart problems, and other maladies.

The seven warning signals of cancer, though well known, are emphasized here. With early detection, the chances of recovery are significantly improved. Here are the warning signs:

1. Unusual bleeding or discharge

2. A lump or thickening in the breast

3. A sore that doesn't heal

4. Persistent change in bowel or bladder habits

5. Hoarseness or cough that is persistent

6. Persistent indigestion or difficulty in swallowing

7. Change in a wart or mole

Problems with the Breast

Infections of the breast are most common in women who are breast-feeding. Otherwise breast infections can occur in women who have had surgery on the breasts, particularly when lymph glands have been removed, or in women with compromised immune systems due to chemotherapy or diseases such as AIDS. Healthy women may also develop breast infections. Mastitis and abscesses are two kinds of breast infection. Mastitis is an inflammation of the breast tissue usually due to milk ducts that are blocked and bacteria grows. The bacteria are in the mouth or skin of the newborn baby. Abscesses are uncommon is an infection (bacterial) that produced a cyst filled with pus due generally to untreated Mastitis in the early breast feeding period. Symptoms of Mastitis are fever and fatigue, breast swelling, redness and heat sensation. Also, breast appears red and swollen in the area of the areola. Antibiotics are used to combat both problems. A physician may drain the abscess to relieve much of the pain. Compresses to the same areas, warmth helps free blocked milk ducts. It is not necessary to stop breast-feeding with either infection but it is necessary to have the milk flowing.

Breast Cancer

Breast cancer is the most common cancer in women. The Mayo Clinic estimates 250,000 women are diagnosed with breast cancer each year (2010). It begins in one spot and grows. It can spread (metastasize) to other body parts via the lymphatic system and the blood stream leading to illness and perhaps death. Earlier detection of cancerous tumors by self-examination and mammograms is the best protection against breast cancer. For those over 40, having a daughter—close kin—or mother who have breast cancer, began menstruating at 12 or younger, or starting menopause at age 55 or older, have not carried a pregnancy to term, using hormone replacement therapy for 10 years or longer, been exposed to radiation or had breast cancer before are at greater risks than those not included here. In pre-menopausal women, high levels of an insulin-like growth factor called IGF-1 may indicate increased risk of breast cancer.

The most common outward sign of breast cancer is a hard lump in the breast that is usually not moveable and may or may not be painful. The skin over the lump may look dimpled (like the skin of an orange) or indented in areas where the cancer has spread. The nipple may be inverted (turn inward) or leak dark fluid. Any lumps you feel under your arm may be cancer that has spread from breast tissue to the lymph glands under your arm. Some cancers are undetectable. Any suspicious Pap smear should be repeated to rule out error and followed up by colposcopy. It is important that women learn to examine their breasts (many middlescent women regularly monitor themselves for other reasons) on a regular monthly basis. Assistance can be readily found in the physician's office (either women or men) and no woman or man should fail, however shy, prudent or painful (rectal examination is painful and for some women the uterus examination is also) to receive some sort of medical attention in this regard. It is recommended that a mammogram should be taken annually after age 40!

STAGES OF BREAST CANCER	SURVIVAL: 5 YEARS AFTER DIAGNOSIS
I Cancer is less than 1 inch (2 centimeters [cm]) and has not spread outside the breast.	95%
II Cancer is 1 to 2 inches (2 to 5 cm) or cancer is smaller than 1 inch (2 cm) but has spread to lymph glands under the arm or cancer is larger than 2 inches (5 cm) but has not spread to lymph glands under the arm.	80%
IIIA Cancer is larger than 2 inches (5 cm) and has spread to the lymph glands under the arm or cancer is smaller than 2 inches (5 cm), has spread to the lymph glands under the arm, and the lymph glands have grown together or attached themselves to other structures.	50%
IIIB Cancer has spread to tissues near the breast (such as the chest wall, including the ribs and the muscles) or cancer has spread to lymph glands inside the chest wall along the breastbone.	50%
IV Cancer has spread to other parts of the body (most often the bones, lungs, liver, or brain) or cancer has spread to the skin or lymph glands inside the neck near the collarbone.	10%

Reprinted with the permission of The Free Press, A Division of Simon and Schuster Inc. from Harvard Medical School Family Health Guide, Anthony L. Komaroff, M.D., Editor in Chief, Copyright 1999, 2005, by President and Fellows of Harvard College.

BREAST CANCER TREATMENT

All kinds of breast cancer can be treated, usually starting with surgery to remove the tumor and part or all of the breast. There are additional treatments that may be used individually or in combination, depending on the extent of your cancer and other factors such as your overall health, gone through menopause, and response to hormones.

TREATMENT OPTIONS	DESCRIPTION
Surgery	Surgery involves removing the tumor (lumpectomy) or removing the tumor and part or all of the breast tissue (mastectomy).
Radiation therapy	Radiation is used after surgery to kill any remaining cancer cells.
Chemotherapy	Chemotherapy is the administration of anticancer drugs. It can be used with surgery and/ or radiation to eradicate cancer cells and prevent them from spreading or to relieve pain and discomfort if the cancer is incurable. Drugs may be taken as tablets, liquids, injections, injections, or intravenous infusions.
Hormone therapy	Hormone therapy is used to treat cancer that grows in response to hormones. Tamoxifen and raloxifene are medications taken (either by themselves or with chemotherapy) to fight tumors that are responsive to estrogen. Hormone therapy has been used most often in women over the age of 50 (although research shows that hormone therapy can be effective in women of all ages).
Biological therapy	Biological therapy is experimental therapy that uses the body's immune system to boost specific types of white blood cells that fight cancer.
Bone marrow transplant	Higher doses of chemotherapy are better at eliminating cancer cells but usually destroy bone marrow, the site where blood cells are produced. Bone marrow transplantation is an experimental approach that replaces destroyed bone marrow after high-dose chemotherapy.

Reprinted with the permission of The Free Press, A Division of Simon and Schuster Inc. from Harvard Medical School Family Health Guide, Anthony L. Komaroff, M.D., Editor in Chief, Copyright 1999, 2005, by President and Fellows of Harvard College.

Mayo Clinic recently claims lobule status (milk produced by the breast) can determine cancer risk. If the lobules aren't largely gone by age 55 the risk of breast cancer triples (2010). This discovery is thought to be an important tendency for risk of breast cancer.

For women a special word should be said about taking the PAP test for with its widespread use (more than 85% American women by the end of 1985 had one Pap smear) the ability to save most sufferers of cervical cancer is at hand. Of the various Pap classifications (I-V) I and II are negative while III is labeled suspicious, classes IV and V are positive. Some research reports use the term dysplasia, to describe pre-malignant changes. Such a report indicates the need for further evaluation by a specialist as does the labels class III, IV, and V. Also women who at their first checkup reported gynecological complaints (bleeding, irregular bleeding, spotting, or discharge) were found to develop cancer three times more often than those with no complaints. The incidences of uterine cancer grow markedly after thirty-five.

For more information: with considerable help, call Multidisciplinary Breast Clinic, (904) 953-0707, www.mayoclinic.org/trastuzumab/

OVARIAN CANCER

No treatment can be affected that cures cancer for sure (no fruit juice cure or drugs, clinics or fortune teller) so do not treat yourself or take the claims of advertised cures or take the word of friends who attempt it for you. Physicians may make misjudgments but they are usually corrected before the final resolution of treatment is made—radiologists, blood analysis personnel, specialists are all usually involved in the diagnosis and subsequent therapy.

Ovarian Cancer

STAGE	LOCATION OF SPREAD	SURVIVAL 5 YEARS AFTER DIAGNOSIS
IA	Cancer is confined to the ovary and no tumor remains after surgery.	After surgery-95%
IB	Cancer is confined to the ovary but some tumor remains after surgery or tumor cells appear to be malignant.	After surgery plus chemotherapy and radiation therapy-80%
II	Cancer is confined to the pelvis.	After surgery-70%
III	Cancer has spread to the abdomen.	Following surgery plus chemotherapy -15% to 20%
IV	Cancer has spread outside the abdomen	After chemotherapy and (in some cases) surgery-1% to 5%

Reprinted with the permission of The Free Press, A Division of Simon and Schuster Inc. from Harvard Medical School Family Health Guide, Anthony L. Komaroff, M.D., Editor in Chief, Copyright 1999, 2005, by President and Fellows of Harvard College.

Vague abdominal discomfort, mild indigestion, has few early signs. Women with children or on birth control pills are less likely at risk.

Cervical Cancer

STAGE	LOCATION OF SPREAD	SURVIVAL 5 YEARS AFTER DIAGNOSIS

I	Cancer is confined to inside the cervix.	
IA		A simple hysterectomy is given (removing only the uterus)-99%
	Cancer has gone beyond the first outer layer of cells of the cervix and measure no more than 5 millimeters (mm), with the affected area smaller than 7 mm.	
IB		
		Radical hysterectomy or radiation therapy-85% if the cancer doesn't spread to the lymph glands and 50% if the cancer spread to the lymph glands; chemotherapy improves survival
	Cancer has spread deeper than 5 mm or broader than 7 mm but is inside the tissues of the cervix.	
II	Cancer has moved to nearby organs.	
IIA		Following radical hysterectomy or radiation therapy-85% if the cancer spread is to the lymph glands; adding chemotherapy aids survival.
	Cancer has spread to the upper two thirds of the vagina.	
IIB		
	Cancer has spread to the tissue around the cervix or uterus but not to the pelvis.	After radiation therapy-5% to 60%; adding chemotherapy improves survival.
III	Cancer has spread to the walls of the pelvis, the lower third of the vagina, or the ureters (connecting the kidney to the bladder).	After radiation therapy-30% to 35%; chemotherapy improves survival.

IV	Cancer has spread to distant organs	
IVA	Cancer has spread to organs nearer to the cervix, as the bladder and rectum.	With radiation therapy or more surgery-10% to 15%; adding chemotherapy increases survival rates.
IVB	Cancer has spread to more organs such as the lungs.	Following chemotherapy or radiation therapy—less than 10% (death can come within 1 year)

Reprinted with the permission of The Free Press, A Division of Simon and Schuster Inc. from Harvard Medical School Family Health Guide, Anthony L. Komaroff, M.D., Editor in Chief, Copyright 1999, 2005, by President and Fellows of Harvard College.

Warning signs: Abnormal vaginal bleeding, genital herpes, many sexual partners, early sex after puberty, tobacco use.

Other Kinds of Cancer

Endometrial cancer: Signs of this approach vaginal bleeding.
Risks: Failure to ovulate
Obesity
Diabetes
High Blood Pressure
Late menopause arrival
Gallbladder disease
Hereditary nonpolyposis colorectal cancer

Can be detected early due to bleeding in the postmenopausal period. Women should get biopsy each year after the mid 39's.

Oral cancer: Early recognition is seen from the change of color inside the mouth, a lump or thickness failing to heal. If you have a sore in your mouth that doesn't heal see a dentist or doctor.
Risks: Male and over 40
Chews tobacco

              Heavy smoker

              Alcoholic

Skin cancer: Appears as a small lesion with irregular border.

A bump from light colored to black anywhere on the skin, dark sores on the hands or feet or even the tips of the fingers, change in a mole, any sore that fails to heal.

        Risk factors: Fair skin

                   Red hair

                   Severe sunburn in childhood

                   Exposure to tar, pitch, creosote, coal or arsenic

                   Blue eyes

                   Family history of birthmarks or moles

If you have sores that relate to the risks listed above, check with your doctor.

Testicular cancer: Indications of trouble are if a lump is found on the testicles or a change in size or a sense of fullness.

        Risks: Hits younger men mainly before forty.

        An undescended testicle one or both

        Men in their late teens check with their doctor and also can examine themselves for any abnormalities.

Throat cancer: Problems with speaking clearly, hoarseness.

        Risks: Constant smokers

        Heavy smokers

        Need to have throat examined once each year, stop smoking and moderate the alcohol consumption.

Urinary tract and Bladder cancer: Indications of its presence blood in the urine, loss of weight, use of tobacco, history of urinary tract problems, age 50 or older, being male.

Regular urinalysis should be made each time you have your yearly examination or perhaps more often.

The estimated new cases for breast cancer (193,000) for 2007 places it in second place behind lung cancer. The estimated deaths for 2009 (NY Times Almanac, 2010) from breast cancer are 194,000 and ranks third behind colon/rectal cancer and lung cancer. The following is a list of the projected new cases and their deaths for 2007 by the American Cancer Society of top ten cancers.

CANCER	PROJECTED NEW CASES	PROJECTED DEATHS
Prostate	218,890	27,050
Lung and bronchus	213,380	180,380
Breast (Female and Male)	F 178,460 M 2,030	F 40,460 M 450
Colon and Rectal combined	213,380	160,390
Bladder	67,160	13,750
Leukemia (All)	44,240	21,790
Non-Hodgkin's Lymphoma	63,190	8,660
Melanoma	59,940	8,110
Kidney (Rental Cell)	43,512	10,857
Endometrial	38,080	7,400

Zollinger-Ellison, a rare type of cancer (tumor) occurs in one out of a quarter of a million people. It is caused by a tumor found in the pancreas or duodenum that creates excessive digestive acid. Information given by American Cancer Society, Atlanta, GA, Facts and Figures 2007. Major studies on this disease were conducted at the NIH in Bethesda, MD.

Of the cancers mentioned above following breast cancer three major types remain, which we will discuss, are: lung, prostate and colorectal.

LUNG CANCER

The information given here is taken from the American Institute for Cancer Research found in their publication Cancer Treatment Today 2007, Washington, DC.

There are four major types of lung cancer—Squamous cell carcinoma, Adenocarinoma, Large Cell Carcinoma and Small Cell Carcinoma. In Squamous Cell carcinoma a third of the cells of the lungs originate on the surface of the lining of the larger airway and are usually found in the central part of the lungs. In time they spread to the lymph glands near the lungs and then to other organs. Adenocarcinoma represents around 40% of the lung cancer cases often beginning in the smaller airways therefore on the outside edges of the lungs. It spreads to the lymph glands near the lung area where it begins to reach other organs. Large cell carcinoma to as little as 10% of the cases to as many as 40%, spread inside the lung before moving to other parts of the body. Finally the last major type, Small cell carcinoma represents about 20-30% of lung cancer cases and is found spreading to the other organs from the original cancer in the lung.

Symptoms and Prevention

Symptoms nearly always exhibit coughing, spitting, sometimes with blood lined phlegm and/or shortness of breath. Accompanied is sometimes raspy, somewhat incoherent speech, nausea, loss of appetite, pneumonia and in the advanced stages pain in the bones, mind disturbances, etc. If you smoke stop, if you don't do not start. If you stopped ten or fifteen years ago, this will stand you in good stead against being inflicted with it, at least the risk is considerably much less. Try to live in a smoke free environment. Your home you can control it! Get your home tested for radon that's important.

If your work place is dangerous with hazardous fumes, asbestos get protective gear and if you need be find other work. Asbestos causes an extremely fatal cancer called mesathelioma. This can develop 20 to 40 years after exposure to it. Recovery depends upon the size and location of the cancer.

Treatment

People with squamous large cell carcinoma or adenocarcinoma are subjects for surgery. The small cell type spread too fast and far too effectively to use surgery for it. The surgeon removes the tumor and the tissue around it. The usual type is called lobectomy in which the involved lobe is removed. A smaller or larger section may be removed or the entire lung may be removed, this is called a pneumonectomy. Along with this the lymph nodes that drain the related lung. Hospital stay is usually five to seven days' recovery or could take longer. Normal activity is possible for many people in four to five weeks or a little longer. Unfortunately few cancers of the lung are discovered before they have spread. Only around twenty-five percent at best can be operated on surgically. It is estimated that around 75% of those not identified early have five more years of life after treatment. After treatment if it recurs then chemotherapy or radiation may decrease the size of the tumor, extend life and reduce the pain.

Small cell carcinomas are typically treated through chemotherapy involving a group of anticancer drugs taken by mouth or intravenously. These drugs are made to reach the entire body to cut off the spread of cancers to places beyond the lungs. Improvements in these drugs have eliminated many bad side effects and are more effective than a few years ago. Radiation is sometimes used. High energy radiation is pointed at the tumor to hit cancer signs. It also assists in stopping bleeding and swallowing problems. Improvements in use of radiation have lowered the complications related to its application though it may still cause inflammation of the lung, scarring and lowering the capacity of the lung.

PROSTATE CANCER

The following information comes from the American Cancer Research Bulletin 2007 on the Prostate used with Permission, Washington, DC.

Next to lung cancer prostate cancer is the leading cause of death. Most prostate cancers grow very slowly. A man's risk of dying with prostate cancer is very low only around 3%. Many men, most in fact, will die of something else before they would of prostate cancer. Risk factors: include ages as early as 55-60 years in most situations. Race with African-Americans shows the highest rate of prostate cancer. Family members who have had prostate cancer confer the risk of ten times on a kinsman who is a close relative also suspect is high fat diet and tobacco and alcohol use.

Diagnosis

In the early stages of prostate cancer there are no symptoms unless it has spread. Cure chances are highly favorable like 95%. Four methods exist—the digital, the PSA, transrectal ultrasound and biopsy. The digital recommended annually for men over forty is done by the physician who uses his finger from a gloved hand, enters the rectum and circles the prostate to feel for nodules, irregularities and size, also the stool for blood presence and other abnormalities.

The other major source is the PSA exam. The PSA is a protein produced by the prostate most of which goes into the semen some however gets into the blood. Through this blood the amount of PSA is measured those with high levels are examined with the digital rectal (DRE) method to find if abnormalities exist.

The transrectal ultrasound is a method in which a probe the size of a finger is pushed into the rectum to check the prostate. It shoots high-energy sound waves off internal tissues making echoes. These echoes make a picture of a group of tissue called a sonogram. This may be used during a biopsy. A biopsy is a medical procedure whereupon a piece of body tissue is removed from the suspected area of disease and is then later viewed by a pathologist under a high-powered microscope. The pathologist checks for cancer cells to determine the Glesson scale. These scores range from 2-10 indicating the likelihood the tumor will spread. The lower the number the better the odds.

Recovery Possibilities Depend Upon:

- Age and health of the person involved.

- Stage of the cancer when discovered.

- Care given including nutrition.

- The time of diagnosis or recurrence.

- The location of the cancer when discovered.

- Gleason Score and PSA level.

If cancer is found in the prostate it usually cannot be found through digital rectal exams nor is it visible by imaging but located by accidentally surgery. This is Stage I. Stage II Cancer is more advanced but has not spread outside of the prostate gland and the Gleason score can be as low as 2 and as high as 10.

Stage III—The cancer has spread beyond the land's outer layer tissue and it may be found in the seminal vesicles.

Stage IV—Cancer has spread to the lymph nodes near or far from the prostate such as the rectum, bones, liver, bladder or lungs.

TREATMENT

1. Watchful waiting—monitoring closely the patient condition without giving any treatment until symptoms appear. This is used with older men with other medical problems.
2. Surgery—Patients in good health are offered several types of surgery: Pelvic lymphadenectomy involving removal of the prostate; then radical prostatectomy means removing the prostate by cutting through the abdominal wall and perhaps taking out close by lymph nodes. Another type called perineal prostatectomy is removal of the prostate through the perineum, area between the scrotum and the anus also taking out lymph nodes if necessary.
3.

Type 3 Transurethral Resection of the prostate—a surgical procedure using a resectoscope inserted through the urethra to remove tissue to relieve symptoms caused by the cancer before other surgery is done.

RADIATION THERAPY

This cancer treatment uses high energy x-rays or other types of radiation to kill cancer cells. Two types are used. One operates externally whereby a machine sends radiation toward the cancer. Internal radiation uses a substance sealed in seeds, needles, wires and catheters that are placed into or near the cancer. Which is used depends on the type of cancer being treated.

HORMONE THERAPY

This therapy removes the hormones or stops their action from growing. The hormones are produced by the patient's body. Some hormones cause cancers to grow these are countered by radiation, drugs or surgery. Hormones used in this type of therapy are as follows:

- Luteinizing hormone
- Antiandrogens
- Drugs—prevent the adrenal glands from producing androgens
- Orchiectomy - removal of the testicles
- Estrogen—not used often because of their serious side effects

NEW TREATMENTS BEING TESTED IN CLINICAL TRIALS

CRYOSURGERY

This is a treatment that utilizes freezing to destroy prostate cancer cells.

CHEMOTHERAPY

This therapy uses drugs to stop the growth of cancer by killing the cells or stop the dividing of them. When taken by mouth or through the veins or muscle it gets to the blood stream and reaches the cancer cells wherever they are. When the drug is placed in the abdomen or wherever it works on the cancer in that area. The manner in which the therapy is used depends upon the type and stage of the cancer being treated.

BIOLOGIC THERAPY

This is a treatment that uses the patient's immune system to counteract the cancer. Enzymes made by the body or in the laboratory are utilized to raise or restore the body's natural defense against cancer. This is called immunotherapy or biotherapy.

HIGH-INTENSITY FOCUSED ULTRASOUND

This treatment uses ultrasound (high-energy sound waves) to destroy cancer cells. To treat prostate cancer, an endorectal probe is used to make the sound waves.

Treatment Options For Recurrent Prostate Cancer
- Radiation therapy
- Prostatectomy for patients initially treated with radiation.
- Hormone Therapy
- Pain medication, external radiation therapy, internal radiation with radioisotopes such as stronium-89 or palliative therapy to lessen bone pain.
- A clinical trial of ultrasound of ultrasound-guided cryosurgery
- A clinical trial of chemotherapy or biological therapy

To learn more about prostate cancer call the National Cancer Institute 'NCF'Ss Cancer Information Service toll-free at 1-800-422-6237 Monday through Friday, 9:00 a.m. to 4:30 p.m. Deaf/Hard to Hear callers with TTY equipment call 1-800-332-8615. The NCL Web site provides online access information on cancer, clinical trials and other Web sites and organizations that offer support and resources for cancer patients and their families.

COLON CANCER
The following data is derived from the American Institute for Cancer Research publication Cancer Treatment Today: Colon Cancer, Washington, DC, 2007.

This cancer is a malignant disease (cancer) which forms in the tissues of the colon. The colon is part of the body's digestive system starting with the esophagus and continues through the stomach and the small and large intestines and ends in the rectum and finally the anal canal. Risk factors are affected by age and health history. They are:

- Age 50 and older.
- A family history of cancer of the colon or rectum.
- A personal history of the colon, ovary, endometrium or breast.
- A history of polyps in the colon.
- A history of ulcerative colties (ulcers in large intestines or Crohn's disease).
- Hereditary conditions as familial adenomatous polyposis and hereditary nonpolyposis colon cancer (Lynch Syndrome)

Signally noteworthy in watching for signs of colon cancer are change in bowel habits or blood in the stool. These and other symptoms may indicate problems which should send one to their doctor to report.

- Change in bowel movement.
- Blood in the stool whatever the color.
- Diarrhea, constipation or feeling the bowel doesn't empty completely.
- Stools that are narrower than usual.
- Frequent gas pains, bloating, fullness or cramps.
- Weight loss for no reason.
- Feeling very tired.
- Vomiting.
-

DIAGNOSIS

After reviewing the health history of the patient, the doctor can perform a number of physical exams to discover the possible size, location and extent of any tumor. Among them are these:

Fecal occult blood exam: A check of the stool for blood to see if cancer cells can be found.

Digital rectal exam: A insertion of a finger lubricated in the rectum to feel for lumps or anything unusual.

Barium enema: A series of x-rays are given covering the lower gastrointestinal tract. The white metallic compound substance is put into the rectum. It coats the tract and pictures are taken (x-rays) called a lower G.I.

Sigmoidoscopy: A procedure to look inside the rectum to search for polyps or cancer. The scope, a thin, lighted tube is inserted through the rectum into the sigmoid colon. Samples may be taken for biopsy.

Colonoscopy: A method for looking inside the colon and rectum for polyps, abnormal areas or cancer. The tube is a thin, lighted tube put through the rectum into the colon and may result in biopsy taken from polyps or tissue.

Virtual colonoscopy: The use of a series of x-rays known as computed tomography that makes a series of pictures of the colon. The pictures that are made create a detailed image that may show polyps and other abnormalities that are unusual inside the colon. This test is called colonography.

The chances of recovery depends on a number of factors principally age, health, location, spread of the cancer, recurrent. To determine spread Cat scan, MRI, Chest x-ray, complete blood count, CEA assay, lymph node biopsy, and surgery are used.

STAGES IN COLON CANCER

Stage 0 – Cancer is found in the innermost lining of the colon.

Stage I – Cancer has spread beyond the inner most layer of the colon wall to the middle layer often referred to as Duke's A Cancer.

Stage IIA – Cancer has spread to nearby tissues beyond the middle tissues around the colon or rectum.

Stage B – Spread has occurred to nearby organs and or through the peritoneum. This stage is often called Dukes' colon cancer.

Stage IIIA – Cancer has spread to as many as three lymph nodes.

Stage IIIB – Cancer has spread to nearby organs, at least three lymph nodes and nearby organs.

Stage C – Cancer has spread to four lymph nodes and all the other places previously mentioned above, colon, rectum, and peritoneum.

Stage IV – Cancer has spread to nearby lymph nodes and to other parts of the body such as the liver or lungs.

TREATMENT FOR COLON CANCER

Local Excision – Cancer found in the early stages may be removed by a tube inserted into the colon and cutting the cancer out.

Resection – If the cancer is larger, a partial colectomy is performed removing the cancer and a small amount of healthy tissue around the cancer and also some lymph nodes and examine them for signs of cancer.

Resection and colonstomy – If the two ends of the colon cannot be attached a stoma-opening will be made on the outside of the body to drain the waste which is collected by a bog. When the lower colon has healed the colonstomy is not needed but if the entire lower colon is removed the colonstomy will be permanent.

Radio frequency ablation – Special probes with tiny electrodes that kill cancer cells are inserted directly through the skin and only local anesthesia is needed.

Cryosurgery –An instrument is used to freeze abnormal tissue as carcinoma in situ, this treatment is called cryotherapy.

CHEMOTHERAPHY

This treatment uses drugs to kill cancer cells or stopping for cells from dividing. When the drugs are placed in the veins, muscles, or taken by mouth, this is known as systematic chemotherapy. When placed directly into the spinal column, an organ or body cavity like the stomach the drugs affect cancer cells in those areas is called regional chemotherapy. Chemoembolization of the hepatic artery may be used to treat cancer spread to the liver by blocking the hepatic artery and injecting anticancer drugs between the blocked artery and the liver. The liver arteries then deliver the drugs throughout the liver. Only a little of the drug reaches the other parts of the body. The blockage may be permanent or not depending on the drugs used. The liver will receive some blood from the hepatic portal vein, which carries blood from the stomach and intestine.

RADIATION THERAPY

This therapy uses high-energy x-rays or other radiation types to kill cancer cells. Two types exist—External Radiation: this type uses a machine outside the body to send radiation to the cancer. Internal Radiation—this type uses a radioactive substance sealed in needles, seeds, wires or catheters that are placed directly into or near the cancer. The therapy given depends on the type and stage of the cancer being treated.

CLINICAL TRIALS

Biologic Therapy—These trials often the forerunners of standard treatment make use of the patient's immune system. Substances made by the body or laboratory are used to boost, direct or restore the body's natural defense against cancer. This type of treatment is also called biotherapy or immunotherapy. Follow-up exams after treatment using blood tests to measure carcinoembryonic antigen (CEA) that may increase when colon cancer is present finding the cancer earlier. For information on clinical trials or cancer contact NCI Web site. Many clinical groups are looking for volunteers—they usually pay expenses, travel, lodging and treatment so don't hesitate to call!

Mayo Clinic announced in their Breakthrough Bulletin (2007) seven significant steps forward toward winning the battle against cancer.

1. Their clinic researchers have enhanced safety and effectiveness of therapeutic virus that fights cancer.
2. Their clinic provides new recommendations for the use of biophosphonates in the treatment of multiple myeloma.
3. That two-faced protein can stop metastasis or promote it, their researchers say.
4. Their researchers discover protein as potential target for preventing tumors.
5. Mayo Clinic Cancer Center is harnessing the measles virus to attack cancer.
6. A Mayo study reports normal aging process linked to lower breast cancer risk.

7. Fresh use of targeted therapy advances treatment of early
    HER2-positive breast cancer.

Emphysema and (COPD) Chronic Bronchitis Chronic Obstructive Pulmonary Disease
Data from the National Institute of Health: Heart, Blood and Lung Institute, Bethesda, MD, 2007.

Another common disease afflicting the middle age population is emphysema. Its victim is most commonly men over 40. Women and young people may also suffer from this respiratory ailment sometimes as an after effect of infections. Unfortunately, since women are increasingly taking up smoking, and smoking has been identified as the major cause of obstructive pulmonary disease they are highly vulnerable. Physicians estimate that there are 5 million Americans with emphysema or bronchitis. Bronchitis is hard to distinguish from emphysema but is marked by excessive mucus in the lungs and air passages. Emphysema progressively cuts off the exchange of oxygen for carbon dioxide by killing air cells little by little, making the chest muscles work harder to try to make up the deficiency. Without oxygen the muscles do not function properly. Thus the disease has a cyclical effect. The symptoms are shortness of breath, a difficulty in breathing or a winded feeling. Chronic bronchitis has the same symptoms.

Our breathing apparatus is constructed in the form of a bush with branches, positioned upside down in the chest. The main tube, the "windpipe" or trachea, is the trunk of the bush; it leads air from the nose and mouth down into the chest. There the trunk divides into two chief branches, the bronchi (a single one is a bronchus). These go right and left into the two tissue sacs that are the lungs. Within the lungs each bronchus branches out as smaller and ever more numerous bronchi. The smaller of these are bronchioles.

Each bronchiole ends in a tiny structure that looks much like a cauliflower, made up of very small air sacs, or alveoli. There are estimated to be 750 million of them. The alveoli are the destination of the indrawn air, and it is in them that the work of the lungs is done. Small blood vessels near the surface take the oxygen into the blood cells by osmosis. If inhaling of air and exhaling through the bronchi is not coordinated so air gets smoothly in and out, air is strapped in the bronchiole eventually breaking down the alveolar walls. What follows is the increasing inability to get oxygen in the body.

The exact causes of emphysema are not known. It is thought that it may result from the accumulated effect of all the lung ailments we have managed to live through as well as the polluted air we have breathed. Cigarette smoking is the most important cause. An inborn tendency making one more susceptible for damage if discovered may help to determine those who are most likely to contract the disease. Environmental pollutants, like excessive acids and corrosive materials in smoke, asbestos fibers from the brake lining of cars, excessive dust and particles in the atmosphere are suspect when we are constantly breathing this type of air. My mother died of this disease after a fifteen-year bout. She never smoked but did live in an industrial town where the air was polluted. She ran a tourist home where she was exposed to considerable secondhand cigarette smoke from the many guests. At times she was also under considerable stress. You should limit air pollutants in your home, use medication like corticosteroids, and learn diaphragmatic breathing techniques to clear the lungs of phlegm.

Suggestions for prevention are: prompt attention to infections of the eye, ear, nose, throat and chest, no smoking and try to escape air pollution. Early detection is most important since doctors are unable to reverse the damage already caused.

Diabetes

The likelihood of becoming diabetic increases with age. Millions of Americans who have diabetes don't know it—although it is one of the most common diseases affecting an estimated 25 million people. According to Dr. Michael Lyon. M.D. the Director of the North American Diabetes Prevention and Research Institute diabetes is not a new disease but only an epidemic in the 21st century - calling it a modern-life problem. Diabetes is fairly easy to detect and if found in early stages, can be controlled but that requires understanding the problem and willing to follow a regimen. With the growing universal problem with overweight (one of two in the adult population) it is crucial that we take note of it. The body handles sugar less well as one gets older.

Diabetes is a condition in which the body can no longer make use of sugar in a normal way. Glucose accumulates in the blood (high blood sugar) making the kidneys work overtime to expel this wasted sugar from the body. Long time inability to handle sugar leads to destruction of renal tissue (kidneys); it can lead to heart attacks and contributes to retinopathy, neuropathy, nephropathy, autoimmune disorders, bacterial infections, and atherosclerosis. Symptoms include: excessive thirst, excessive urination, hunger, loss of weight, easy tiring, slow healing of cuts and bruises, changes in vision, intense itching, pain in fingers and toes and drowsiness.

TYPE I Diabetes (known as Insulin-dependent diabetes) begins in children or young adults. None of the insulin-producing cells functions properly. Daily insulin injections are necessary for the diabetic to stay alive.

TYPE II Diabetes (known as Non-Insulin dependent diabetes) has its onset in adults when some insulin-producing cells stop functioning. This type of diabetes can be controlled with diet and oral medication. About 90 percent of all diabetes is Type II.

Symptoms of Diabetes

- Increased urination
- Loss of appetite
- Breath smells fruity and sweet
- Weakness
- Drowsiness
- Nausea
- Abdominal pain
- Weight loss
- Confusion
- Rapid breathing

Treatment of Diabetes

Major medical health clinics (such as Mayo, NIH, and Harvard) agree in general on the following treatment options. The main factor in treating diabetes is in your hands. Several health care professionals may also be involved. First the individual must monitor their blood sugar level (their physician, nurse or an endocrinologist's nurse will instruct them). Secondly, you must eat a healthy diet. Thirdly, stay active—exercise. Fourthly, maintain healthy weight. Fifthly, take medicine as prescribed and finally have regular medical checkups. The word sugar when related to diabetes is similar to glucose and the word glycemic.

Diabetics typically are treated with diet (low carbohydrates, high mineral-vegetable food) calorie reducing diet programs (typically 1800-2500 calories per day depending upon the person). Accompanying this is the use of insulin particularly for those diabetes prone to ketosis (a poisonous substance where the body uses fat for a substitute for glucose to provide energy) and had its onset in youth (Type I Diabetes). For the older diabetic who are ketoacidotic, weight reduction (also for Type II—adult onset) exercise, both very important, and insulin are used when patients cannot control their weight or diet according to the Mayo Family Health Book 2003.

Insulin should be used for all Type I (Insulin Dependent Mellitus) persons, for those actively ill, the pregnant, those under stress from surgery infection or use of cortisone-like drugs and the symptomatically diabetic with fasting hyperglycemia of over 300 mg per dl. Medicine for increasing production of insulin by the pancreas are the Sulfonylureas Glipizide and Glimperide are about 65% effective with Type II diabetes.

Oral Medications:

- Those that stimulate the pancreas to produce more insulin.

    Amaryl   Glyburide   Glipizide

    Diabrinace   Micronase   Tolbutamide

- Those that cause rapid but short-term release of insulin by your pancreas.
  Prandin

- Those that improve the body's response to insulin by decreasing insulin resistance.
  Glucophage

- Those that delay the digestion of carbohydrates slowing the rise of blood sugar after a meal.
  Precose   Glyset

- Those that reduce resistance to insulin.
  Actos   Avandia (currently under investigation for serious side effects)

The use of sugar of various kinds (lactose, milk, fructose—fruit, galactose—milk component, sucrose—any sugar) relate in some way to hyperglycemia and hypoglycemia (hyper-over hypo-under). The former, too much sugar in the blood; the latter, too little. As a method of handling the high and low sugar problems, diet for weight reduction is a prime importance. Typically for the low sugar blood problems, a diet of high-protein and low carbohydrate is indicated with complex sugars some fruit (like dates or raisins) plus frequent feedings five to six times a day to maintain an adequate blood sugar level. Mealtime schedules must be strictly maintained for these people. For a suggestive diet plan, ask your physician or request literature on this form your public health agency.

Treatment includes proper diet, insulin and exercise. There is a high tolerance in the body for glucose where exercise is taken regularly and vigorously. Care should not be sporadic and left to chance and it must be done in coordination with other remedies. With today's treatment methods, diabetes may be controlled and the diabetic may lead a normal life but it continues to be the fifth leading cause of death by disease. For uncontrolled diabetes, one can forecast eye problems leading to blindness and kidney problems leading to kidney failure and hardening of the arteries and other problems like neuropathy, retinopathy and scarface ulcers. Therefore it is important to recognize its symptoms early and seek medical treatment.

OBESITY

America's #1 health problem is being overweight or obese. Obesity has been defined as a disease and as a major cause of physical problems in middle age. Estimates are that about 65% of adults in America are overweight. The American Diabetes Association estimates that 57 million Americans are pre-diabetic! The main cause is over-eating and under-exercising with metabolic disorders accounting for only one or two out of every 100 overweight persons. Diabetes and heart problems and strokes are close friends of overweight adults.

The causes for over-eating are varied ranging from (1) family habits, (2) economic and cultural factors, (3) pregnancy, to (4) psychological factors including tension, anxiety, depression and frustration. Studies have shown 9 out of 10 persons over-eat when they are nervous, worried, or idle. The side effects of being overweight range from heart disease and hypertension to hardening of the arteries; from diabetes to osteoarthritis (breakdown of the lower spine, hips and knees).

If a middle-aged person is 10 pounds overweight the danger of death is increased by 8%; a 20 pounds it rises 18%; at 30 pounds to 28%, and at 50 pounds 56%. Hypertension, circulation problems and diabetes are all possibilities for those exceeding 20 pounds. Prevention is the best approach to obesity. Treatment, of course, is to follow medical advice to reducing safely. For those slightly over the norm a routine of daily vigorous exercise should be initiated (running, tennis, swimming, weight lifting, brisk walking exercise routines, body bends, etc.). Sharply curtailing fats, starches and sugars in our food selection is indicated. It is not recommended that you diet by using patent medicines, pills or any other kind of drug on your own. Smoking is a dangerous and unreliable substitute for long-term weight reduction. A general estimate of your weight class follows; how does your weight fit? A discussion of food and the balanced diet is dealt with under preventive medicine.

BODY MASS INDEX

To estimate body mass index (BMI), identify your weight (to the nearest 10 pounds) in columns across the top. Then go down the column until you come to the row that represents your height. Inside the square where your weight and height intersect is a number that estimates your BMI. If you weigh 170 pounds and are 5'8" your BMI is 26. You are overweight slightly, of course, muscle weighs more than fat and you may be healthy with this BMI.

BMI INTERPRETATION

Underweight	Under 18.5
Normal	18.5-24
Overweight	25-29
Obese	30 and over

HEIGHT	100	110	120	130	140	150	160	170	180	190	200	210	220	230	240	250
5'0"	20	21	23	25	27	29	31	33	35	37	39	41	43	45	47	49
5'1"	19	21	23	25	26	28	30	32	34	36	38	40	42	43	45	47
5'2"	18	20	22	24	26	27	29	31	33	35	37	38	40	42	44	46
5'3"	18	19	21	23	25	27	28	30	32	34	35	37	39	41	43	44
5'4"	17	19	21	22	24	26	27	29	31	33	34	36	38	39	41	43
5'5"	17	18	20	22	23	25	27	28	30	32	33	35	37	38	40	42
5'6"	16	18	19	21	23	24	26	27	29	31	32	34	36	37	39	40
5'7"	16	17	19	20	22	23	25	27	28	30	31	33	34	36	38	39
5'8"	15	17	18	20	21	23	24	26	27	29	30	32	33	35	36	38
5'9"	15	16	18	19	21	22	24	25	27	28	30	31	32	34	35	37
5'10"	14	16	17	19	20	22	23	24	26	27	29	30	32	33	34	36

Height																
5'11"	35	33	32	31	29	28	26	25	24	22	21	20	18	17	15	14
6'0"	34	33	31	30	28	27	26	24	23	22	20	19	18	16	15	14
6'1"	33	32	30	29	27	26	25	24	22	21	20	18	17	16	15	13
6'2"	32	31	30	28	27	26	24	23	22	21	19	18	17	15	14	13
6'3"	31	30	29	27	26	25	24	22	21	20	19	17	16	15	14	12
6'4"	30	29	28	27	26	24	23	22	21	19	18	17	16	15	13	12

Problems associated with being overweight are legion such as, those overweight by 40% are twice as likely to die prematurely as those of normal weight; raises the rate of getting Type II diabetes and heart problems—high blood pressure, stroke and certain kinds of cancer. In men overweight prostate cancer is a threat, in women breast and uterine cancer. Both women and men are likely to develop colon and rectal cancer, also gallbladder diseases and gallstones, osteoarthritis and gout. In addition there are also psychological and emotional maladies in a culture that equates slimness with attractiveness. Those obese persons may run up against bias and job discrimination. Treatment for overweight usually involves diet, exercise, behavior modification, perhaps medicine, and in a few cases surgery. The overweight and obese must eat fewer calories than they burn: exercise can reduce weight also provides the strengthening of the heart:

1. Better cholesterol level LDL (harmful type) can be reduced while the HDL (good) is increased.
2. Stronger lungs help to use oxygen more effectively and ups the breathing capacity.
3. Makes for strengthened bones and muscles particularly for women at menopause and afterwards when lowering levels of estrogen can contribute to osteoporosis.
4. Lower blood pressure thereby reduces risks for stroke and heart disease.
5. Provides protection against cancer B reduces time passage of waste through the colon and may help against breast cancer and endometrial (abdomen) cancer.
6. Protection against diabetes — and reduces the long term risks and associated problems of neuropathy, eye and kidney failure.
7. Reduces appetite — true some exercise increases the desire for food but sustained regular exercise at a sustained clip takes away appetite in the long run—it also reduces sugar (glucose) levels and weight and makes for better circulation.

A Healthy Diet

1. Eat a variety of foods to get energy, vitamins, protein, minerals and fiber.
2. Keep a healthy weight. Look at the charts presented in this section.
3. Use a diet of low saturated, trans-unsaturated fats, and cholesterol.
4. Choose a diet with plenty of vegetables and fruits that provide complex carbohydrates, minerals, vitamins, and fiber.
5. Use a small amount of sugar.
6. Use a small amount of sugar.
7. Use salt (sodium) sparingly.
8. Drink alcoholic drinks limited to 1 or 2 drinks that amount has a salutary effect on atherosclerosis (hardening of the arteries). No alcohol if pregnant.
9. Eat no more than 4 ounces of lean meat—poultry with the skin off and fish (one or no more than twice a week). Including fish several times a week is a good antioxidant.
10. Check your glucose every day with a meter that gives a cumulation mean (average) of daily takings over several months. This will be fairly similar to the AIC tests taken by your physician.

One should eat at least as much vegetables and fruits as the grain, bread, pasta (basically carbohydrates), carrots, beets, corn, potatoes have considerable amounts of carbohydrates in them for those turn quickly into sugar. The 50% to 60% of a daily diet (recommended by some diets) is too much carbohydrates (sugar to add to your diet). Wheat bread is better than white. Eat no sugared cereals but choose from 100% wheat from those with low sugar (seen on the nutrition facts found on food product labels) and saturated fats. If you are 40 to 45 years old, you should also take a multivitamin supplement. Many studies have shown the importance of multivitamins containing additional Vitamin C and if you are over 50 , Silver Centrum multi-mineral vitamins or the equivalent are recommended.

As we talk about diet keep in mind that according to the experts (Dr. Murray, and Dr. Lyon) 80% to 90% of individuals with Type II diabetes are overweight

The following Food Pyramid shows the proper balance of foods to consume on a daily basis to maintain the most healthy diet.

Anatomy of MyPyramid

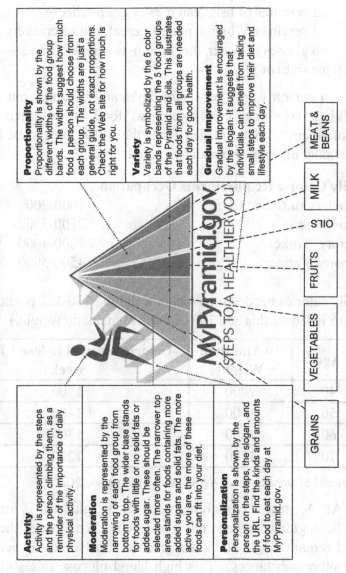

Proportionality
Proportionality is shown by the different widths of the food group bands. The widths suggest how much food a person should choose from each group. The widths are just a general guide, not exact proportions. Check the Web site for how much is right for you.

Variety
Variety is symbolized by the 6 color bands representing the 5 food groups of the Pyramid and oils. This illustrates that foods from all groups are needed each day for good health.

Gradual Improvement
Gradual improvement is encouraged by the slogan. It suggests that individuals can benefit from taking small steps to improve their diet and lifestyle each day.

Activity
Activity is represented by the steps and the person climbing them, as a reminder of the importance of daily physical activity.

Moderation
Moderation is represented by the narrowing of each food group from bottom to top. The wider base stands for foods with little or no solid fats or added sugar. These should be selected more often. The narrower top area stands for foods containing more added sugars and solid fats. The more active you are, the more of these foods can fit into your diet.

Personalization
Personalization is shown by the person on the steps, the slogan, and the URL. Find the kinds and amounts of food to eat each day at MyPyramid.gov.

MyPyramid.gov
STEPS TO A HEALTHIER YOU

GRAINS VEGETABLES FRUITS OILS MILK MEAT & BEANS

Suggested Daily Diet for the Boomer

2 servings of fresh fruit or fruit juice
2 servings of green or yellow vegetables
2 servings of fish, lean meat, eggs or cheese
3 servings of bread, potato, cereal, roll or crackers (6-8)
6 glasses of water, diet or non-sweetened drinks—coffee
(caffeine free) or tea.

If a person works very hard physically by doing much lifting, walking, climbing, etc., additional food is indicated. Calorie requirements can be judged from the following tables; however, individual differences should be noted.

Daily Caloric Requirements Occupation

Secretary or Office Clerk	1000-2000
Housewife	2500-3000
Factory Worker	3000-4000
Laborer, Farmer	4500-5000

Daily calories needed for Women weighing 130-132 pounds. (If 10-15 lbs. over this add 100 calories to maintain weight.)

Age	To Maintain Weight	Calories needed to lose 1 lb. per week
40	2000	1500
50	1900	1400
60	1800	1300
70	1700	1200

Source: U.S. Department of Agriculture, Washington, DC, 2007

An A_{1C} test reveals how much sugar (glucose) is attached to the hemoglobin in your red blood cells. The longer the glucose level remains high, the more glucose attaches to the hemoglobin and other substances. This high blood glucose raises the risk of complications (cataracts, hardening of the arteries, heart problems, stroke and kidney diseases).

How blood glucose can affect A₁c¹

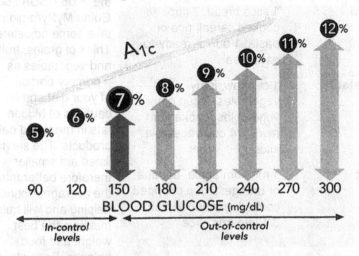

A fasting blood glucose test shows how you're doing during that period of the day. An A_{1c} test shows where your blood sugar level has been over the past two months.

National Institutes of Health (Heart, Blood and Lung Institute) Bethesda, MD 2007

Food Choices and Helping Sizes

FOOD GROUP	ONE SERVICE SIZE
Grain	1 slice bread; 2 cup cooked cereal, rice or pasta; 1 ounce ready-to-eat cereal
Vegetable	1 cup raw, leafy vegetables; 2 cup other vegetables (cooked or raw); 3/4 cup vegetable juice
Fruit	1 medium apple, banana, or orange; 2 cup chopped, cooked, or canned fruit; 3/4 cup fruit juice
Meat	2-3 ounces cooked lean meat, poultry, or fish (1 egg or 2 tablespoons peanut butter counts as 1 ounce of meat); 2 cup cooked dry beans
Dairy	1 cup milk or yogurt; 12 ounces cheese; 2 ounces processed cheese

Eating according to the 2005 USDA Food Guide MyPyramid may take some adjustment. Think of grains, fruits, and vegetables as a primary portion of your diet and be cautious of hidden fats in meat and dairy products. The servings listed are smaller therefore better than the average American helping and will help maintain the best weight and food balance. Eating less is better.

Types of Fat

Different kinds of dietary fats are shown below. Some are better for your health than others. Fats you eat should be in the main food categories.

DIETARY FAT	USED FOR	INGREDIENTS	
Polyunsaturated fat	Needed by the body to help form the membranes covering every cell	Natural vegetable oils; soft (tub) margarine	**GENERALLY GOOD FOR YOU**
Monounsaturated fat	Needed by the body to help form the membranes covering every cell	Natural vegetable oils; soft (tub) margarine	
Omega-3	Protective against coronary heart disease.	Fish and marine foods	
Saturated fat	Raises blood cholesterol and increased heart disease if eaten in large quantities	Animal fats (fatty meats, butter, whole milk, chicken skin)	
Cholesterol	Plax accumulates on carotid arteries cause strokes if excessive	Animal fats	**WORKS AGAINST YOU**
Transunsaturated fat	A type of unsaturated fat that has recently been found to be probably harmful	Animal fats; stick (hard) margarine	

U.S. Department of Agriculture, Washington, DC, 2007

83

Daily Calories for Boomer Men Weighing 160-165 pounds:

Age	To Maintain Weight	Calories needed to lose 1 lb. per week
30	3000	2500
40	2900	2400
50	2500	2000
60	1800	1300

Source: U.S. Department of Agriculture, Washington, DC, 2007

Recommended Practices for Boomer Health Protection

1. Vaccination against Influenza and Pneumonia for foreign travel. This is particularly needed where one has a chronic health problem such as diabetes or bronchitis. A variety of shots are needed for those going to equatorial regions and other countries depending on the purpose of your travel and the length of your stay.
2. Immune globulin injections for those contacting persons with hepatitis.
3. Wearing of seat belts when driving particularly when driving on the open road at considerable speed. Automobile accidents are a major cause of death.
4. Periodic Tuberculosis testing or chest X-rays to identify contact with this disease in time to reduce its ulterior effects on the body.
5. Periodic Pap testing and breast examination are a must as early warning is the best protection against the possible ravages of cancer. A suggested schedule for mammograms is as follows:

- At no extra risk for breast cancer:

- Baseline at age 35; then again at 40. Followed by every 2-3 years up to age 50, then once every year starting at 51.
- At risk for breast cancer:

  - Baseline at 25-30; then every 2-3 years until 40 and yearly from then on.

6. Heart Disease: A program approved by Massachusetts General Hospital and others indicates that to help prevent heart disease, cancer, and stroke one should:
   - Be a non-smoker
   - Have a cholesterol level of below 200 mg/dl
   - Less than 20% of daily calories to be from fat
   - Have blood pressure less than 130 mm Hg systolic and 80 mm Hg diastolic
   - Exercise vigorously for 20 to 30 minutes 5 to 6 times a week.
   - Minimize exposure to environmental or occupational toxic substances.

7. Avoidance of noxious fumes—acids, gas, etc., and other air impurities such as smog, smoke, dust, asbestos, coal dust, etc. Your home should have carbon monoxide detectors and fire detectors.

8. Avoidance of foods which have been labeled carcinogenic—such as cyclamates, betel nuts, smoked fish and meats.

9. Avoid taking laxatives habitually as these can lead to rectal problems. A proper diet including plenty of fruits, fibrous foods as cereal, lettuce, celery, etc., liquids (mainly water in quantity) and vigorous exercise will usually suffice to allow avoidance of medicines which in time get the body out of its natural rhythm.

10. Avoid taking pills on your own advice. No drug should be taken even aspirin for a long period of time without consultation with the physician. You are usually just treating the symptoms. The use of analgesics (painkillers—Demerol, Meperidine or Codeine) have

the potential to cause dizziness, abdominal distress, nausea and impaired consciousness. Anti-depressants like Siequan, Tofranil and Vivactil can work wonders but should be administered by the physician. The sedatives like Phenobarbital, Amobarbital, Membutal and Butisol are agents which reduce anxiety and promote sleep but over-dosage is a constant threat particularly when allied with alcohol. The diet pills (as Dexedrine, Tenutate) are also contra-indicated without the doctor's advice. For information on pill taking conditions and generic drugs check with your doctor. Beware the use of illegal drugs and alcohol for depression, etc. These can kill.

11. Have a regular routine of exercise. To be in good physical condition by keeping your weight down, burning up excess calories and possessing good muscle tone, one must work the body, exercise and stretch the muscles. Get the heart beat up (typically 150 beats per minute for the 40-year-old, fewer for those over 50 to 60). The routine you use can be jogging, tennis, brisk walking calisthenics, swimming or whatever puts some strain on the system. Remember, build up the pace of exercise gradually and only after you have conferred with your physician. As an idea of how many calories are burned per minute of activity, consider the following:

> Mopping the floor 5.3 cal/min
> Chopping wood 4.9 cal/min
> Brisk walking 6.0 cal/min
> Shoveling snow 9.0 cal/min

Dr. Kenneth Power, Chief Behavioral Epidemiology, Division of Health Education says exercise benefits prevention and control of hypertension, osteoporosis, diabetes and certain psychiatric and psychological conditions. Even low level physical activity, he says, reduces the risk of coronary heart disease. It is believed that no more than 20% of Americans participate in a physical fitness activity.

Best Medical Care

The rule based on evidence from the American Journal of Medicine, Journal of Urology and Northwestern Medical School states that those hospitals that do procedures in greater numbers such as coronary bypass, angioplasty, carotid (endutectomy), pediatric heart surgery, prostate surgery, abdominal aortic aneurysm repair, mastectomy, major liver surgery and pancreatic cancer surgery provide less risk of death.

Beyond this, to get the best care one has to be aggressive. Insurance companies cover hospital care but they sometimes will "cut deals" to minimize administrative costs (discount/with certain hospitals when doctors agree to send their patients to specific hospitals). You may have to fight your insurance company by enlisting the aid of medical staff in the hospital where you want to be treated. Also, your own doctor can look into top hospitals who have physician-to-physician referral lines. Your physician might help you find a specialist at Mayo Clinic, Johns Hopkins, UCLA Medical Center, Los Angeles, to list a few examples. You can get information on choosing the right care—quality care through the Web page www.healthfinder. org. The latter provides information on how to get managed care to work on your behalf.

Outstanding hospitals and medical centers are important because they are usually at the cutting edge of advance knowledge in studying major diseases and investigating rare and potential devastating ones. The National Institutes of Health funded by the U.S. government is thought by many to be its best investment. Its purpose is to discover cures for diseases, find ways to mitigate suffering, and short circuit progressive maladies.

In the early sixties a new rare disease known as Zollinger-Ellison (Z-E) was identified – a genetic defect affecting one in a quarter million people. The NIH organized a protocol to study it through its Endocrinology Department. In the next 30 years they learned what was needed to treat it and control it. Some Medical Centers early on such as Mayo Clinic and Duke Medical Center began to study it also. Z-E was not contagious but deadly if not treated. This is an example of what the superior hospital and centers do. There are many of these.

When patients are in need their doctors or specialists can identify a suitable hospital relative to the special and effective care needed. Most folks may know of major hospitals like John Hopkins which is noted for Eye, Nose and Throat, Heart, and Cancer. They may know of Mayo Clinic for Heart, Rheumatology, Neurology, Hormonal and Heart Specialties. They are also building a large center equal to their Rochester, MN in Jacksonville, FL. Most doctors know about the University of Texas Cancer Center, the MD Anderson in Houston. Duke Medical Center is also well know. The late Senator Kennedy went there for a brain operation. Massachusetts General is another hospital with a fine reputation also the National Jewish Center in Denver. There are many lesser known that are competent and even great centers for various specialties which doctors and certainly specialists can recommend when needed.

There are many fine hospitals looking for patient volunteers. Many of these centers offer clinical trials or protocols for the purpose of research and study of disease. This is usually handled on an outpatient basis although some bring you into the hospital, clinic or center for a week or so each year for complete check-ups, etc. There are usually no costs associated with these arrangements. Your physician can locate one of the places for you. Typically documentation is required which the physician can assist you, also in-services, may be over the phone. These trials frequently provide funds for travel, food, lodging for a night or two awaiting admission and provide medicine incident to your malady. Kinds of trials are varied but include diabetes, neurological illnesses, cancer, AIDS, and other problems. For example, Bristol-Myers Squibb sponsors a clinical study if you are a Type II diabetic (uncontrolled through a medicine), call 877-897-2025. The National Institute of Health, Bethesda, MD (U.S. government controlled) offers two ways to find out about trials through the patient recruitment line and Public Liaison Office, call 800-411-1222 or go to http://www.cc.nih.gov.

•

Women's Health Care Pre and Post Menopausal

Information from the National Institutes of Health, Bethesda, MD 2007.

Hormone replacement therapy (HRT) in some form has been available for almost 50 years since it became apparent that many menopausal symptoms were due to failing estrogen production. HRT is the artificial introduction of estrogen to compensate for the body's falling production levels. In this way, many of the symptoms of menopause can be alleviated. Despite some on-going concerns over side-effects, HRT can be extremely effective for many women, but only after careful attention to your medical and family history, route of administration and dosage. In this way it is usually possible to achieve optimal hormone replacement quickly and without safety concerns or side effects.

As researcher Marcelle Pick, WIS, 2007 points out, while we agree that women should consider alternatives to synthetic HRT, most of the fear and confusion is unnecessary.

First, note that the majority of studies published to date have concerned synthetic HRT, specifically Premarin and Prempro. Very few have involved or say anything about *bio-identical hormone replacement therapy.*

Second, the women in the Women's Health Institute (WHI) studies were on HRT after menopause, which is most often unnecessary therapeutically and obviously unnatural. The most common therapeutic use of HRT is for perimenopausal symptoms. So we can't say the WHI studies really predict the health risks for women in their 50's who are the typical users of synthetic HRT.

Third, there clearly are women who want HRT – even synthetic HRT. We believe they are entitled to make that choice for themselves.

Study after studies reveal that women using HRT run a higher risk of acquiring breast cancer, heart attack, stroke, blood clots and dementia. The overall benefits must be considered whenever making a decision to take HRT. The first consideration should include an in-depth review your family history before making a choice.

Studies are under way to evaluate alternate methods for hormone delivery, low-dose hormone therapy, and selective estrogen receptor modulators (SERMS) in reducing cardiovascular risks in perimenopausal and postmenopausal women. Implications for clinical nursing practice include education as well as assessment and counseling related to individual risk factors. Gerontology Nursing (2007, Mayo). There are few fields in which approaches to therapy are changing so rapidly and controversy is so rampant as in the field of menopause and its treatment.

MENOPAUSE

In the life of women, prior to menopause, the menstrual cycle sets the rhythm of daily activities. It influences her work life, her entertainment, her mood sometimes and colors many other things such as sex, etc. Beginning with onset of menopause (the average American woman begins at age 48-51) may begin for many at 45 and extending to 60, the ovaries secrete fewer hormones, gradually ceasing altogether. Menopause is defined as 12 months in succession without a period. The climacteric (from the Greek meaning rung in a ladder, which relates to a stage in development) is the period encompassing menopause and the average time in 5 years from the time ovaries start to decrease follicle development (estrogen is produced in the ovary follicle) to the time a woman has passed through menopause and her body has adjusted to the change in hormones. The circulating levels of estrogen and progesterone hormones dwindle and the body registers this fact. The menstrual flow diminishes becoming of less duration, lighter in color and the periods come further apart until it's over. For many women this is all there is, but for others irregular periods of heavy bleeding accompanies the menstruation. It can lead, if prolonged, to anemia. This is not normal, although irregularity is characteristic of menopause. Heavy bleeding carries the threat of uterine cancer or provides evidence to the physician to investigate of samples of tissue from the lining of the uterus gained by D & C surgical procedure (dilation and curettage) and from which one of the diagnosis can be fibroid tumor (non-cancerous) as seen in the illustration shown later. Sometimes a tumor, polyp or cyst can be removed without taking out the uterus. The decision to remove the uterus, etc., should be made in consultation with the gynecologists and your personal physician.

Menopause - Scenario

Women experience menopause in different ways. Your body is influenced by your general health, nutrition, stress level, exercise routine, heredity, and life style.

The following chart lists the most common symptoms. Most women do not experience all of them and many women experience only a few.

WHEN	SYMPTOM	DESCRIPTION
Menopause beginning	Irregular periods	Menstrual cycle shortens and is irregular, you may still be fertile.
Menopause	Hot flashes	Dramatic changes in body temperature that could begin several years before periods stop.
	Insomnia/night sweats	Sleep problems, possibly caused by nighttime hot flashes.
Post-Menopause	Vaginal dryness; urinary irritation or incontinence	Thinning of the vaginal wall and bladder, along with decreased vaginal secretions, can cause vaginal dryness, pain during intercourse, also risk of vaginal or urinary tract infections, and urinary incontinence.
	Sexual problems	Loss of libido due to low testosterone (produced by the ovary before menopause) levels but can result in vaginal irritation because of vaginal dryness.
	Mood changes	Irritability, anxiety, stress, and depression are not caused by lower estrogen levels, but may occur as a result of disturbed sleep.
Long-term	Bone loss	Bones become more porous, with risk of breaking a bone.
	Heart disease	Blood vessels are less flexible and cholesterol levels rise, causing the risk of having a heart attack.

Source: National Institutes of Health, Bethesda, MD - 2007

After Menopause – Scenario

Revitalization (Hormones and Replacement Therapy) for Sex Glands

Outside of recognizable disease affecting the major ductless glands (endocrine glands composed of the pituitary, sex glands [testes and ovaries] thyroid, parathyroid and adrenals are the islets of langerhans-pancreas (insulin related) the hormones secreted are sufficient to carry one to old age, 80 or more. However, by the time many women are 50 and many men are 60, there is a functional loss in gonadal hormones provided by the sex glands (testes) in men and (ovaries) in women. Though whatever the cause (usually due to the running out of eggs in women, eggs produce estrogen), the tendency exists for men and women in the latter middlescence period 55-65 for men to produce less testosterone and women less estrogen. When gonadal reproductive activity fails so does the sex steroid production. This does not mean that life is over by any means, perhaps less sex drive for men and little change of potentia in women, but for them it may be improved with the fear of pregnancy removed. Women manufacture estrogen from adipose tissue so some do not need replacement therapy. Sex activity may suffer from lack of partners, rather than desire to engage in sex. Sex hormones replacement which has been sometimes used for both sexes to improve and perhaps forestall the diminishing large supply of hormones is in a ratio of 20-1 (in milligrams) of testosterone (essentially male hormone) over estrogen (essentially a female hormone). Replacement use is under the physician's direction. Estrogen shortage can lower libido and cause vagina dryness. Recent controversy over estrogen and patches has bothered many women. Alternatives exist in locally applied creams such as Premarin, Estrace, and vaginally inserted drugs like Estring and Vagifem are helpful. Women treated in this manner will generally find there is no breast tenderness, vaginal bleeding will not occur nor will there be a lowering of the voice or excess hair growth. Most medical experts have concluded that estrogen replacement therapy (ERT) is safe when properly used. This means low doses—usually 3 milligrams or 0.625 milligrams used for two years. These doses are combined with progesterone, the other women's sex hormone. The estrogen builds up the uterine lining and the progesterone prepares the lining to be shed just like the menstrual period for the next part of the month. These kinds of uses protect from osteoporosis also helps with heart disease and reduces the risk of uterine and breast cancer. There are two types of hormone therapy:

> **Estrogen replacement therapy (ERT).** ERT is estrogen alone. Because ERT may increase the risk of cancer in the lining of the uterus, it is usually prescribed for women who have had a hysterectomy.

> **Hormone replacement therapy (HRT).** HRT combines estrogen with progestin, another female hormone. Progestin reduces the effect of estrogen on the uterine lining and protects against cancer of the uterus.

>

Hormone therapy reduces the discomfort of menopausal symptoms such as hot flashes and vaginal dryness. However, hormone therapy can have unpleasant side effects, including bloating, cramping, nausea, breast tenderness, and periodic vaginal bleeding.

Hormone pills are taken every day. Some forms of hormone therapy are available as skin patches. There is very little risk in taking hormone therapy for a year or less to manage symptoms of menopause. However, hormone therapy is not usually recommended for women who have had breast cancer, trouble with blood clots, liver disease, or undiagnosed uterine bleeding.

Hormone therapy though used for a long time or in increasing amounts does not protect against heart disease (Women's Health Initiative study showed this). It might help with osteoporosis. Talk to your doctor before deciding whether or not hormone therapy is a good idea for you.

Long term risks associated with progesterone use are unknown at the present time. There is some evidence of lipid metabolic effects. Men treated on this formula will not develop breasts, protein wastage nor the dangerous state of relaxed blood vessels (vasodilation). Treatment of men with this mixture has had far less beneficial results than treatment of women. Also there is only limited data to suggest that men benefit from this treatment. Estrogen prescriptions are used for three main reasons only; (1) vasodilation instability, (2) changes in vaginal mucus, (3) osteoporosis. Women with pre-existing cancers shouldn't take estrogen at all. Some decline in sexual function may occur towards the end of the middlescence period but physical causes should always be investigated, as these are frequently at fault, for example diabetes, hypertension medication, prostatic problems and fatigue. About half of the men 75 years old can achieve satisfactory intercourse.

Help is now coming to the aid of women. The problem for men it is erection in the middle years, for women it is libido or desire to have sex. Recent drugs are now on the market with others coming most of these for women. With billions spent on Viagra many companies are reproducing the same kind of success. For men, the newest drug is Levitra being touted as more vigorous than Viagra. Sex can be had for 24 hours and is alleged to have 6 to 9 times more potency. It takes effect in 15 minutes and works for nearly 82% of men. Another drug Cialis known as the weekender for it works up to 36 hours. Clinical Trials data says 64-92% of men find it effective—works in 16 minutes. Some side effects, headaches, facial flushing, upset stomach and nasal congestion. But it doesn't cause blurry vision or eye trouble experienced by some Viagra users.

SEX

Viagra heads the list, unbelievable but true. A recent study found women treated with Viagra for four weeks showed improvement in arousal, orgasm and sexual enjoyment. If so, its use for this purpose has not found wide acceptance. It may improve lubrication problems better than libido problems, which for women tend to be more about hormones and psychology than blood flow. Scientists have discovered the basic functioning of men's sexual format but they haven't as yet discovered all that's involved in women's physiology leading to a quick libido booster.

A rather new birth-control pill, Seasonale (Jolessa is a generic of Seasonale, Barr Pharmaceuticals) developed by Eastern Virginia Medical School in Norfolk, Virginia in its Jones Institute for

Reproductive Medicine (the nation's first vitro fertilization clinic), reduces women's menstrual periods from 13 to four per year. This medical school has become an international leader in women's health. Typically women using oral contraception follow a 28-day regimen. They take "active pills" for 21 days, then switch to placebos for a week. Stopping the hormone regimen causes "withdrawal" bleeding that resembles a period, even though ovulation hasn't occurred. In what is known as an "off-label use," doctors have advised women to delay their periods by starting a new pill pack at the end of three weeks. Because they don't skip any active pills, they forgo withdrawal bleeding that month.

Seasonale is thought to work in a similar way. Women take a pill with the same hormone level for 84 days and placebos for seven days, during which time they have their periods. The reduced frequency of periods is at the heart of Seasonale's appeal.

Oral contraceptives influence hormone levels. Most birth control pills contain estrogen and progesterone hormones, producing even hormone flows during the month in eliminating the trough at 14 days that come with ovulation. These pills also control menstrual flow, which can be sped by stopping the pills a few days early or put off by taking the pills a few extra days at the end of the month. The difficulty with the pill is for a few women it has ulterior effect, their contraception problems can be solved by other methods. The medical profession has not in the past prescribed the use of hormones for cosmetic purposes, to delay softening of bones, preserve breast fullness, youthful feminine tissues, to combat masculinizing facial hair, loss of hair, etc. This however is changing at the present time. Estrogens are used (Premarin, Ethinyl Estradiol or Menest) for prevention and treatment of vascular instability (hot flushes, flashes, vaginal dryness and osteoporosis). Artificial progestational agents may be prescribed like diethylstilbestrol or sometimes Provera tablets. Some of these hormones have been linked to vaginal and breast cancers and the decision to use them should be a matter of serious thought in consultation with your doctor. Birth control pills are not prescribed after 35 because of the high incidence of cardiovascular and thrombotic problems associated with their use after this age. However, the woman who is still ovulating can get pregnant, and contraception is a major concern (especially now that the IUD is not being advised by some physicians). Most IUD's are not off the market. A new IUD, ParaGard, is marketed primarily to doctors. ParaGard is aimed at only women who have no history of pelvic inflammatory disease, are involved in stable mutually monograms relationships and have had at least one child. This IUD (Model T380A) is marketed by Gynophorma of Somerville, New Jersey. The manufacturers claim it is safe. For those over 35 who do not wish to bear children, sterilization is a safe option and either the man or woman can undertake the operation.

It is true, according to the physicians to whom I talked, that the menopausal woman is frequently emotionally upset and given to crying spells. It may be a depressing time for many women because the ovaries no longer supply the body with enough estrogen and progesterone. These hormones along with some other (thyroxine, adrenalin, etc.) and along with the nervous system, influence behavior. The hormone upheaval upsets body control with flushes of heat causing sweating without apparent reason and feeling of suffocation. They sometimes occur during eating, sleeping or exercise. The problem here lies with a hormone (gonadotropin) released by the pituitary (master gland) which serves to control and adjust body level of estrogen and progesterone. At menopause the ovaries secrete less and less of these female hormones so in order to counteract this the pituitary gland pours more hormones into the system with the resultant effect of creating the "hot flash." The pituitary levels of FSH and LH (gonadotropic hormones) remain high for life but at menopause the temperature control is upset affecting some women. Replacement therapy (by tablet or injection) of the missing hormones can be used but should be attempted only with your physician's guidance. For the woman with a normal menopause, the ovarian function diminishes gradually and the symptoms mentioned above are few and spread over two or three years and sometimes longer. National Institutes of Health, Bethesda, MD, 2007.

A hysterectomy is sometimes given to correct a uterine fibroid tumor. The tumor when it occurs usually begins early in the life of a young woman and by the later thirties or forties has become a problem that is large enough to be removed. Dilation and curettage (D&C) is a way to diagnose and control causes of abnormal bleeding, i.e., post menopausal bleeding. Surgery for fibroids is the more common way to treat them. In many instances, if the woman is through childbearing and the fibroids are getting larger, the surgeon will do a vaginal hysterectomy. Brigham Hospital& Women's Hospital, Boston, is trying a non-invasive method without surgery. The ovaries are often removed (called oophorectomy) in conjunction with a hysterectomy and sometimes the fallopian tubes are removed (called a bilateral salpingectomy). In a D&C performed under anesthesia, the cervix is widened and the uterus lining is scraped to get a sample of cells. This is the third most frequently performed operation in the United States and it is simple. It has been claimed that a sizable number of these operations mentioned above are not needed. Even though much is probably done for preventive measures, second opinions should be obtained. If abnormalities exist suggesting removal of the womb, then losing the uterus or fallopian tubes will cause few menopausal symptoms but the ovaries lost will create some difficulties as outlined above.

Androgen

Androgen is basically a male hormone but women possess some which usually helps in menopausal time with their potentia. According to Irvin Goldstein, M.D., Director of the Institute of Sexual Medicine at Boston University, estrogen imbalance isn't even half the problem. There are 10 sex steroids only three are estrogens, the other seven are androgens. Three of four women who they see in their clinic is for lack of desire have serious androgen shortages. Therapy focuses on upping female levels of Testosterone, the biggest emphasis is on DHEA, a chemical cousin of Estrogen and Testosterone. DHEA use shows large improvements in their self-evaluated sexual performance. This drug should not be taken on one's own. Side effects of Testosterone can include weight gain, clitoral enlargement and hair growth. DHEA has been linked to cancer. More research is needed such as the unsolved mystery of women's sexual functioning. It is coming!

For the upper middle age (60-70) middlescent person, use of certain drugs have a good effect upon fatigue (sometimes it is principally a psychological phenomena—boredom, lack of activity, etc.). Frequently among the overweight, the lack of thyroid hormones may cause the drowsiness—that can be remedied. For women during the menopause some estrogen used with progesterone is beneficial; it helps the body retain calcium. For older men some thyroid extract aids overcoming fatigability particularly where the basal metabolic rate is low and the cholesterol level high. Iron deficiency, a common cause of lack of energy, in women and men can be treated with iron tablets. The use of these type drugs at present time, on a chronic basis, is only in documented cases of narcolepsy or cataplexy. These conditions are sleep disorders leading to fatigue. Caffeine may work as well and has less side effects but limited use is suggested for it has side effects of its own. Stimulant drugs are not given where blood pressure is chronically high, in the presence of coronary, artery disease and other vascular disease. One should remember that there are more people who complain of "being tired" who do not have enough to do than those who work very hard. Let us not lose sight of the fact that an important cause of fatigue in middlescence is depression (see Chapter II). This problem can be readily helped by medication and by becoming more involved with outside interests and less involved with one's self and therapy.

The material that follows comes from Our Bodies Ourselves, Pregnancy & Birth, Boston Women's Collective 2008.

It should be emphasized that some danger lies in the administration of hormones, particularly the sex related hormones. Use of androgen for men with prostate problems is questionable and certainly the use of the "pill normally for birth control," as a tonic stimulation or replacement has some hazards for women. The fact remains, that there are no "monkey glands" or elixir which will bring the forty or fifty-year-old man back to twenty or the 35-45 year-old woman back to eighteen. Beware of quacks and promises of being made over functionally! A good face-lift may be worth it but your physician will give you the advice about the "fountain of youth." When responding to claims for "making you over" make sure you go to a medical doctor (M.D.) (Plastic Surgeon). Many bogus degree-holding people claiming to be doctors or specialists are bilking the public with degrees in everything (like N.D. Doctor of Natureopathy) to poetry. Check the licensure displayed and give the local Public Health Department a call to validate the credential and specialties claimed if there is some doubt. Women may have need of the following tests:

Cervical Biopsy

Removal is made of a piece of tissue from the cervix for analysis under a microscope. A punch biopsy used collects a small circle of tissue. This can be performed in a doctor's office without anesthesia. Cramping and spotting may occur following this procedure. A core biopsy is used for diagnosis and treatment in a hospital using anesthesia. Core section is removed from the cervical opening and closed by stitches and by applying heat (cautery).

Colposcopy

The use of a small binocular magnifying glass that reveals cell changes that might indicate a tendency to development cancer. This approach helps identify the best site for a biopsy. Does not usually require anesthesia.

Endometrial Biopsy

A sample of tissue is removed from the lining of the uterus. A plunger is inserted and pulled back, some small pieces of the endometrial tissue is sucked inside the catheter. The biopsy is performed in the doctor's office or nurses causing some discomfort and produces spotting a day or two afterwards.

FSH and LH Blood Tests

These tests measure the level of follicle-stimulating hormones (FSH) and luteinizing hormones in your blood. These two hormones help determine the cause of abnormal menstrual cycles, lack of ovulation and infertility also may determine onset of menopause.

Hysteroscopy

This is a thin wand inserted through the vagina and cervical canal to the inside of the uterus. A light source to show the uterus along with a device that sprays carbon dioxide or a saline solution to inflate the uterus to keep the wall of the organ from touching a scalpel, laser or scissors can be inserted into the hysteroscopy to perform the surgery. This procedure is usually formed on an outpatient basis.

Mammogram

This procedure, that takes about fifteen minutes, is an x-ray of the breasts. With the breasts exposed one stands before a machine with a camera positioned above the breasts. A technologist positions the breasts on the lower of two compression plates and slowly brings the top plate down to flatten your breast. Side and front views of the breast are made and then the procedure is repeated on the other side. Another view may be required particularly if the woman has had breast implants. The American Cancer Society recommends annual screening after age 40. In December 2009 the U.S. Preventive Services Task Force recommends the start of screening at age 50. This will certainly be debated and may influence some to drop screening altogether.

Pap Smear

This test makes it possible for the doctor to recognize and treat abnormal cells in the cervix before they become malignant. A speculum is inserted in the vagina to bring the cervix into view. A spatula is brushed along the outer surface of the cervix. A small brush is put into the cervical opening and moved around to collect cells from inside the cervical canal. The cells are placed on a glass slide, which is sent to a lab for analysis. This procedure is painless.

Breast, Pelvic and Vaginal Ultrasound

The use of ultrasound is painless and used to see the internal reproductive organs and breast. A cool gel is spread on the skin and then a transducer moves over the area that's being inspected. The vaginal ultrasound uses a wand-shaped transducer (about the diameter of a tampon) which is inserted into the vagina to get a close look at the uterus and ovaries.

Source: Our Bodies, Ourselves, Pregnancy & Birth, Boston Women's Collective 2008.

Testing for Fungi

Vaginal infection with yeast or with Trichomonas (parasitic) can be recognized by examining vagina secretions under a microscope.

Common Vaginal Infections: Symptoms and Treatments

This chart lists the common vaginal infections, their causes and symptoms and tells how they are treated.

INFECTION	CAUSED BY	SYMPTOMS	TREATMENT OPTIONS
Vaginosis	Bacteria	Genital itching or burning; gray vaginal discharge with an unusual fishy odor that may be especially noticeable after intercourse	Antibiotics in tablet form taken by mouth or as a cream inserted into the vagina; sexual partner should be treated also
Candida	Yeast-like fungi	Intense burning and genital itching; clumped, white, cottage cheese-like discharge; possible pain during sexual intercourse	Prescription or over-the-counter antifungal cream or suppositories inserted into the vagina soothe the burning and itching for some women; antifungal tablet taken in one dose by mouth
Trichomonas	Protozoa, which are single-celled organisms that are sexually transmitted	Genital itching and burning; possible frothy, gray-green discharge with an unusual odor	Antibiotic in table form taken by mouth; sexual partner should be treated also

EYE DISEASE

The two most common eye ailments occurring during the middle years are cataracts and glaucoma. There are no symptoms, vision stays normal and there is no pain. Detection is found by the use of the "air puff" test or other tests used to measure eye pressure in an eye examination. But, this test alone cannot detect glaucoma. Glaucoma is found most often during an eye examination through dilated pupils. Two other common problems lie with Diabetic Retinopathy and Macular Degeneration. More people fear these diseases, according to a recent Gallup Poll, than any other excepting AIDS and cancer. Cataracts, which may occur from thirty-five onward, are opaque spots which form on the lens of the eye. The lens becomes milky and cloudy not allowing the light to pass through to form a clear image in order to focus on the retina. This impairment affects the picture carried by the optic nerve to the brain. The cause of cataracts besides age related changes include heredity, eye injury, and some medicines like corticosteroids, health problems and diabetes mellitus.

Cataract Surgery

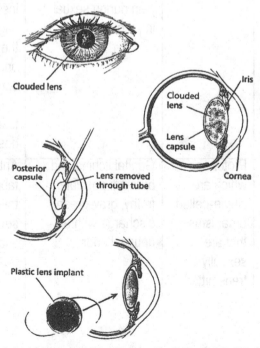

Diagram: Copyright 1999 & 2005 by Harriet R. Greenfield - Medical Illustrator

The only effective cure involves removing the clouded lens and replacing it with a plastic implant. Diagnosis of cataracts doesn't mean immediate surgery, if the vision is only slightly blurred. A correction to the prescription of their glasses and better lighting may be sufficient to help. Some medicines that dilate the pupils help some people. Some people delay surgery for years. Risks for cataracts involve smoking, drinking alcohol in excess, exposure to ultraviolet radiation, have diabetes at an early age and have used corticosteroid for a long time. By the time people are 75, 45% will need surgery. Only 2 of 100 from 45-54 and 5 of 100 55-64. Surgery is painless and is done on an outpatient basis and the operation requires an hour or slightly less and most are effective.

In glaucoma (hypertension of the eye) extreme internal pressure is exerted within the eyeball causing it to harden. In acute cases considerable pain is noted along with dimming of the vision. The most damaging type of glaucoma doesn't cause pain, but injures the vision silently and very slowly. Sometimes an indication of this disease is accompanied by the appearance of colored rings and halos about bright objects, or vision remains good centrally but dims on the periphery. Half of all blindness comes from this disease and it seems particularly to affect women in the middlescence years. There are now non-painful tests for glaucoma. If diagnosed early vision can be almost always be spared.

Eye problems are serious and should not be left unattended. Those twenty-five years of age should see an eye specialist at least every two to three years. Those over fifty should see an ophthalmologist (eye physician) once a year. Eye injuries should be treated promptly, one should avoid, glare; using lighting along with television viewing and do not try to treat infections of the eye yourself. Most of these minor infections like pink eye (conjunctivitis) can be cleared up by using ophthalmic ointment containing antibiotics. Boric acid is not as good as it used to be thought for eyewash. No wash should be used frequently unless professionally advised. One should rinse eyes every morning to rid eye of the granules (sleepers) which cut the eyelids and tend over time to have them turn in to the eyeball. Eye drops such as Refresh (Tears) have been found to be effective.

In Glaucoma there is usually an increased pressure in the aqueous humor (the fluid that fills the chambers of the eyes). This pressure causes damage to the optic nerve. Aqueous humor is always being produced and excess fluid is always being eliminated through the canal of Schlemm to keep a good balance of pressure in the eye. If the drainage system becomes blocked and pressure rises, pressure in the blood supply of the optic nerve increases. If it continues the nerve fibers that carry optical messages die and vision begins to fade. Vision loss might also occur by the blocking of very small blood vessels that feed the retina and optic nerves. Nerve fibers on the outer edge are affected first, so vision loss begins with peripheral vision and gradually closes until the cells supplying central vision are killed. The damage done is not reversible so early identification is important. Glaucoma does run in families. Those most likely to get glaucoma: Blacks over age 40; everyone over age 62 especially Mexican Americans; people with a family history of glaucoma.

Glaucoma

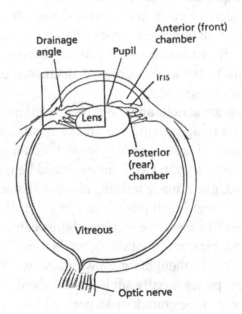

Diagram: Copyright 1999 & 2005 by Harriet R. Greenfield - Medical Illustrator

Most Glaucoma is open-angle type (90% of cases) sometimes called simple or chronic Glaucoma. The angle in the front chamber of the eye remains open, yet the aqueous humor drains out too slowly leading to a backup but a gradual but persistent rise in pressure. Closed-angle glaucoma is known by a rapid rise in eye pressure over hours as the drainage angle suddenly becomes blocked preventing the outflow of fluid.

Most ophthalmologists start with medicine that is the lowest Glaucoma medicine to reduce the side effects. This requires people taking these medicines to see their physician once every three months.

Diabetic Retinopathy

This condition involves deterioration of the blood vessels of the retina in people with diabetic mellitus. It usually occurs in both eyes. The longer one has diabetes the greater the risk. The symptoms though limited at first reaching an advanced stage without notice can be observed by an ophthalmologist. A dilated fundus examination involves placing eye drops in the eye in order to dilate (widen) the pupils and your retina as seen through an ophthalmoscope. Sometimes a fluorescein agniography is performed. In this case a dye is injected into the vein in your arm, the dye travels through the blood vessels to the retina and photographs are taken to determine whether or not the vessels are leaking. In case of leaking blood vessels and enlargement of the macula, laser surgery is used. The laser is focused on the damaged retina to close the ruptured vessels. This procedure is done in a doctor's office. Where new and fragile vessels have developed, the use of laser surgery is utilized. The beam is spread on the damaged retina creating scars that stop the growth of blood vessels and protect the retina to the back of the eye. A local anesthesia is used and procedure is performed in an office.

Another circumstance exists where the vision from bleeding occurs. Freezing therapy is indicated. This shrinks new blood vessels until blood settles then laser surgery is used. It is sometimes performed in an operating room requiring a local anesthesia. Advanced proliferative retinopthy removes the vitreous gel and replaces it with a clear solution. This operation is performed under a powerful microscope in an office or operating room using local anesthesia. In the case of retinal detachment repair surgery is performed re-attaching the retina to the back of the eye. This repair work is done in an operating room.

Age-Related Macular Degeneration (ARMD)

Generally age related, ARMD is the leading cause of blindness in people over 60. The problem is the macula, the area on the retina responsible for sharp, central vision when it deteriorates gradually causing blurred vision making reading difficult and finally leaving a blind spot in the center area of vision. Risk factors are smoking, exposure to bright sun light and ultraviolet radiation, light colored eyes, farsightedness, hypertension, high cholesterol and coronary artery disease.

The ARMD occurs in two forms—wet and dry. The majority of people have dry or atrophic form—it may affect one eye producing a gradual distortion of vision mainly in the dry form. Blurred vision and difficulty reading or distinguishing faces are usually the first symptoms. The second is affected. One-eyed vision masks their perception of vision for they seem to have normal sight. Wet ARMD is more severe. It results when blood vessels develop in the choroid layer, the back layer of tissue under the retina and extends like tentacles toward the macular. The new vessels tend to leak fluid and blood which injures tissue and photoceptor cells. Distorted vision is a first symptom, straight lines seem wavy, colors seem faded and a blind spot may develop in the center of the focus area. People with ARMD do not go blind they retain peripheral vision. Treatment for dry macular degeneration unfortunately doesn't exist however this form of ARMD progresses very slowly and people manage well in daily chores even with central vision loss. Laser surgery is sometimes used in wet ARMD with the laser aimed at the leaking blood vessels to seal them. This procedure works better when accomplished on newly formed vessels that have not grown over the Fovea. It is not a cure but slows down the progress of the disease. It is thought diets high in vegetables and antioxidants (Vitamins C & E) slows the progress of wet ARMD.

Age-Related Macular Degeneration

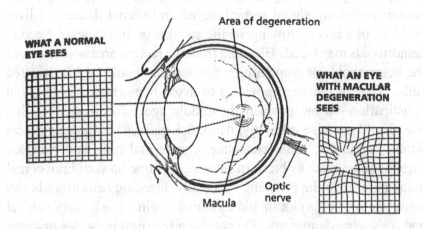

Diagram: Copyright 1999 & 2005 by Harriet R. Greenfield - Medical Illustrator

Detached Retina

Detachment of the retina happens when the retina lifts away from the Choroid, which contains an inner layer of blood vessels. If treatment is delayed the pulling away continues until the retina hardly hangs on the cilicry body and the optic nerve. Both eyes may be affected. The separated retina is a serious situation that can lead to permanent loss of vision. Middle age and older people are most likely to be smitten. Near sightedness increases the chances of detachment. Cataract removal increases the risk of retinal separation. Notable occurrences that signal detachment are flashes of light and floaters—small black bits go across the field of vision.

Hemorrhoids

A problem many Boomers may have is hemorrhoids which are sometimes called piles. They are enlarged veins situated inside or just outside the rectum. Prolapsed hemorrhoids are recognized because of the mass protruding from the anus. They can move back into the canal or you can push them back gently. Internal hemorrhoids are permanently prolapsed become inflamed and may issue a watery discharge. They cause itching, pain and sometimes bleeding. They are like varicose veins in the legs. Usually they can be controlled by medicine or surgery. There are two reasons for seeing the physician promptly if you think you have hemorrhoids. First, though rare hemorrhoids may signal something as an internal disease (a liver problem or cancer growing in the rectum or intestines). Second hemorrhoids may bleed. Bleeding from the rectum area whether from the hemorrhoids or something more serious should be investigated fully. One of the best remedies to avoid hemorrhoids is to avoid constipation—a big problem in middle age. To circumvent this one should exercise regularly, drink 6-8 glasses of water daily, eat fruits, vegetables, some chocolate, cheese and milk and complex carbohydrates such as bran. In some people one bowl of bran cereal a day may solve the problem. Secondly, bleeding hemorrhoids can cause anemia or if a clot should form in the vein it can be very painful and somewhat dangerous. Do not use advertised remedies or cures instead consult your physician. For some help in emergency, apply very cold (ice) water or witch hazel (it eases the pain) or hydrocortisone cream (controls the inflammation) on a cloth directly to the anal area, continuing for five to ten minutes until relief is obtained. Hot baths in the morning and at night often help as well as certain over the counter aids like petroleum, lidocaine. The doctor may use a anoscope, which has a light at can see any difficulty internally up in the intestine such as cancer, internal hemorrhoids. Bathing in warm water helps so does drinking 6-8 glasses of water a day and eating a lot of fruits and vegetables. Increase fiber in the diet is recommended. Bathe with unscented soap and when using the toilet, use unscented tissue. Also important is taking Kegel exercises and promptly attending to the first sign of bowel movement activity.

Incontinence

This is a disorder found mainly in women involving the leaking of urine when laughing or straining. A muscle weakening or relaxing in the genital area creates this condition. Metabolic problems such as diabetes, neuropathy, damage from infections, or anatomic abnormalities may be the cause of incontinence. Sometimes this happens due to some infection. Treatment depends upon the cause and usually consists of proper exercise and in many cases surgery upon the advice of a specialist.

There are four kinds of incontinence called stress incontinence, urge, overflow and transient incontinence. Ten million people are affected with one type or the other. A majority (90%) could be helped or cured, however, only 1 in 4 seek a physician. Many people resign themselves to wearing adult diapers, many think incontinence is part of growing old or are embarrassed to acknowledge the problem.

Kinds of Incontinence

Stress - This is seen in the leaking of small amounts of urine when coughing, lifting heavy objects, sneezing, exercise or put pressure on the bladder. This is more common in women after childbirth and in men after prostate surgery. Among women whose age is under 60 this is the most common type. The Harvard Medical School Health Guide (2005) gives the following information on types and treatment for incontinence follows:

Urge - The bladder in this case develops a spasm. A sudden contract makes the urine flow with little warning. For men and women this is the most common type.

Overflow - This can occur with women after pelvic surgery or men who have prostate enlargement. With partial blockage, the bladder cannot empty completely so urine dribbles frequently. Urological problems can cause weakening of the bladder and unsolicited urine flow.

Transient - Is caused by a temporary condition and most often in people older than 65. The causes that predominate are low estrogen levels, medicine (sedatives and channel blockers), delirium, urinary tract infection, drinking great amounts of fluids, drinking diuretic beverages as coffee or alcohol, heart failure, difficulty getting to the toilet when the urge to urinate, and fecal impact occurs.

Keep a daily log on the daily urination, the circumstances, etc., for a week. Having this information the doctor will perform a genital examination and one on other simple reflex and muscles. If your bladder is usually full it may mean you are not able to completely empty the bladder. The Harvard Medical School Health Guide (2005) suggests the following for stress incontinence - which can be alleviated 50% to 75% of the cases by:

- Performing exercise to strengthen the urinary sphincter.

- Learning biofeedback to help you contract the correct muscles.
- Holding weighted cones in your vagina to strengthen pelvic muscles.
- Wearing a tampon or pessary while you exercise to prevent leakage. They press against the vagina wall and compress the urethra.
- Taking drugs such as pseudoephedrine (unlabeled use) can increase the urinary sphincter ability to contract. This helps up to one out of every three women.
- Using a vaginal estrogen cream or taking estrogen pills (by mouth) particularly if through the menopause as it acts to close the sphincter.
- Having collagen implants. Purified collagen from cows is injected into the urinary sphincter. The body breaks down the collagen and forms scar tissue, which in turn bolsters the muscles.
  About half of the women taking this procedure find improvement but in men, it's less successful.
- Having surgery to strengthen the pelvic muscles or to lift the bladder. Many surgeries require only a small incision in the abdomen others are done through the vagina.

Urge incontinence can be improved up to 75% in people who have it. Increasing the capacity of the bladder by learning to suppress sudden urges and prolonging the intervals between urination for 1 to 2 hours then 3 to 4 hours. Or another way is to set time schedules. Drugs can improve urge incontinence like Oxybutynin, Propantheline anti-depressants. Side effects like dry mouth are common with this drug. Overflow incontinence may improve with blockers Prazosin, Terezosin or Doxagosin if the problem is an enlarged prostate. These drugs are often used for high blood pressure, they can also help relax urethral muscles and the fibers of the prostate. Implants can be used which stimulate coordinated activity of the bladder when medicines provide no relief. The Simon Foundation for Continence provides further information about causes and treatment of incontinence (call 800-237-4666).

Preventing Incontinence by Taking Kegel Exercises

For women, start on an empty bladder, contract the muscles you use when you try to stop urinating. An effective Kegel exercise will also tighten the vagina. Pull in the muscles and hold for a count of three. Then relax for a count of three. Work up to 10 to 15 repetitions each session. For best results do the exercise three times a day in different positions standing, sitting and lying. In several weeks results will come.

Preventing Incontinence by Taking Kegel Exercises

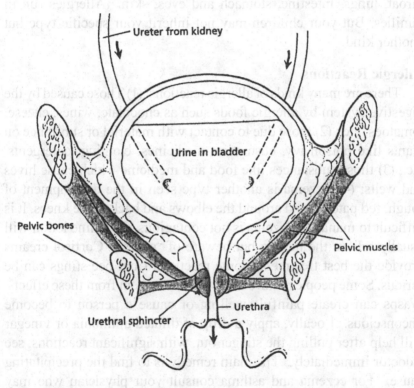

Diagram: Copyright 1999 & 2005 by Harriet R. Greenfield - Medical Illustrator

For men, two muscles are involved—one muscle you use to stop a bowel movement and those at the base of the penis that you use when you get rid of the final drops of urine. So tighten the muscles you use to stop bowel movement. Tighten the muscles at the base of the penis. Hold both muscles as tight as possible for a count of 10. Relax for one minute. Repeat the exercise six times. Then do the exercise once a day at night before going to bed, preferably in a sitting position or while lifting. Once you have urinary control continue this exercise to keep control.

Allergies

Allergies are groups of symptoms caused by contact to substances that are usually harmless but are viewed by the immune system as being hurtful to the body. The immune system overreacts to these substances (allergens) releasing histamines, etc., that causes runny noses, itchy eyes. Allergies affect one or more systems as nose, throat, lungs, intestine, stomach and eyes, skin. Allergies run in families. But your children may not inherit your specific type but another kind.

Allergic Reactions

There are many kinds of allergic reactions: (1) Those caused by the digestive system by allergic foods such as chocolate, wines, cheese, tomatoes, etc.; (2) those due to contact with material or substance on plants like poison ivy, cosmetics, medicines, clothing, detergents, etc.; (3) those substances like food and medicine which cause hives and welts; (4) Eczema is another type seen in the development of rough, red patch found around the elbows and back of the knees. It is difficult to manage. Eczema is not contagious. Calamine lotion will usually relieve the itching but beware of "cures." Cortisol creams provide the best treatment. Some reactions from bee stings can be serious. Some people require shots to protect them from these effects. Wasps can create painful swelling or cause a person to become unconscious. Locally, apply a drop of diluted ammonia or vinegar will help after pulling the stinger out, with significant reactions, see a doctor immediately. The main remedy is to find the precipitating cause. For eczema and asthma consult your physician who may suggest an allergist.

Food Allergies

Many people are allergic to foods. Those some on those foods are intolerant to the body. Nearly everyone at some time has a food they do not digest well. A common food milk (lactose) is an intolerant food. In these cases an enzyme is lacking that is needed to digest milk sugar lactose. Food allergies are an abnormal response of the immune system as in other categories of allergies is usually causing a reaction to a small bit of food. The reaction occurs when a body manufactures antibodies causing a reaction, which includes itching, swelling of the mouth, lips, or airways, sometimes causing extreme breathing problems, itchy skin, rash, wheezing and though rare loss of consciousness. Symptoms appear in minutes up to 1 hour later after eating the offensive food. The most reliable test for the culprit is the elimination diet. In this situation all possible offending foods (dairy products, grains, caffeine, alcohol, red meat and sugar) one at a time for 2 weeks then gradually reintroducing them one at a time. Blood tests are also utilized, one kind is the radio allergo sorbent test also an assay used to indicate the presence of IgE antibodies in the blood. The foods responsible for 90% of all food allergies are: cow's milk, eggs, wheat, peanuts, soy, tree nuts, fish and shellfish. In some people kissing someone who has eaten a peanut recently may cause a severe reaction.

Treatment is solely avoidance of the offending food. Those at risk of severe reaction should carry portable injections of epinephrine for use at the first indication of an anaphylactic reaction.

Hay Fever (Rhinitis) Allergy

This allergy is triggered by pollen in spring, summer and early fall though some people have it all year round. These people may be affected by indoor allergens such as dust that harbors mites that produce irritating substances especially in warm humid weather. Molds, hair of skin cells known as dander is shed by animals. Most rhinitis allergens come from the air. At 50 years of age most allergies any less severe the symptoms are nose running, eyes become red and itchy, may produce mucus, frequent sneezing and irritated throat and skin. Treatment—some medicines like Beta blockers, oral contraception pills, and thyroid hormones can cause nasal symptoms. If allergy is suspected skin testing—scratch tests or an injection just under the skin may confirm it. Decongestant pills (non-prescription) with the medicine pseudoephedrine can also help. If you have high blood pressure, diabetes, coronary artery disease, narrow angle glaucoma or trouble urinating check with a physician about its use. Non-prescription antihistamines such as Chlospheniramine or diphenhydramine are cheap and very effective also in some people they may cause drowsiness, blurred vision, trouble urinating, etc. If these do not work your doctor will prescribe a more powerful drug that's non-sedating like Cetirezine, Lasatadine or Fexofenadine. People with liver disease should be careful with other non-sedating antihistamines Terfenadine and Astemizole can cause heart rhythm abnormalities. Nasal sprays on a short period basic may be help.

Allergies to Medicines

Some adverse reactions to medicines are caused by an allergic problem in which your body produces antibodies to a drug. The antibodies bind to the drug to rid it from the body. In this operation the clumps of antibody bound to the drug travel through our blood and can harm body tissues or interfere with normal body functions. Allergic reactions are most often outbreaks of minor problems involving the skin they may also attack cells in the kidneys, liver, joints and blood. Inform your doctor if you think you are having an abnormal reaction. The worst type of reaction comes from anaphylactic shock that lowers the blood pressure and the airways become so narrow you cannot breathe, this requires emergency treatment. Sun exposure may cause photosensitivity of a drug you are taking like antibiotics, Tetracycline, Sulfa antibodies. Alas some birth control pills have the same affect, as does NSAIDS (nonsterodol anti-inflammatory drugs). Everyone needs to ask the doctor what are the side effects to his prescribed medicine and how do they interact with my other medicines.

Eczema and Dermatitis

These allergies are forms of reactions that are interchangeable for several situations that cause inflammation of the skin. Most common ones listed here they have like caused but common symptoms, red areas of skin, red lumps, blisters itching, rash and scratching. This type is called atopic dermatitis. If one has this type of problem its likely another family member has another type of allergy. This allergy usually goes away on its own and usually is confined to one part of the body such as the hands.

Contact Dermatitis

Touching or rubbing a substance which creates a rash or is marked with blisters. Contacts may be with laundry detergents. Metal from jewelry, clothes fasteners, some rubber products (gloves or condoms), some cosmetics, plants (poison ivy) and some drugs. In rare cases a person contact with another body. The reaction usually occurs one or two days after contact.

Stasis Dermatitis

Occurs on ankles, calves and feet also in people who have varicose veins or circulatory problems. Symptoms include mild redness and swelling along with itching. It the swelling is not treated the rash will become crusted and leak fluid. Infection can occur and injury to the area can lead to ulceration. Treatment starts with wearing compression stockings.

Seborrheic Dermatitis

Typically observed at scales over red patches which most commonly appears on the scalp in the form of dandruff. It also affects the eyebrows, eyelids, ears and folds near the mouth. The cause of this condition is not known.

Perivral Dermatitis

Often confused with Rosacea the small red papulses and pustules are limited to the skin around the mouth, nose and under the eyes. Young women are the most likely to be affected. It usually clears up in 1 to 3 months with an antibody; its cause is unknown.

Treatment to these problems can be treated by the individual involved through using hydrocortisone cream and skin moisturizers. Dandruff can be treated by medicated shampoo. Antihistamine can help the itching and can be purchased across the counter.

Information from Asthma and Allergy Foundation of America, 1233 20th St., N.W., Washington, DC, 2006.

Asthma

This disease is a disorder of the airways, inflammatory that is marked by recurring bouts of breathlessness and wheezing. The symptoms are caused when the breathing tubes of the lungs clamp down and fill with sticky mucus, making it difficult to get air in and out of the lungs. Some 5 million people in the USA, a third being children, are affected. The researchers do not fully understand the cause of asthma. Aspects of the environment especially allergies. Adults who have had asthma as children have a 10% reduction in lung capacity.

Common causes of Asthma are as follows:

Allergens
    Cockroaches and dust mites
    Feathers, molds, animal dander, saliva or pollen
    Foods containing sulfites (used in wine, beer, on salad bars, and on dried fruit).
    Foods using coloring dyes.
Strenuous Exercise
    Too much at one time and by cold, dry air
Polluted or Cold Air
    Air pollution outdoors
    Tobacco or wood smoke
    Indoor polluted air as fumes from dry cleaning, new carpeting, cleaning materials (never mix bleach and ammonia), and wood finishing products.
Medicine
    Aspirin and other non-steroidal and inflammatory drugs as Ibuprofen or Indomathacin, Beta blockers, cholinergic drugs used as eye drops in glaucoma or bladder contraction
Viral Respiratory Tract Infection
Flu and common cold
Occupational Substance
    Metal salts, wood or vegetable dust, solvents, and certain plastics

Asthma Triggers - Stress and Emotional Upsets

Stress worsens with the coming of impending Asthma attacks. Allergies caused by insects can be countered with repelling devices you can buy from Wal-Mart and other like stores an Ultrasonic Pest Repeller to rid one of spiders and roaches. The small machine is put in each room. As a result their high vibrations will kill these insects. A trade name of one such device is Wettich. Also filters are now on the market which placed in a room will rid the air of 30 or more percent of the dust and dust mites. These hold promise for the Asthma patient.

Treating Asthma involves four aspects—evaluation, medicine, environmental control, and education about the problem.

Treatment - Evaluation of the Problem

Measures of lung capacity and volume are made to gauge the severity of Asthma. Many physicians like patients to monitor their lung function with a device called a peak flow meter. Inexpensive, portable it can be used at home to measure your peak expiratory flow rate, this gives you advance warning of an impending attack setting off the reminder to take medicine or see your doctor. Getting a baseline level, measures when you are feeling well and when you are under duress. Measures should be taken every day. These baselines can tell you how well you are doing. Seventy-two percent of those monitoring their Asthma as opposed to 42% who do not require days off within four months—three levels describe the peak flows—Green, 80 to 100% the ideal level—non-symptom; Yellow level, 50-80% take medicine regularly—may not have symptoms; Red levels—unacceptable, i.e., 50% less than your ideal level get help immediately (your doctor or emergency center).

Medicines

Drugs can prevent and reverse inflammation while treating narrowed airways. Medicines for long-term control help to achieve and maintain better levels of lung functions. Some anti-inflammatory medicines include: Cortisosteroids, Cromolyn, Nedocromil, Leukotriene and Antagorids, bronchodilators designed to open airways by relaxing the 8 mouth muscles are Beta-agonist, methylxanthines, and immunotherapy.

Environmental Control

Those measures that help control factors that bring on asthma attacks heretofore mentioned in this section.

Asthma and Allergy Foundation of America, 1233 20th St., N.W., Washington, DC, 2006.

Education

Learning about the nature of your problem through American Lung Association publications or other medical hard books such as *The Harvard Medical School Family Health Guide,* available now in 2005; *American Association Medical Guide,* and *The May Clinic Family Health Book, 2005.*

ARTHRITIS

Some 15 to 20 million Americans seek treatment for one or more of a 100 different conditions which fall under the category of arthritis. The word means inflammation of the joint. The three major concerns of middle-age people are rheumatism, osteoarthritis and gout. There are seven main types of arthritis:

1. Rheumatoid - The most serious type that affects nearly 3 million people in the America according to Harvard Medical School reports in 2005. It is an inflammatory disease that damages the synovial tissue connecting bones and joints and it is chronic. Women are affected three times as often as men. However, very few are severely disabled because of it. It is not known what triggers the immune system to produce the substances that cause the inflammation which can in time all the components of the joint, the synovial tissue normally smooth, becomes grainy and rough invading the joint cavity eats into the cartilage bone, tendon areas of tissues (called pannus causing the bones to fuse). If tendons rupture, it will create floppy joints.

Treatment - Taking a part in your treatment is important—following the plan for therapy, recognizing the flare-up and drug side effects and exercising. Nonsteroidal anti-inflammatory drugs, like Aspirin or substitute. If this isn't effective then methotrexate or hydroxychlaroquine in large dosage can improve your situation. Some other disease changing drugs are antirheumatics—gold therapy, penticillimine and sulfacalazine. One needs to pay attention to diet, rest and exercise, protecting joints and saving energy. Diet—recommend two servings of fish per week rich in omega-3 polyunsaturated fatty acid found in salmon, mackerel and sardines—taken in capsules form is beneficial also.

Rest and Exercise - During periods of flare-ups you may need 8 to 10 hours sleep. Short naps may be needed for during hiatus periods some people will overdo their activities becoming very tired—rest is preventive. Exercise reduces pain, relieves stiffness and fatigue.

2. Rheumatic fever - A generalized inflammatory disease affecting the whole body; may cause heart damage. It usually follows a streptococcus infection such as tonsillitis or scarlet fever. (This disease causes only transient arthritis in most cases and rare in itself.) This is seen mainly in children. Aspirin helps if more serious involving streptococcal antibodies are used to combat this is used.

3. Gout - a situation where the uric acid accumulates in the blood attacking the small joints, especially the big toe; occurs most frequently in men. This disease is due to a deficiency of a substance needed in breakdown of certain meats and therefore a build-up of uric acid develops because of this deficiency and creates the problem. The kidney cannot handle an overload of uric acid leaving the joints vulnerable irritating the synovial tissues during pain and swelling. Drink plenty of water, less alcohol. Foods such as liver, anchovies, kidney, herring, sardines rich in protein—foods, which prevent kidney stones, should be eaten.

4. Infectious arthritis - A joint inflammation caused by a bacterial infection; the most common of which is gonorrhea, a sexually transmitted disease. Thousands of cases each year, untreated gonorrhea can spread through the blood stream can cause infections in the joints, bones and skin. Women have no symptoms so need to be tested

to ascertain this situation—in several weeks' discharge from the urethra or vagina and painful urination. Men have discharge from the urethra, which is clear or white or thick yellow or pus like. Treatment is with antibiotics, which cure the problem and keep it from spreading through the body. Sexual partners should be warned about their situation. Not common in middle age, however, it is seen as a non-GC (gonorrhea coccus) (Chlamydia) seen in young women and men or inflammatory problem in people with immune system problems, diabetics or damaged joint (Rheumatoid arthritis, Trauma).

5. Bursitis - The inflammation of a bursa (sac) filled with fluid that lies between a muscle and bone. Pain occurs outside the elbow where the tendons are connected to the bone. The sac assists the movement of the arm. Frequently this is called tennis elbow (only 10% get Bursitis in this manner) but can also occur in the shoulders and knee by people who garden a lot, job related lifting and screw driver use or wrist overuse, the muscles of the forearm. Rest and medical or surgical procedures can effect a cure. (Injection of cortisone frequently helps this problem.) Nonsteroidal inflammatory drugs relieve the pain. Physical therapy and shoe insoles use can improve the problem.

6. Reiter's Syndrome - This is a non gonorrheal cause of arthritis which is most frequently due to an altered immune response to a venereal disease type organisms known as chlamydia. It has a genetic component. This syndrome affects joints, eyes and urethra (the tube that connects the bladder to the outside world). Many times antibiotics cure the disease. Some forms of Reiter's syndrome are chronic and others may be recurrent.

Signs and symptoms which often occur in middle-age by nearly everyone sometimes need to be recognized and treated early regarding arthritis: The symptoms include:

- Persistent pain and stiffness on arising.
- Pain and tenderness in joints.

- Swelling in joints.
- Tingling sensations in fingertips, feet, hands.
- Unexplained weight loss, fever, and weakness.

Physicians are aware that Arthritis victims are continually exploited by quacks with useless remedies, usually anti-inflammatory such as aspirin and other drug therapy. They are not only wasting money but valuable treatment time. The American public is paying over a billion dollars a year for quick relief, which doesn't occur. For more information contact the Arthritis Foundation in Atlanta, GA or go to www.arthritis.org.

Treatment includes special diets and dietary supplements, aspirin, exercises, rest, special supports, drugs and climate change. Additional advice includes guarding against cold and dampness, avoiding strain, fatigue (don't do all your house or yard work or ironing at one time). Unfortunately, there is no cure for most forms of arthritis.

Dental Problems

Tooth decay, periodontal disease and gingivitis are common ailments during middle years. Teeth play a vital role in our nutritional health and must be free of disease to continue their proper function. More serious than decay is periodontal disease caused by plaque organisms from it-secretions of toxins damage the ligaments as a result gums become inflamed and pull away the teeth from the gums. Over time they can damage gums, the roots of the teeth and finally the bone. This infectious ailment of gums can have serious side effects such as heart disease by causing infection of the heart valves. It is an ailment of major proportions in the United States with one out of four American being seriously affected. This disease affects some ninety-percent over 50 years of age. Progressive stages and symptoms include redness and swelling, bleeding when gums are pressed, pink after brushing with toothbrush, bleeding and painful gums. Pain is killed by Aspirin, Tylenol, Acetaminophen or Ibuprofen. Vitamin deficiencies, improper brushing and flossing, and malocclusion, contribute to the disease. Treatment for advanced and serious cases involve surgery

Prevention by proper dental care flossing and brushing regularly and professional cleaning are of single importance is the best cure. We should regularly visit our dentist thereby forestalling the unexpected and for receiving preventive maintenance. Replacing broken teeth or lost ones can easily be done to make your teeth appear normal by your dentist by capping teeth, making bridges to avoid loss of teeth, using implants and braces, crowns and partials.

Deafness and Loss of Hearing

The ability to hear begins to fade with age. Say what? By twenty-one our hearing of certain frequencies peaks. By middlescence it is estimated that some 25 to 30 million have some degree of hearing loss. Sensitivity to high pitches is the first to go. Deafness may be caused by disorders such as vitamin deficiencies, infections, metabolic and glandular disorders, head trauma, inheritance, or even wax build-up. Deafness also may be inherited.

Types of deafness are as follows:

1. Inherited deafness (otosclerosis) this is a common form of trouble usually beginning in younger adulthood becoming more pronounced during middle-age. One of the middle ear bones experiences abnormal growth, which prevents vibrations from activating the nerve leading to hearing. Surgery is sometimes necessary to correct this disorder of the middle ear.
2. Catarrhal deafness is a conduction problem which sinuses, tonsils, adenoids, etc., create the inflammation of the Eustachian tube connecting the throat and the middle ear. These conditions act as sound insulation and interfere with the sound transmission through the middle ear to the inner ear where the hearing apparatus is located even though the nerve endings may be normal. Medicine to sure infection is a treatment and/or surgery.
3. Nerve Deafness is seen when sound is sent to the hearing nerve but the hearing organ has degenerated (the nerve that transmits impulses to the brain, or the brain itself).
4. Mixed deafness may be a combination of any two types of deafness. Hearing aids are available and can be

costly. Check with an ear, nose and throat doctor for a recommendation. Hearing aids do not eliminate all the peripheral noise entirely but do help if properly fitted.

The Most Important Medical Advice You Will Ever Receive:

Keep in touch with your doctor! A doctor is not solely responsible for your health, you are. Don't wait until you are really sick to go to see one. Try to get a thorough health screening at least once a year. Those with chronic health problems will need to see the doctor regularly—at least every three months if they are under control, like with diabetes, high blood pressure, or anemia.

When you see your doctor, you need to know what questions to ask and what information you may need to tell.

Tell About	Ask about
Any fever and how long it lasted	Eating habits, diet, and medication
Any pain, or tingling in the arms or legs	The state of your health - sugar level, blood pressure, are my
Any change in weight or swelling	lungs clear
Bleeding (unexplained)	Exercise routine
Coughing or shortness of breath	Mountain climbing trip or
Change in urine color or amount	undertaking a project involving
Vision difficulties	physical strain
Marked weakness or fatigue	Doubt, worries, or questions about
Change in bowel habits	your health
	Use of tampons, contraceptives

As important as it is to know about the problems and rules of health, one should recognize that a seasoned body that has been carefully tended in young adulthood greatly increases the chances of surviving ailments of the middle age and reducing the effects of the aging process. The natural aging process can be slowed with sensible everyday living patterns. Most of our bodies don't wear out; we wear them down. The person who follows sound health maintenance programs—adequate nutrition, sufficient mental and physical exercise, rest and moderation in living habits would respond better to an unusual physical or emotional stress than those who have not. The latter person, though free from impairment, may not have the built-in reserve, which can handle an emergency situation. Complete wellbeing in the middle years may be defined as a state of maximum resistance to disease, injury, or other abnormal stress.

Capabilities, in order to be kept at their peak, must be used. The muscle that is not used will weaken. Mental capabilities not employed to their fullest will decline. The circulatory system not subjected to the demands of regular exercises may decrease in pumping capacity. Capabilities must be constantly used to remain at their prime throughout one's life.

Survival of the Boomer Years Depends Upon:

1. Sleep between seven and eight hours each night
2. Eat breakfast
3. Stay within 10 percent of your proper weight
4. Don't eat between meals
5. Don't drink alcoholic beverages excessively
6. Don't smoke cigarettes
7. Exercise regularly

The greater the number of rules a person follows the less likely he or she is to have an illness. The two most important health rules, this research says, relate to exercise and avoiding cigarettes. The good life during the Boomer years can be yours!

CHAPTER FOUR

CARING FOR OUR PARENTS

"Tending to Ma and Pa"

For the Boomer generation, one of the biggest toll taking aspects of life involves caring for parents. It is energy sapping and emotionally draining. It is said that young people growing up today do not feel they need to care for their parents in a special way. After all their parents have Social Security, Medicare, Medicaid, pensions, etc. Many youth it is said, are not planning on building houses or having apartments with an extra bedroom for the visiting parent to settle in old age. They are in many cases moving far away from home. But for most of us, we feel an obligation to help our aging parents in many ways—providing money, emotional support, decision-making, and help in planning, etc. For persons 35-40, their parents are somewhere near 60-70; for those of 45 with parents at 65 or 75; for those of 50-55, 75-80, helping our mothers and fathers is an omnipresent concern. For most of us there will be only one parent who will be with us beyond 70-75, usually the mother. But if we are married it would likely leave possibly three parents, certainly two, to concern ourselves with. Some may also have a responsibility for their grandparents who are in their eighties and nineties. The author knows of one couple who had the responsibility for four parents and though it was very difficult they managed to survive by utilizing a nursing home for two of them and taking the other two into their home. Deciding who will go where could be a problem!

I am not suggesting that as soon as retirement comes, usually at 65, or maybe a couple of years earlier, we will have the immediate burden of our parents. Most of our parents will want to maintain their independence as long as they can; in fact some will not leave their home even under the most extreme circumstances.

We should note that most gerontologists and psychiatrists believe that all people, including the old and the sick, are entitled to control over their own lives in so far as this is possible. This means choosing the way they live and how they are to die. We as concerned children have no right to impose on a frail parent solutions that they will not accept—even where it seems clear-cut that we are right. As some individuals get older they become less and less concerned about the feelings of others and the impact their behavior has on those that provide care for them. Physiological impairment and the loss of vitality can amplify this. The pressure on us to act on their behalf is constant. Most families do not have a complete plan on what to do with our parents in emergency and crisis situations. This is the reason that so many times social service agencies are called upon to help. Trying to decide what is best when our father is stricken with paralysis, or our mother cannot drive to do the shopping and procure provisions necessary to sustain life, is a calamity of the first order. Or, our mother dies suddenly and our father cannot face the emotional stimulus, the reminders the old home brings, and no longer being able to remain in the house; so he must be cared for immediately. In these situations, where there are other persons in the family involved (sisters and brothers), we feel we have to take action and make arrangements as the situation pressures us to do something. These feelings run the gamut from depression (how can I handle it with the other aspects of my life) to guilt (I should have done more or something concrete before now) to anger (how could my parent be so insensitive and in denial of the need to plan for the inevitable); reason struggles with ego. It may be between you and your parent, or other kin as to who is number one to mother or father, my brother or sister or me? And what reference does caring for the parent have for the division of property and money after their demise? Hostility, duty, the need for family approval, all attends our attempts to help our parents. No amount of advice and outside assistance will ever satisfy what is needed nor make up for the investment of your life in caring. This is unfortunate but usually true. In the long run, it will be satisfaction you get from being a "real person" upon being responsible that makes the difference.

Let us turn our attention to the broader view of changes that take place between ourselves and our parents—attitudes, roles differentiation and what specific help can be given. It is interesting that true friendship between parents and grown children is rare. In many cases, unfortunately there is little or no relationship at all between parents and their children. Partly due to the fact that parents continue the parent-child relationship and the young need to be independent and emancipated. Also they may misunderstand the love codes of each other. Parents, however, generally play the dominant, granting and giving role, while children continue in the submissive, receiving and taking role. For the parent who is able, the use of the checkbook is a very powerful weapon and he or she may use it as a form of control on a married child. The author will not forget his first attempt to get married (he was nineteen and a junior in college), both his grandfather and his mother said that if he got married he would have to support the new wife and pay for his education. This threat along with another thing or two convinced him not to take this step. It was possibly better for the young lady for he was too immature for marriage. But for many the parent-child role continues until in one case he knew of the ninety-year-old father, in reasonably good health, and living with his son 65 years of age, forbade him to go with his wife for a day or two visits with friends. The father's complaint was, "I'll be alone and have nothing to do. You can't go." And they didn't.

This type of thing is not an unusual case for persons of this vintage for most rely, due to infirmities, etc., almost totally on their children for emotional and material support. When our parents become dependent for health and/or economic reasons upon us, the role of the parent-child tends to reverse itself. Our parents opinions and views should be respected and taken in consideration in decision making. This is said in view of "honor our father and mothers" and veneration due them. Typically cultural attitudes and economic circumstances will dictate what is done for our parents when it is essential that we take over their lives—decide the living arrangements, responsibility sharing, establishing a general routine, and taking on the financial burden if needed.

There are many cultures and groups; the Amish, Chinese, Catholics, Greeks, Jews, and Native Americans who have a tradition of the three-generation and extended family living together. Some build additions to their homes in anticipation of accommodating the elderly. Even split-level housing in the suburbs is being advertised as mother-daughter homes. We assume these are for any age but certainly for the boomer female and her mother and/or father. These are some who are affluent enough to maintain the residence of their parents and provide nursing or a maid to help look after them. If, as in most cases this cannot be done, the parent or parents become a part of the household and they may care for the grandchildren if their parents have to be out working. This is a good arrangement for it gives the older parent something to do. However, many older persons do not want to live with other members of their families. They feel that they will physically be in the way, or financially they will be a burden, or they don't like the other members of their family all that much. This could be true; however, reassurance on this matter should be given our parents. Recent studies indicated a longer life for those maintaining independence by living alone or with a spouse rather than with family or in some other type of care facility.

The Family Round Table

The question often arises who will take care of aging parents who are widowed or ill? In an attempt to solve the issue—enter the family round table. Daughters are the most likely to be assigned to the task due to the former nurturance role, the physical care of the parents, while sons give financial assistance and "moral" support. Whether or not it is the most well off or the poorest child who take the parent depends upon the circumstance. Each son or daughter should take part in making a contribution to the welfare of their parents - in a perfect world. Approximately what can be expected should be decided early in family discussions about parental care. The personality of the children according to Silverstone and Hymen in this book, *You and Your Aging Parent* (2008) is important in how responsibility is assumed. A child who feels very close to a parent will logically accept the keep and extra burden of the parent. On the other hand, a daughter or son who feels guilty about their past feelings, the neglect of their parents and lack of concern, may think that by taking over the caretaking role he or she can win approval and in so doing expunge their guilt. Self-centered children may find it easy to break away from caring for their parents. Few, however, are so alienated from their parents that they turn their backs on them completely.

We should remember that many older people do not want to accept their condition. To admit they can no longer care for themselves, be mobile and manage their affairs is too painful to consider. They desire to be independent so they will ignore physical problems, housekeeping, personal hygiene, and reject assistance in order to continue their lives as usual. They may struggle between their need for assistance and their desire to be self-sustaining. You must try to sift through conversations, perhaps over months and years, to help your parent accept the reality of their situation and what should be done. And those things done in haste are often regretted later. Hence take your time to decide what is to be done.

At some point in the lives of our parents they are willing to become the child—when they can't manage getting or carrying the groceries, walk for the newspaper, are afraid to go out of the home in a ghetto neighborhood or can't get service on plumbing or electricity. Sometimes these irritations keep the blood circulating for our parents. However, when these types of things get too much for them, they will usually ask us to intervene. The author's mother gave up driving at seventy-seven when she recognized it was more than she could safely handle. But in no way would she give up her home, even though her only daughter who formerly lived with her had died and she was now alone. The principal questions about relocation of our parents is how they regard the quality of life where they are? Frequently when one of the parents dies, the children quickly decide that the bereaved parent should be moved into one of their homes. This movement away from familiar surroundings, friends, activities and sometimes a job, is usually over-reacting, for once things settle down and the shock of loss wears off they become first class burdens, particularly if the parent is in reasonably good health. One such situation existed in one of the author's family where the aunt's husband died. Her son insisted she move in with him and his wife and young daughter. Shortly afterwards they built a one floor duplex with an adjoining connection, the living room being the central point between them. The son was transferred to another city where the mother then shared a bedroom in the house. By this time the young granddaughter had grown up and married, leaving—since the son's wife didn't work—the mother-in-law and his cousin's wife were together most of the day for weeks on end. This lasted for twenty years and was a constant source of strife judging by amount of injury transmitted to him by the wife and aunt. The aunt incidentally was in rather vigorous health and was mobile until 93. The son was caught in the middle. The lesson we think is to be sure you want to accept the sharing of your home before you make a commitment and consider other options. Remember also that parents often would rather be less well cared for in their our homes than be with you feeling they are beholden to you for everything you do for them. The respect, generally, given old people is not lost on our parents. There are countless situations where parents, old-maid aunts or uncles who have added immensely to the quality of family life, education of children and joy in general, but these are still in the minority. Frequently when we involve ourselves in a new role with our parents we wonder how our children will behave toward us in similar circumstances.

Getting Help

When we need help in a critical situation in dealing with our parents who may be 1000 miles away and suddenly one is immobile, where should we look? There are a variety of help agencies both public and private who will assist you in making short-term or long-term arrangements. If your mother living alone has broken her hip and you are unable to leave your home for a long period of time to aid her, you can receive assistance from Private Social Agencies or Local Governmental Agencies. Catholic Family Services, Protestant Federation of Welfare Agencies and Jewish Family Services organizations don't require you be of their faith to get help nor do agencies require persons to be poor. However, one should perhaps start by getting information from friends who have experienced these kinds of problems, from their own physicians, ministers and social workers. You can call one of your local agencies like the United Fund for information. Any city or county with 50,000 population should have social service to help aged persons in their area. Social workers can help arrange, when your parent is a distance away, for meals through "Meals on Wheels," to visit your parent regularly, check on what needs to be done for his or her comfort and keep you informed. They will make necessary arrangements because you cannot be there. And importantly they know what part you are entitled to freely receive from the local, state and federal government. Securing a practical nurse, a temporary shelter and many other services are part of their work. There may be a required payment or donation for this service but you will have peace of mind not otherwise affordable. Private and government agencies are usually found in the white or blue pages of the telephone directory under Professional, Business and Organizations, whereas in the yellow pages you will find such agencies as Senior Citizens, Nursing Services, Health and Welfare Agencies, United Way, Social Service Agencies and Homes for the Aged. If you have trouble finding a person or agency that can give you an answer about your specific problem call a city councilman, the mayor, or a town alderman. Human Resources Commissions in larger cities can tell you what the Medicaid eligibility requirements are in a given state. There are organizations such as the Red Cross and others that can make provisions for transportation, day-care centers, meals for the homebound, financial assistance and legal aid. Individual churches usually make some provisions for assistance, though they are generally limited; They frequently give assistance to people of their own faith who are sick and aged through peer visitation, gifts, reading material, pastoral visits and sometimes meals and counseling.

Nursing Homes and Homes for the Elderly

Most people think of nursing homes as institutions where old people can live and be cared for regularly. To qualify as a nursing home the home must offer facilities that meet the standards and regulations of Medicaid and Medicare as U.S. Agencies. The Skilled-Nursing_Facility (SNF) provides 24-hour supervision by a licensed vocational nurse or a registered nurse, the nearest service to hospital care available. Normally a physician has to prescribe admission. At minimum SNF's provide medical, nursing, dietary, pharmacy and activity services. Another nursing home is the Intermediate Care Facility (ICF) which cares for people who aren't well enough for independent living and are not sick enough to require constant medical and nursing attention. They are required to provide 8 hours of nursing. Those licensed nurses are not always available. An ICF should give patients help with bathing, dressing, eating, walking, and other personal needs and provide programs of social and recreational activities. These kinds of institutions usually have agreements with close-by hospitals and health centers to supplement their services or to secure provisions they do not have. This should be checked into when looking into a nursing facility. Medicare and You 2010, U.S. Department of Health and Human Services, Baltimore, MD.

Skilled Nursing Facilities for Special Disabilities

This is a facility that provides a protective environment for themselves and others or persons who have mental disabilities. Some have long-term care facilities. Besides these types of institutions Old-Age Homes and Retirement Homes abound that are operated by state and private agencies. A number of these are non-profit, frequently caring for the well and not-so-sick old. Many are run by church groups. Before you place your parent or parents in any of these institutions you should investigate the institutions thoroughly. When my brother, who was a minister, and I considered moving our mother to a nursing home, we looked at a number of places in her local area. He was convinced that some of them offered what she wanted (congenial settings, concerned staff, and adequate support facilities). However, my separate visits did not validate this view. The proprietary interest of these nursing homes appeared to be the dominate concern rather than patient-centered care. Subsequently, instead of moving our mother, we found a helper to live with her. This was the first of many such arrangements, which kept us constantly worried as we lived 400 miles away, for sometimes mother would keep a helper only a week before something would happen. On one occasion, the lady housekeeper insisted upon having her boyfriend into her room! Our mother strongly objected to this and consequently invited her to leave. "No hanky panky here! Not her kind of people," she said.

BEWARE – Be cautious as to hidden costs (nursing, refreshments, games, magazines, shampoo, etc.) and the financial involvement. Sometimes a home will charge two dollars or more for tissue—toilet or facial. The administrator of a home may want a large down payment or commitment of the estate at the person's death—though this is common, however, one should evaluate the agreement before giving a sizable holding, house and/or money. Robert Bua's *Inside Guide to America's Nursing Homes* (1999), available from Amazon. com, was one of the first to explain nursing home alternatives and rates for all certified nursing homes in the U.S.A. This book will help you in making a decision on choosing the right nursing home. Some general recommendations for the choosing of a nursing home are as follows:

Care giving and Eldercare from *The Harvard Medical School Family Health Guide* (2005)

1. Be sure that the home is accredited, licensed by local and state authorities. If there are any questions, call your local health department. The home you are considering should be certified for Medicare or Medicaid if need be.
2. The nursing, medical, therapy, rehabilitation, and social services should be appropriate for your parent's needs.
3. The home, buildings, and yards should be well-kept and attractive. In addition it should be clean, safe, and meet federal and state fire codes and not located in condemned structures however approved.
4. The room for sleeping should be uncrowded with enough room to allow separate seating, dressing tables, and closet space. The furniture should be appropriate, as should the bathing arrangements.
5. Food should be prepared under the sanitary conditions, appear appetizing, and possess adequate variety in order to cover numerous dietary needs.
6. Staff personnel should be well-trained and in sufficient numbers to look after the patients. It should be clear who is

the chief and subordinate administrators. In other words, to whom do you look for information and input about the care of your parent or parents. A readily available structure for discussing problems is a necessity.

7. If possible, visit the home with your parents in advance so they can meet personnel and see the sort of living conditions that will prevail. Also this gives an opportunity for them to get accustomed to the surroundings; perhaps several trips would be better, particularly where some reluctance to enter exists on the part of your parents.

8. Make sure that the legal conditions under which the nursing home operates are clearly spelled out; that is, reduced to plain English. Of course the responsibility of financial obligation and support should clearly be understood by all.

9. Observe if attention is paid to the patients' morale.

- Are they addressed with dignity?
- Do they have privacy?
- Are they dressed in nightclothes or street clothes?
- Are beauticians and barber available?

10. Expect the level of available Medical services to be clearly spelled out according to the type of plan you select. For example:

- Do they have a staff physician available 24-hours a day?
- Does the staff physician make the rounds of the residents?
- Are provisions for dental and foot care available?

11. Do they have group activities, i.e., trips, group discussions, a variety of programs, citizenship participation, and social services available?

Make a list of the nursing homes thought suitable in your area and, if applicable, near enough for family and friends to visit. Learn as much as possible about each nursing home by talking with people that have loved ones in nursing homes, ministers, health professionals such as doctors, social workers, or nurses, a Long Term Care Ombudsman, and even nursing home employees. If you have general concerns you can even review the state survey inspection reports for each facility which should be posted in each facility as required by federal law. Also the inspection reports should be listed on the Medicare web site.

Visit and Evaluate Each Nursing Home

According to Robert N. Bua who is an expert on American nursing homes, look for the following:

- Do patients appear happy and well taken care of?
- Is the building clean and well maintained?
- Are wheelchairs and other equipment in clean working order?
- Are activity calendars posted with a variety and sufficient number of activities for patients to choose from each day?
- Are patients involved in activities or just sitting around bored with nothing to do?
- Does the food look appetizing and are patients eating most of their meal?
- Does the dining room and kitchen look clean and are cooks wearing hairnets?
- Do the patients look well fed?
- Are the rooms neatly arranged and individually decorated with personal possessions of patients?
- Do staff members interact cheerfully with patients and each other?
- Are patient call lights responded to quickly?
- Does the facility overuse physical restraints (devices that tie patients to chairs or beds)?
- Are staff members responsive to patient or family needs and requests?
- Are staff members visible?
- Are patients treated with dignity and respect?
- Does the linen look clean and not old and thin?

- Is patient privacy protected during patient care and treatment (are room doors and privacy curtains used)?
- Do staff members stop and knock on room doors prior to entering patient rooms?
- Is the facility well lighted?
- How much time alone with a nurse does the patient receive?

Find out
- Are call lights sounding for a long time before being answered?
- Are patients calling out for help?
- Is patient care and information being discussed within hearing range of others?
- Is there an excess amount of noise in the facility caused by staff, intercom, etc.?
- Notice if nurse relation to patients is friendly, supportive and helpful.

Smell
- Do patients smell clean when standing five feet away?
- Are there any strong odors in the facility?
- Are rooms well ventilated and kept at a comfortable temperature?

Taste
- Ask to eat a meal and evaluate the quality and taste of the food.

As increasing numbers of our parents are living to their eighties and nineties, we may be called upon to assist them in relocating their homes. In the past several decades there has been a movement to the Sunbelt—Florida, Arizona and California. The decreasing metabolic ability of the body as we age makes it difficult for older people to keep warm; the warmer climate compensates for this. Many older people suffer from heart disease, emphysema, and rheumatism which makes physical exertion difficult, hence these locations serve to reduce needed labor—shoveling of snow, handling coal, putting up storm windows, etc.

Dr. Robert Havighurst, Human Development Specialist associated with the University of Chicago, states that the principal values older people look for in housing are (1) quiet, (2) privacy, (3) independence of action, (4) nearness to relatives and friends, (5) residence among own cultural group, (6) low cost, and (7) closeness to transportation lines and communal institutions—libraries, shops, movies, recreational centers, churches, etc.

The best types of housing arrangements for older people other than independence in their own homes according to Dr. Havighurst seem to be:

1. Small villages or communities in warm climates specially planned for old people. The communities should have shops, movies, churches, a library, restaurants and allow children and pets.
2. Housing units specially designed for older people in all parts of the city, with laundry facilities, adequate protection, and special ramps for the wheelchair persons, elevators, etc.
3. Dwelling units (small apartments) in single-family residences designed for three-generation families. The grandparents have a small apartment of their own which gives them quiet and privacy, and yet they are in the same house with the rest of the family and can help and be helped as need arises.
4. Cooperative housing projects for older people with communal eating, laundry, and other facilities. The Federal Housing Authority has built and is building such projects. Many of these will be close to their children.
5. Old people's homes that are specially equipped to handle those with limited ability to care for themselves.

Most of the non-institutionalized disabled persons receive all needed assistance from the primary family and friends. Nearly half of nursing home care payments made are private and direct out-of-pocket expenditures. Catastrophic costs of long-term nursing homes require in many cases that the patient spend down their resources to become eligible for Medicaid. When Medicare runs out and when all the resources are used up Medicaid becomes the payer. The elderly frequently believe that Medicare alone or combined with private insurance will cover most or all of their long-term care. Unfortunately, this is not usually the case.

Recently some communities have developed what are called not-for-profit Life Care Communities or Continuing Care Retirement Communities (CCRS). These provide housing, health care, social activities, supporting service and meals. The typical campus consists of independent living units, a nursing facility, a contract with the residents which guarantees health care for more than a year and where the long-time care is shared by the entire community. No one, therefore, has catastrophic expenditure or goes on Medicaid for the expenses are paid from pooled funds from monthly fee of $2,600 or yearly $32,000. To move in a community site, entry fees range from $60,000 to $120,000 and monthly fees from $1,800 to $3,000 in 2007. There are hundreds of these facilities in the United States and by 2010 these are expected to expand to thousands. Unfortunately, few elderly can afford this type and level of care. New York State prohibits these contracts in order to protect consumers from unscrupulous operators.

Another type of care arrangement is the Life Care at Home (LCAH). Entry fees range from $5,000 to $10,000, monthly fees from $200 to $300 per month. The service provided is for the lifetime. Therapies at home are provided, such as physical, speech, occupational, electronic monitoring, respite and day care, personal care, and homemaker services. Physician and hospital care is also given to the elderly.

Another arrangement is Group-Shared Homes. These allow from 5 to 15 persons to buy a building, renovate it, or build another. Share-a-home began in Florida as a non-profit organization banding compatible persons together to pool their resources to pay their living costs. A smaller version of this is where two or three women rent an apartment and share the expenses. The work required is shared as is cleaning responsibility and meal preparation. The group is supportive of individual members' problems and health needs. A greater degree of independence is available in this setting as opposed to the institutional home or to live with children or other relatives. The secret here is to find persons of common background, flexibility and interests. Saving a large entry fee payment to a Care Community such as the LLC or LCAH's is a distinct possibility.

A second type is the Congregate Community. This arrangement provides a studio apartment with one bedroom. There is a monthly fee covering rent, two meals a day (noon and night), housekeeping services and a variety of social, recreational, and cultural programs. A person must be over 62 and ambulatory to enroll. Individuals have the freedom to come and go as they want and the community has a residence council composed of the renters which meets once a month to discuss programs and problems of the group.

Another type of arrangement allows for the individual to remain in their home (28 million live in their own home or a realty one—8 million alone) and use the mortgage equity of the home to pay their living expenses. This plan is known as the Home Equity Conversion plan. It usually pays rates adjusted to the forecast of the owner's longevity. The money is given on a monthly basis and begins once the contracts are signed following examination of the deed and appraisal of the home. These opportunities have been available in Buffalo, NY, in Wisconsin and California and are available in other places. However, due to the possibility of heir suits contesting the sale of the home and lenders concern for fixed rates many are wary of this type of loan.

The Mobile Home Pool is a situation where many elderly persons are now living. It is not age specific and not organized for the elderly but many retired and older persons (often a majority) are living there despite the high density. There is the advantage of paying low rent, opportunity for developing friendships and finding a support group. Usually located near towns and cities where there is access to supplies, health facilities, churches, and recreational opportunities.

Alternatives to Nursing Homes

Assisted-living facilities: If your loved one doesn't need the level of medical care offered by a nursing home, consider an assisted-living facility, where residents get help with tasks such as cooking and laundry. These facilities are listed in the Yellow Pages of your phone directory. But be aware: They are less tightly regulated than nursing homes.

Home Health Care - Advocates of this approach claim it's more efficient than nursing home care and more supportive of elderly dignity and independence. For more information check the National Association of Home Care and Hospice www.nahc.org/SunCity (Arizona) and Leisure World (California) for those who can retire early. They require early age and too much money for most age required 45-55, children under 18 not allowed. One may purchase a condo and pay homeowners' fees. Climates and recreation are the calling cards. There are other communities besides these around the country.

A Naturally Occurring Retirement Community (NORC) is where residents remain for years and age as neighbors. A NORC may refer to a specific apartment building, or a street or block of single family homes. Residents have just stayed in their homes or apartments for many years and it has evolved into a senior community. It is possible to band together and develop, or seek help to develop, access to services to aid those needing assistance, to retain the highest quality of life as they age. Some 27% of seniors live in a NORC. Fair housing laws provide for a complex with 80% of its residents over 55, to become officially age restricted.

Care giving and Eldercare Harvard Medical School Family Health Guide 2005

For many years the law required an age restricted community to offer significant amenities and services if it was age restricted. That is no longer the case, but to compete and attract residents, we still see most age restricted communities offering amenities and services to serve their residents. Significant amenities and services may include:

- Social and recreational programs
- Continuing education programs
- Information and counseling
- Outside maintenance and referral services

- Emergency and preventive health care programs
- Meal Programs
- Transportation on a schedule

Nursing Home Availability and Cost

Among Americans turning 65 today 69% will need some form of long-term care whether in the community or in a residential care facility. What is available, its costs and pay for the services rendered are shown below. Various kinds of care are addressed later in this chapter.

Availability in the U.S. - Source: Robert Bau, author of *America's Nursing Homes.*

- There are 16,100 certified nursing homes - down from 17,000 in 1999.
- There are 39,500 assisted living facilities.
- There are 2,240 continuing care retirement communities.
- Accounting for about 40 percent of total expenditures on nursing facilities, Medicaid's payments cover the care of more than half of all nursing home residents. (aahsa. com 2007)

For information from Medicaid about programs that may help you, 1-800-633-4227 (Medicaid, PACE).

Information for Veterans

Veterans Administration	Nursing Home	Home Care
Facility on a space available basis for eligible veterans. If you are a veteran, call 1-800-827-1000 for available services.	Skilled nursing care for veterans provided only in Virginia.	Chronically ill veterans eligible for medical nursing, and rehabilitative care.

The BIGGEST FEAR of Boomers is the Loss of Independence and Mobility

In an AARP survey, older Americans with disabilities expressed their biggest worries about the future to be:

1. Loss of Independence
2. Loss of mobility
3. Being unable to pay for the cost of care services
4. Becoming housebound or confined to living quarters
5. Loss or decrease of financial assets

About Healthcare Costs and Finances

(Source: Survey of large and small sites by F.R. Jones, et al, 2009)

Costs (Reported by AARP 2008):
- The average monthly cost for a private room in a nursing home is $6,234, or $74,806 annually.
- The average monthly cost for a semi-private room in a nursing home is $5,448, or $65,385 annually.
- The average monthly cost of living in an assisted living facility is $2,714, or $32,572 annually.
- The average monthly cost of living in a not-for-profit Continuing Care Retirement Community is $2,672, or $32,064 annually.
- To move into a community, individuals must also pay an entry fee ranging from $60,000 to $120,000.
- The average hourly rate for a certified home health aide is $32.37.
- The average hourly rate for an uncertified home health aide is $19.00.
- The national average daily rate for adult day centers is $61.
- The national average hourly rate for homemakers/ companions is $18.

- **Who Pays**
  Private Payment
  - Nearly 40 percent of long-term care spending is paid for by private funds. (Dr. Robert Bau)
  Medicare
  - Medicare, which covers rehabilitation services after an individual is discharged from a hospital, pays for 19 percent of all long-term care spending.
  - Medicaid, which covers health care costs for low-income individuals, pays for 49 percent of all long-term care spending.

What you pay if you have Original Medicare

MEDICARE PART A

Part A helps cover inpatient care in hospitals. This includes critical access hospitals and skilled nursing facilities (not custodial or long-term care). It also covers hospice care and home health care. You must meet certain conditions to get these benefits.

Part A Costs for Covered Services and Items

Blood - In most cases, the hospital gets blood from a blood bank at no charge, and you won't have to pay for it or replace it. If the hospital has to buy blood for you, you must either pay the hospital costs for the first 3 units of blood you get in a calendar year or have the blood donated.

Home Health Care - You pay:
- Limited part-time skilled nursing care
- 20% of the Medicare-approved amount for durable medical equipment

Hospice Care:
- Hospice care is given in the home to the terminally ill
- Prescription for outpatient prescription drugs for pain and symptom management
- Medicare approves the amount for inpatient respite care (short-term care given by another caregiver, so the usual caregiver can rest)

Medicare doesn't cover room and board when you get hospice care in your home or another facility where you live (like a nursing home).

Hospital Stay - In 2010, you pay:
- $1068 deductible and no coinsurance for days 1-60 each benefit period
- $267 per day for days 61-90 each benefit period
- $534 per "lifetime reserve day" after day 90 each benefit period (up to 60 days over your lifetime)
- All costs for each day after the lifetime reserve days
- Inpatient mental health care in a psychiatric hospital limited to 190 days in a lifetime

Skilled Nursing Facility Stay - In 2010, you pay:
- $0 for the first 20 days each benefit period
- $133.50 per day for days 21-100 each benefit period
- All costs for each day after day 100 in a benefit period

Note: If you are in a Medicare Advantage Plan, costs vary by plan and may be either higher or lower than those noted above. Check with your plan.

Medicare Part B

Part B helps cover medical services like doctor's services, outpatient care, and other medical services that Part A doesn't cover. Part B is optional. Part B helps pay for covered medical services and items when they are medically necessary. It also covers some preventive services.

Part B Costs for Covered Services and Items

Part B Deductible - In 2010, you pay the first $135 yearly for Part B-covered services or items.

Blood - In most cases, the provider gets blood from a blood bank at no charge, and you won't have to pay for it or replace it. However, you will pay a copayment for the blood processing and handling services for every unit of blood you get, and the Part B deductible applies. If the provider has to buy blood for you, you must either pay the provider costs for the first 3 units of blood you get in a calendar year or have the blood donated by you or someone else. You pay a copayment for additional units of blood you get as an outpatient (after the first 3), and the Part B deductible applies.

Clinical Laboratory Services - You pay $0 for Medicare-approved services.

Home Health Services - You pay $0 for Medicare-approved services. You pay 20% of the Medicare-approved amount for durable medical equipment.

Medical and Other Services - You pay 20% of the Medicare-approved amount for most doctor services (including most doctor services while you are a hospital outpatient), outpatient therapy (within limits), most preventive services, and durable medical equipment.

Mental Health Services - You pay 45% of the Medicare-approved amount for most outpatient mental health care.

Other Covered Services - You pay copayment or coinsurance amounts.

Outpatient Hospital Services - You pay a coinsurance or copayment amount that varies by service for each individual outpatient hospital service. No copayment for a single service can be more than the amount of the inpatient hospital deductible.

Note: All Medicare Advantage Plans must cover these services. Costs vary by plan and may be either higher or lower than those noted above. Check with your plan.

Additional Medicare Part B Coverage

Ambulance Service – When you need to be carried to the hospital or skilled nursing facility and it would be the most appropriate means available. Medicare will pay.

Ambulatory Surgery Center – Facility fees are covered for approved services if completed in 24 hours.

Bone Mass Measurement – Helps to see if you are at risk for broken bones—covered for once every 24 months (more often if medically necessary) for people with Medicare who meet certain medical conditions. You pay 20% of Medicare approved amount.

Cardiovascular Screenings – Every five years test for cholesterol, lipid and triglyceride levels to help prevent heart attack or stroke. Pay 20% for each visit.

Chiropractic Service – To correct a subluxation (when one or two or so if your bones in the spine moves out of position using manipulation of the spine. Subject to limits. Pays 20% of approved amount.

Clinical Laboratory Services – Includes blood tests, urinalysis, some screening tests and more. No cost.

Clinical Trials – To help doctors and researchers to find better ways to diagnose or treat diseases. Routine costs are covered if you take part in a qualifying clinical trial. No cost.

Each of the following items listed down to and including Transplant Services will be covered by Medicare for 80% of the approved cost.

Diabetic Self-Management Training – Diabetics with written orders from a doctor for teaching how to handle diabetic control.

Diabetic Supplies – Includes glucose testing monitors, test strips, lancet devices and lancets, control solutions and therapeutic shoes. Syringes and insulin if used with an insulin pump.

Doctor Services – One time welcome to Medicare physical exam.

Durable Medical Equipment – Items such as oxygen, wheel chairs, walkers, and hospital beds needed for use in homes.

Emergency Room Services – When in serious condition you get treated in emergency room and its services immediately.

Eyeglasses – One pair with standard frames after cataract surgery that implants an intraocular lens.

Flu Shots – One flu shot a season to prevent influenza.

Foot Exam and Treatment – If a diabetic with nerve damage and/ or meet certain conditions.

Glaucoma Tests – To help find eye disease glaucoma one every 12 months for people with high risk of glaucoma. High risks are people with family with glaucoma, African American age 50 and over or Hispanic 65 or older. Test for to be confirmed by an M.D. legally authorized to perform this service by the state.

Medical Nutrition Therapy Services – For diabetics or people with renal disease not on dialysis or had a kidney transplant or with a doctor's referral 3 years after a kidney transplant.

Occupational Therapy – Services given to help you return to usual activities.

PAP Test and Pelvic Exam – Check for cervical and vaginal cancers every 24 months—high risk women 12 months.

Physical Therapy – Use of heat, light, exercise and massage.

Prostate Cancer Screening – Test to help find prostate cancer—
PSA every 12 months.

Prosthetic/Orthotic Items – Arms, legs, both, neck braces,
artificial limbs, eyes, prostheses devices body parts, ostomy supplies
and physical therapy.

Smoking Cessation – Counseling to help stop smoking.

Telemedicine – Rural area rendered aid in a practitioner's
office.

Transplant Services – Includes heart, lungs, kidney, pancreas,
liver, under certain conditions. Also bone marrow and cornea under
certain conditions. Patient must be entitled to Part A.

Travel Care – Medical services is covered if travel to or from
Alaska to U.S. or on board ship if in territorial U.S. waters and U.S.
protectorates, Guam, Puerto Rico, Virgin Islands, etc.

Medicare and You 2010, U.S. Department of Health and Human
Services, Baltimore, MD

For more information on Medicare call 1-800-633-4227.

Part C and D   Medicare Health and prescription drug costs.

Part D	2010
National Base Beneficiary Premium	$31.94
1% Penalty Calculation	.32

Long Term Care Insurance

Of those 65 nearly one in three will spend three months or more
in a nursing home, and one in four will spend one year or more.
Nursing home care can cost $30,000 to $70,000 a year! The problem
with long term care is the lack of preparation for the costs incurred
when someone you love requires assistance. Some people can pay the
bill themselves, others will qualify for Medicaid (welfare), but most
will fall somewhere in between. According to Dr. Bau, Medicaid
pays most of the bills, private insurance pays only 2%.

When shopping for long-term care insurance, keep in mind the
high cost of care. If your funds are sufficient for care no need for
insurance otherwise get coverage.

Components of a Good Long-Term Care Policy

In looking for a policy several plans should be examined, they are different in many ways—when they apply, how benefits are paid, what they cover, etc. You should see what the benefits are in writing, the costs, the limitations and restrictions. Any special features should be noted to see if they are worth the cost. You might look into adding a rider onto your present health insurance policy. Some companies provide free quotes by mail or by Internet. The Federal government offers its employees long-term insurance and also sometimes to their parents at discounted premiums (at pre-tax dollars) contact www.LTCFeds.com or call 800-582-3337. Veterans Administration provides free or low-cost nursing home care and medical care. Call U.S. Department of Veterans Affairs, 800-827-1000 or www.va.gov.

If your employer offers a plan still look at other plans and compare for it may not be the best for your parents.

Things to Consider in Buying a Policy:

1. Is it offered by a creditable, well-established, stable company. Check your local Credit Business Bureau at www.gov.org. Check rating with one of the stock exchanges—Standard & Poor's www.standardandpoors. com, or Moody's www.moodys.com. Find one that is in the top two categories on financial strength.
2. Does It Provide Inflation Protection? A policy should allow for 5% inflation protection compounded annually. This is important for younger adults 15 to 20 years from retirement.
3. Fixed Premiums - Once a policy is purchased vs. changes in cost. Check to see if there have been recent premium raises.
4. Waivers - Policies should have a waiver excluding your parents from premium payments while in long term care. Find out any holds on this like number of days of care, type of care that one has to get before premiums are waived.

5. Is there protection from cancellation? Most all policies guarantee long term care renewable but check to make sure of this.

6. Is Alzheimer's Covered? Nearly all policies cover Alzheimer's and organic brain disease but not alcoholism, mental illness, drug addiction. Check to be sure.

7. Protection if premium skyrockets or buyer decides to withdraw from policy.

8. Rates for married persons if both buy policies split the benefits or adds benefits of the departed mates.

Who Needs Long-Term Care Insurance

Long-term insurance helps protect assets and preserves inheritance. Who should consider buying a policy?

1. Those with large assets - A policy would protect assets from the excessive cost of long-term care. Your parents should not buy a policy if he or she would be eligible for Medicaid within twelve to eighteen months of entering a nursing home. Nursing home costs vary widely so look at costs in the area. Roughly as a guide your parents should have $100,000+ in assets (excluding their home and personal belongings) before considering a long-term care insurance policy.

2. Those with sufficient income - If they can afford to pay $300 to $700 a month without affecting their standard of living providing they can obtain long-term care that cost no more than 5 percent of their total income. Also if they get less income in the future that they can still pay the premiums.

3. Those with borderline income - This class of people need insurance to pay for their long-term needs for the finances will not allow out of pocket payment for care. Regular payment and saving for eventuality is a must. Search for bear bone insurance that covers their essential needs. Investigate the companies you consider buying a policy from.

4. Those probably needing long-term care - The odds after 65 of going to a nursing home are about 40% and on average the stay is two and a half years. Nearly 50% stay three months or less. Most stay less than a year.
5. Those with no plan to move to a continuing retirement community.

The Parent in the Home with Children

For one reason or the other, be it custom, or economics, or compassion, we decide to move our parents into our home. Frequently, we have at the same time preteen or teenage youngsters to look after. And, to compound the difficulties, it happens in the middle years when we are also trying to forward our own interests. As mentioned earlier, we are destined to serve a middleman function. Few baby boomers can withstand this sort of appeal.

Many of our parents can make a good adjustment when moved to our home. Helping services in the home offer an advantage in that they are free due to the use of unpaid labor of household members. The children often love listening to the grandparent or playing cards and games with a companion. Grandparents frequently relate well with the young, even teenagers; for one thing they do not have the ultimate responsibility and sometimes they form an emotional tie with your children against the establishment, meaning you and/or your spouse, unfortunately. This comes out usually as being more permissive with your kids or a desire to rearrange something in their daily schedule or to do something special for them. One lady told me that her mother lived with her for twenty years—we had to take her in because she couldn't afford to live by herself. "My mother," she said, "followed me around from room to room always wanting to know what I was doing. So I grabbed every opportunity to get out of the house. But my husband was a 'saint' with her. My five children loved her dearly and they all came to her funeral when she died." Some youngsters!

It does require some planning to make things go reasonably well. In the first place, our parents need privacy. If an apartment or additional room can be built to your home for them, then this can serve as a retreat and a place to visit with their friends who come to call. One thing about our older people is that they require a routine; irregular meals are a no-no; the same is true of noise, a lot of people coming and going, the slamming of doors and revving up a car motor are taboo. This is not because old people are cranky. Their sensory systems do not accommodate to high decibel and cacophony of sound like the young. Even though this is true, it isn't fair to re-organize everything around the life of our parents and require younger members of the family to re-style their lives to accommodate our parents. A good place to start is prior to their becoming a part of the household if this is possible. This conversation should include expectations freely given—you have your life, they have theirs and the children have theirs. Hopefully with a good deal of respect, you can have but a common life and individual ones and things will go smoothly. The following are some general principles, which could help in these matters:

1. It should be understood that you have some things to do; social affairs, church obligations, visiting, vacationing time for children, and work tasks which will have to be attended to by you and/or your spouse without them being included many times. The close-knit family of the Waltons rarely exists, in fact, but if it does with you then you have less concern here. Syndicated columnist Ann Landers once reported a situation where the wife's husband's mother and grandmother moved in with them. They had an apartment built off the kitchen for Mama and Grandma with complete cooking facilities. They prepared their own breakfast and lunch. The wife cooked the dinner for all of them. The problem was that the wife worked all day surrounded by people. When she got home, she wanted peace and quiet—time to be alone. But Mama and Grandma insisted on having the door open all the time so that they "could feel a part of the household." It drove the woman crazy for they not only watched her, they asked questions by the dozen which interfered with the dinner preparation. She writes to ask is she selfish to want some privacy? The reply was that Mama and Grandma need to know this is one of your ways to get some relaxation and

you need peace and quiet when you prepare the meal; therefore, the door will have to be closed.

2.   It is not selfish to ask for some respite and to be alone because you need some peace to survive. Many, many different kinds of irritations like this one occur in these situations—husbands and wives both need some time when they are not on call and this should be understood by our parents. (If not, a talk about this will generally insure their cooperation and support.)

3.   When one accepts the role of caretaker they may not realize the understanding is as demanding. For a moment forgetting how much you care, you love, you feel responsible month after month you or your family have to attend to your cared person's need. To go on vacation or anywhere someone has to be there. Day after day meals to plan to prepare, medicine to procure and delivery, clothes to get, wash and help dress at some point. Bath, toiletry and etc. you do it but you'll need help. It's there—perhaps some family, senior centers, day care, senior elderly care sitters, Kelly Girls, Meals on Wheels, Friends, others such as friends or kin. It won't be easy but it will be rewarding.

4.   For many, many caregivers your home will need some additional fixtures even enlarging doorways, changing bath rooms, certainly fixtures for elderly to use the bathing facilities showers or bathtubs, toilets and washing bowls perhaps special chairs, tables and mobile equipment such as wheelchairs, electric motor vehicles or such. Even beds, ramps leading to the entrance to the home and special lifts for getting into vans, etc. Also a variety of other things.

Rules When Parents Live With Us

1.   If your parents can help financially, accept it, for it will give them a feeling of self-respect by knowing they are helping. If they want to give this on a regular basis, do not spurn it.

2. In the same manner, the help that can be given with the chores around the house should be welcomed; this tends to ward off their over-dependence and has the effect of bolstering their egos.

3. Privacy should be given—children, should along with other adults, respect our parents and allow them to have their own social and individual lives. This means also that our children do not have access to their possessions and belongings.

4. Do not give advice except as a last resort. When your idea is wanted or needed, your parents will come to you. Remember, they respect you for taking your own medicine—so don't give any more advice than you yourself are prepared to take—in short, be gentle with criticism.

5. It should be understood by both parents and children that sharing is expected and that no one is a privileged character in the home. Rules for meals, times to do certain things, use of the bathroom, tidying up, consideration by youngsters at night or loud talk and c.d.'s playing and the reverse for older parents in the morning when they are about earlier than most everyone else in the household

6. It has been said that "no roof is big enough for two families" and there is some truth to this saying. When irritation builds, as it will from time to time, maybe a visitation to other relatives and friends can be arranged. I remember a situation where a mother once or twice a year would say she and the daughter-in-law were at an impasse (she had it up to her throat), so she'd go visit a sister or friend for a couple of weeks. When she got back, the air would have cleared and life once again was livable.

The understanding of these rules should be accomplished early in anticipation of moving parents in with your family. Our children may need to be reminded of these rules, initially cooperative, they may come to view, when frustrated by certain restrictions, their grandparents as interlopers. We know, however, that older folks may need more psychological stroking (praise and kind words) than do the young. They have fewer friends, activities and opportunities through which to be complimented. As they get very old or sick, their perceptions turn inward due to increased body monitoring—their sleep, digestion, pain and irritations from being unable to get around as well as they would like. The physical needs come increasingly to dominate their lives like an infant whose needs make him completely oblivious to his social surroundings—he cries, vomits, urinates, and defecates at will with little control, no concern. The very old at some point approach this situation—by choice or by accident. So we need patience to tolerate and function—in short to survive. Understanding of their potential problems should prepare their sons and daughters mentally to undertake the care and assistance that is needed. Hopefully, good luck!

Abuse of the Elderly

The last thing a person would want to do, we hope, would be to abuse his mother or father. Nevertheless it happens one way or the other with a spouse, son or daughter being equally the perpetrator. The elderly are often like children, they have limited perspectives and should be treated with care. We need to remember that abuse is often just simply neglect. Neglect, such as; depriving the parent of medicine, food or care. Doing so ten times a week is considered abuse through neglect. Remember 4 hours a day for each patient is the usual standard for one-on-one care in a nursing facility. This time includes bathing, personal hygiene and grooming.

Physical abuse can range to being pushed, grabbed, shoved to being assaulted with a gun or knife. A national survey of state adult protective agencies released in 2006 turned up, in one year, 565,747 reports of abuse of vulnerable adults—larceny, neglect and cruelty of all sorts. With 89 percent of reports occurring in domestic settings, it's a disturbing snapshot of mistreatment of people in their own homes, mostly by their own kin, who are also likely to be their caretakers.

Many experts believe the survey revealed only the iceberg's tip. According to a yardstick developed by researchers, only one instance of abuse in 14 becomes known; in fact, a U.S. Senate committee has estimated the number of victims at 5 million yearly. Whatever the measure, the number is bound to multiply now that the first of 78 million boomers have passed age 60. AARP Bulletin, Vol. 28 no. 7, 2007 page 20.

When you are having a problem due to long-time frustration, sick/lack of resources or burn-out and are peaked to strike out or deny care to your kinsman you should counsel with a minister or call other family members or an agency for instant social agency whose number you can find the phone directory. The crisis help-lines is another source of help. Some relief is needed in these cases or assistance to get these cases or assistance to get things going normally again. Guidelines on these matters follow:

Suspicion or knowledge of abuse or neglect should be reported immediately to the following:

- Nursing supervisor on duty.
- Nursing home Administrator and/or Director of Nursing.
- Local police.
- State Department of Human services, Adult Protective Services.
- State Ombudsman.
- State Survey Agency.

Definitions

Abuse - the willful infliction of injury, unreasonable confinement, intimidation, or punishment with resulting physical harm, pain, or mental anguish. Many states have laws requiring reports of abuse and neglect.

Neglect - the failure to provide goods and services necessary to avoid physical harm, mental anguish, or mental illness. Neglect occurs when nursing home staff fails to monitor and/or supervise the delivery of patient care and services to assure that care is provided as needed by the patient. Some examples of neglect might include: lack of assistance in eating, drinking, walking, bathing, toileting, or ignoring call bells/lights. Neglect can cause depression, dehydration, incontinence, and/or pressure sores.

Verbal Abuse - the use of oral, written, or gestured language that willfully includes disparaging and derogatory terms to patients or their families, or within their hearing distance regardless of their age, ability to comprehend, or disability.

Sexual Abuse - includes but is not limited to, sexual harassment, sexual coercion, or sexual assault.

Physical Abuse - includes hitting, slapping, pinching, and kicking. It also includes controlling behavior through corporal punishment.

Mental Abuse - includes, but is not limited to, humiliation, harassment, threats of punishment or deprivation.

Involuntary Seclusion - the separation of a patient from other patients, or from her/his own room, or confinement to her/his room against the patient's will.

Misappropriation of Patient Property - the deliberate misplacement, exploitation, or wrongful, temporary or permanent use of a patient's belongings or money without the patient's consent.

Warning Signals
❖ **Physical and sexual abuse**
Suspicious bruises and other injuries. Rope burns or other signs of restraints. Sudden change in behavior. Caregiver's refusal to allow visitors.

❖ **Emotional or psychological abuse**
(insults, threats, social isolation) Elder is extremely upset, withdrawn, unresponsive; other unusual behavior.

❖ **Neglect:** Dehydration, malnutrition, untreated bedsores, weight loss, unattended health problems or lack of necessary aids, such as eyeglasses or dentures. Unsanitary living conditions (lice, soiled bedding). Inadequate clothing; no heat or running water.

❖ **Financial exploitation**
Unexplained bank withdrawals, unauthorized use of a

credit or ATM card, or stolen or "misplaced" cards or checkbook. Checks written as a "loan" or "gift." Abrupt changes in a will or other documents. Unexplained transfer of assets to a family member or someone outside the family. Disappearance of valuables. Ill-advised investments. Sudden appearance of a previously uninvolved relative claiming a right to an elder" affairs or possessions. AARP, JULY/AUGUST 2007 Vol. 48 No. 7 www.aarp.org/bulletin

If and When Problems Arise in the Nursing Home

- Speak directly to the individuals involved. Many times individuals fail to realize there is a problem. Speaking up in a nonthreatening way can help focus the staff on the problem and bring about a quick resolution. If the staff indicates the problem is out of their control or too big of a problem for them to handle alone, ask what you can do to help or whom else you should go speak to about the problem. Above all, remain calm and in control of your emotions. Anger will bring nothing more than a negative reaction from others.

- Speak to a Supervisor of the Individuals Involved in the Problem. Ask to speak with the immediate supervisor of the staff members involved. If it is a Certified Nurse Aid, speak to the charge nurse. If it is a charge nurse, speak to the Director of Nursing. Follow the same pattern for other disciplines.

- Obtain a Copy of the Nursing Home's Grievance Policy/ Procedure. Medicaid regulations and state law require nursing homes to have a written grievance or complaint handling policy or procedures. Follow the procedures outlined. The procedure will designate a staff person, usually a Social Worker, to review and follow up on grievances brought to their attention. Sometimes the policy will outline other individuals to contact within the nursing home, such as the administrator, if you are still not satisfied after speaking with the Social Worker. The policy may further list individuals outside the nursing home, but still connected to the nursing home, such as an owner or company official.

- Contact the State Long-Term Care Ombudsman. These types of Ombudsmen are interested in protecting the aged and those with health problems. They are versed in state law and licensure of nursing home facilities and will readily intervene for you with those charged with your family member to bring about improvement. The services of Ombudsmen provided by the state or federal government are offered without cost.

- Report Problem to State Survey Agency. This agency is required to investigate complaints involving the health or safety of patients within two working days. The agency can only take punitive action against a nursing home when during their inspection/visit they prove a problem exists and it violates nursing home regulations. This agency licenses nursing homes and inspects nursing homes on a yearly basis. When surveyors are in a nursing home, take advantage of the opportunity you have to speak with them regarding your concerns. Surveyors are required to interview patients concerning the quality of care they are receiving from the nursing home.

- Don't Ever Give Up! It can be frustrating at times when you feel no one cares or is listening to you. Don't give up. Find that person in the center or government agency that will listen and help you.

About Our Parent's Money and Documents You Should Know About

There are legal aspects that relate to our parents if they become senile, are terminally ill, or have mental distortions. In 1976, the Tax Reform Act was passed making gifts given in the last three years of a person's life subject to estate tax laws. Monies, gifts, and endowments, etc., given away before this time (three years) will be excluded from tax liability. Inheritance tax can be a very sizable amount. If wills are not made, then the state where you reside will determine how the estate is settled - and no one wants that to happen! You should gently, tactfully discuss this with your parent and/or parents. Also it is of dire necessity that you insist that they keep or get the records of their stocks, deeds, savings bonds, wills, trusts, social security numbers, bankbooks, statements and insurance policies, etc., and you should know of any contracts they have made. The physician of my mother's father put a tremendous lien on our family estate for bills that we thought had been paid. We had sometimes paid the bills ourselves. But in the absence of all but meager evidence we "paid in full." Sometimes our parents decide they would like to give their money (it maybe little) away to a venture, charity or an evangelist. This is a touchy matter, it may be all right in fact commendable, but frankly in many cases it amounts to bilge and smooth glove swindle. The best tactic here is to be persuasive but careful, not losing your cool over it; if it is impossible to convince your parents, then attempt to get them to agree to temporize the matter, to put off the decision, time will usually be a good ally and often circumvent the useless giving away of funds that the parent will need or you in their service.

If in the event the situation arises when a parent is not able to make a decision or is incapacitated, then the state will make the medical decisions for them unless they have given a trusted person durable power of attorney or drafted a living will or an advance directive. Parents should be urged to grant someone power of attorney for them in the event they are stricken with some mental or physical impairment that prevents the normal conduct of their affairs. Of interest to note is that more mothers grant power of attorney to sons or daughters than do fathers.

If you are going to be responsible for your parents there are some facts which can assist you in planning. The requirement of funds is a necessity and whether or not we are in the middle income bracket $30,000 to $60,000 or higher, we need all the help we can get from outside sources—agencies, local, state, and federal.

The typical woman will live nearly 18.7 years after she is 65; for the man at 65, 14.5 years. At age 75, seventy percent of the men still living are married whereas seventy percent of the women are widowed. With two parents (man and wife) it may be more economical to keep them in the home and to supplement their care needs through you. Since forty percent of the homes of the elderly were built before 1939, upkeep could be helped and/or agencies.

Additional Sources of Help

Day Centers

The Older American Act provides services to frail elderly in homes and adult care centers. It provided reimbursement or supplements to centers serving 60 persons or more per day including health education programs. The authors visit to a senior center recently (funded by the state) had a well organized program of activities running from 8:30 to 1:30 five days a week; including a good lunch, health care information and clinics, recreational trips, tax help and an opportunity to learn a new skill. Besides helping care for an elderly person caretakers have a break to manage their own affairs and business.

Adult Day Care

Most towns of moderate size 25,000 upward have adult day care usually operating from 9 to 5. Services offered include monitoring cardiovascular, nutrition, medicine taking, some therapy, information on tax, exercise programs to entertainment. Usually one meal is given plus snacks. Some centers are limited to a place to play games, socialize, have a meal and a special program and recreation.

Some adult day care centers are supported by state or the Federal government and are free to the indigent and low-income person. Some centers take daily collections to help defray the expenses. Many of these centers are private and non-profit and should be less expensive and many not be licensed so this may affect the overall quality.

Home Care

Typically a nurse comes to the home at least three times a week but, if needed, will come one day a week or every day. The cost runs from $16 to $23 an hour and may be less in smaller towns or cities. The duties of the caregiver include personal care, daily activities and household help such as cooking meals running errands, grocery shopping, light housekeeping and occasional transportation.

Kelly Girl Assistance

Help is available as nurses or help with house hold duties such as meal planning and cooking, house cleaning, clothes washing, taking to doctors' appointments, leisurely walks, grocery purchases and errands, etc. The cost is $18.95 with a four-hour minimum time required.

Intermediate Care Facility

A care service designed at meeting the needs of people who are not quite ill enough to go into a hospital but not quite well enough to manage their own home. Increasingly these facilities are incorporated into skilled centers or hospitals. Service provides short term rehabilitation to enable users to regain their optimal levels of independence. A variety of therapies are provided speech, physical, vocational, etc., with close supervision of medical care. Cost can run up to $200 a day.

Rehabilitation Centers

Most often operated on an outpatient basis. Nevertheless are quite costly unless underwritten by private or public funds. Medicare pays for initial rehabilitation cost for long term cost around 20% of cost. Without insurance the cost easily runs from $200 or more a day. Find out the quality of nursing service provided. Typical cost runs from $85 for a 15-minute visit to several hundred dollars for 30 minutes depending on the doctors and the insurance available. Prices do vary so look and inquire around. The Center for Comprehensive Service with outlets in 34 states offers help for speech, vocational, brain injuries, occupational and cognitive trauma. The costs are expensive and range from $500 a day to $1000 depending upon the nature of the therapy and supervision required. Typically $200 an hour services are provided by a psychiatrist with the care ordinarily running three to six months.

Nutrition of Elderly Persons

The importance of nutrition cannot be underestimated and caretakers should be aware of the need of a proper diet. The table below prepared by the Journal of Geriatrics indicates the medical conditions and social factors that related to poor diets.

The elderly need a balanced diet and almost all can profit by foods taken from the basic food groups: meat (red and white), fruits and vegetables, milk products, for protein, carbohydrates, fat, calcium, vitamin A & D, breads and cereals, Vitamin A & B complex - 4 servings per day - (cereal, potatoes, etc.). Many elderly have lactose intolerance and this may lead to avoidance of dairy products resulting in lower intake of protein, calcium and Vitamin D but this has to be compensated for by other foods. The chronic alcoholic may get by with the calories from alcohol but gets inadequate protein. People who eat plenty of fats and carbohydrates may still have a protein deficiency. Some causes of protein calorie malnutrition are: low socio-economic status, loss of dentition, gastrointestinal malabsorption and other functional impairments. These nutritional problems may be characterized by inadequate intake of both calories and proteins or sufficient calorie intake at the expense of a high carbohydrate, low protein diet.

Common Problems of the Elderly Frequently Associated with Poor Nutrition

---

Medical Conditions	Social Factors
Arthritis	Living alone
Dementia	Poor dietary habits
Drug-nutrient interactions	Bereavement
Depression	Alcoholism
Post-gastrectomy or after surgical procedures	Low socio-economic status
Hypothyroidism	Housebound elderly with poor exposure to sunlight

Dysphasia
Neurologic impairment; stroke, Parkinsonism
Malignancy
Vascular insufficiency of the intestines
Chronic pulmonary

Some problems of nutritional deficits are reviewed here.

Vitamin and Mineral Deficiency

Toxicity potential — Vitamin supplements have been suggested for the elderly based on survey studies showing subnormal blood levels or low dietary intake, even in the absence of any clinical signs or symptoms of deficiency. Recent surveys suggest that many elderly take vitamin and mineral supplements. Because these supplements are rarely considered by either patients or physicians as drugs, they are frequently overlooked in the patient's evaluation or are taken in excess. Therefore, the elderly patient may be at risk for toxicity, as well as for vitamin deficiencies.

For example, high doses of the fat-soluble vitamin D with calcium can promote hypercalcemia. Although the exact does at which this occurs varies among individuals, elderly persons are particularly prone to develop this complication due to increased fat stores. Large doses of vitamin C may interfere with the absorption of vitamin B12 and has also been associated with a higher incidence of renal calculi. High doses of vitamin A can cause bone and joint pain, skin or hair changes, hepatomegaly, and benign intracranial hypertension.

Vitamin C Deficiency — Blood ascorbic acid levels decline with age in both sexes. This is usually due to decreased intake, although aging may also have an independent effect on blood ascorbic acid levels. Although severe vitamin C deficiency with clinical scurvy can occur, it is uncommon.

Supplemental vitamin C increases plasma and leukocyte ascorbic acid concentrations in those already receiving adequate amounts of vitamin C in the diet. No bad effects have been noted from this but low intake is a problem.

Vitamin D Deficiency — Vitamin D deficiency has been shown to be present in over 45% of non-supplemented elderly individuals living in institutions. Low plasma 225-hydroxy-vitamin D levels have also been reported in elderly persons in the community.

Even though dietary intake of vitamin D has been found to be lower in the elderly, diminished sunlight exposure and declining ability to metabolize vitamin D at both hepatic and renal levels are also important reasons for marginal vitamin D status in many older persons. In addition, a variety of drugs may interfere with vitamin D metabolism or actions, resulting in a deficiency. Examples include prednisone, phenobarbital, and phenytoin sodium.

Clinical Features — Clinical features of vitamin D deficiency are usually secondary to bone demineralization. It is important, therefore, not to consider bone pain, fractures, or loss of height as inevitable manifestations of aging or due necessarily to osteoporosis. Despite a relatively lower incidence in the elderly compared with the young.

Minerals — Apart from calcium, phosphorus, and iron, exact daily requirements for many minerals and trace elements have been difficult to establish. A notable exception, of course, is that decreased intake of calcium has been widely recognized in the elderly and undoubtedly contributes to the high prevalence of osteoporosis. Calcium alone has been shown to reduce the rate of fractures in patients with osteoporosis and to reduce the rate of bone loss. In addition to calcium, a variety of other elements is clearly essential for the maintenance of health.

The situation with other trace elements can become very complicated, however, because a number of them interact between themselves and/or act synergistically with vitamins. Even if coexistent vitamin A deficiency is present, night blindness will not improve until both vitamin A and zinc are in harmony. Zinc deficiency may also play a role in the anorexia often observed in aged patients.

Clinical features of deficiencies of some minerals are listed in the following table. It is clear from that list that many common clinical problems in the elderly including anemia, poor night vision, impotence, glucose intolerance, and cardiomyopathy can result from these nutritional deficiencies.

Fortunately, deficits of trace elements usually do not occur as isolated events, but rather in the setting of generalized malnutrition, malabsorption, or a requirement of long-term nutritional support. Particularly in these settings, assessment of trace element status by appropriate laboratory measurement is essential.

Conclusion — Deficiencies of a variety of nutrients including protein, calories, vitamins and minerals, are not uncommon in the elderly. The clinical signs and symptoms of these deficiencies may be subtle, and often mistaken as either inevitable accompaniments of aging or secondary to disease conditions often present in geriatric patients. Since correction of nutrient deficits can have a major impact on the health of the elderly, all physicians must monitor dietary intake and overall nutritional status of their patients.

Recommended Daily Dietary Intake of Nutrients for Healthy Elderly Persons

Nutrients	Age	Male	Female
Calories (kcal)	51-75	2000-2800	1400-2000
	76+	1650-2450	1200-2000
Protein (g)	51+	56	44
Vitamin A			
(Fg retinol equivalents)	51+	1000	800
Vitamin D (µg)	51+	5.0	5.0
Vitamin E			
(mg a-tocopherol)	51+	10	8.0
Ascorbic acid	51+	60	60
Thiamine (mg)	51+	1.2	1.0
Riboflavin (mg)	51+	1.4	1.2
Niacin			
(mg niacin equivalents)	51+	16	13
Vitamin B_6 (mg)	51+	2.2	2.0
Folacin (µg)	51+	400	400
Vitamin B_{12} (µg)	51+	3.0	3.0
Calcium (mg)	51+	800-1000	800-1200
Phosphorus	51+	800	800
Magnesium (mg)	51+	350	300
Iron (mg)	51+	10	10
Zinc (mg)	51+	15	15
Iodine (µg)	51+	150	150
Vitamin K (µg)	Adult	70-140	70-140
Biotin (µg)	Adult	100-200	100-200
Pantothenic acid (mg)	Adult	4.0-7.0	4.0-7.0
Sodium (mg)	Adult	1100-3300	1100-3300
Potassium (mg)	Adult	1875-5625	1875-5625
Chloride (mg)	Adult	1700-5100	1700-5100
Copper (mg)	Adult	2.0-3.0	2.0-3.0
Manganese (mg)	Adult	2.5-5.0	2.0-5.0

Fluoride (mg)	Adult	1.5-4.0	1.5-4.0
Chromium (mg)	Adult	0.05-0.20	0.05-0.20
Selenium (mg)	Adult	0.05-0.50	0.05-0.20
Molybdenum (mg)	Adult	0.15-0.50	0.15-0.50
Water (ml/kcal)	Adult	1.0	1.0

Source: *Adapted from Food and Nutrition Board, National Academy of Sciences 2007*

Diseases and Symptoms of the Elderly The number of calories per pound for older adults should range between 16-18 per day meaning 2200 calories a day for the average man and 1800 for the typical woman. A 150-pound man would need approximately 2500 calories per day. A woman of 100 would require 1700 calories per day.

A number of the common diseases are described in the appendix of this book. Also presented are a number of symptoms frequently observed in the older adult.

COMMON DISEASES AND SYMPTOMS
OF OLDER PEOPLE

National Institute of Health Bethesda, MD 2007

Some of the following diseases may occur earlier in life but are much more likely to appear in the later years. Listed below are a number of common diseases that affect the elderly and some ways in which they may be treated. All patients should, of course, consult their physicians for diagnosis and treatment of their own individual conditions.

ALZHEIMER'S DISEASE

About 4 million older Americans have Alzheimer's, a disease that usually develops in people age 65 or older. This number is expected to triple by the year 2050 as the population ages. Although there's no cure for Alzheimer's disease, researchers have made progress. Treatments are available that improve the quality of life for some people, more drugs are being studied, and scientists have discovered several genes associated with Alzheimer's, which may lead to new treatments to block progression of this complex disease.

The telltale mark of the disease in the beginning is forgetfulness. As the disease progresses there will be increasing memory loss. Some personality and behavior changes appear: confusion, irritability, restlessness. Judgment, concentration and speech may be affected. Finally, many may eventually become incapable of caring for themselves. A breakthrough at the Mayo Clinic and their collaborators (2009) have found that agents known as gamma-secretase modulators (GSM) work to reduce production of long pieces of the amyloid beta protein (Abeta). This protein readily sticks together and forms clumps and it increases production of shorter Abeta that can inhibit the longer forms from sticking together. This is critical because only when Abeta aggregates and accumulates is it harmful and can trigger Alzheimer's disease.

When these compounds lower the amount of the bad, longer sticky Abeta peptides in the brain, they increase the quantity of shorter Abeta peptides that may protect against development of Alzheimer's disease.

Not only that, GSM agents actually stick to the Abeta already in the brain, keeping it from aggregating. A hallmark of Alzheimer's is formation of "plaques" and other assemblies of Abeta protein in the brain, which are believed to damage neurons in complex ways that are not yet fully understood, researchers say.

This means that these compounds may do three things that may be beneficial with respect to Alzheimer's disease: they inhibit production of long Abeta, block aggregation of Abeta and increase production of shorter Abeta peptides that may in turn inhibit Abeta aggregation.

Researchers were able to diagnose Alzheimer's correctly, using software that detected the difference between MRI brain scans of those with Alzheimer's and those without the disease with accuracy as high as 96 percent. The study also revealed that the computer-based diagnostic method could successfully differentiate patients with Alzheimer's disease from those with frontotemporal lobar degeneration, a form of dementia involving degeneration of gray matter.

ARTERIOSCLEROSIS (ATHEROSCLEROSIS)

National Institutes of Health, Bethesda, MD 2007

Arteriosclerosis is a general term for hardening of the arteries. Atheroscleria, a type of arteriosclerosis, causes the narrowing and closing of a blood vessel due to accumulation of fats, complex carbohydrates, blood and blood products, fibers, tissues, and calcium deposits in its inner wall.

Arteriosclerosis is also related to hypertension (high blood pressure) and diabetes. The extent of arterial involvement in arteriosclerosis increases with age and can affect all the arteries of the body, especially those of the brain, heart, and lower extremities. When the blood supply to the brain is reduced by narrowing of the arteries supplying the brain, disturbances in behavior and cognition may result.

Arteriosclerosis in the aged is treated by attempting to lower the blood fats by diet when they are significantly elevated. Drugs to lower blood fats at this age are not of proven value. Elevated blood pressure should be treated with a lot-salt diet and, when necessary, the milder antihypertensive drugs. Cigarette smoking should be discontinued. A program of supervised physical activity is helpful, as is the control of obesity and diabetes. Surgical procedures to relieve or bypass obstructed blood vessels in the chest, neck, heart, and extremities may be of value after careful work up and evaluation of the benefits and risks involved.

ARTHRITIS

Arthritis is a general term referring to any degeneration or inflammation of the joints. It is classified according to its acuteness or its chronicity and also according to the joints involved and specific laboratory and X-ray findings. Many older persons suffer from arthritis, some to a mild degree and others severely.

The most common form, called osteoarthritis, involves primarily the weight-bearing joints and is due to the wear-and-tear process that accompanies aging. Osteoporosis, or thinning of the bones with aging, which occurs more often in women, contributes to collapse of the backbone as well as hip and wrist fractures. Inflammatory involvement of the joints, rheumatoid arthritis, is less common in the aged. Gout, a metabolic disease of the joints accompanied by severe pain and signs of inflammation, may also be seen in the aged.

Treatment of arthritis varies with the cause and includes physiotherapy, use of certain anti-inflammatory medications, and orthopedic devices. The use of female sex hormones for treating osteoporosis may be beneficial, but warrant careful discussion with a physician.

BRONCHITIS AND LUNG DISEASES

Bronchitis is an inflammation of the cells that line the bronchial air tubes. It may be caused by infection, or by chronic irritation cigarette smoke or following the inhalation of some harmful substance. Infectious bronchitis may be treated with antibiotics. In the case of chronic bronchitis, cessation of smoking is, of course, imperative. If untreated, chronic bronchitis may progress gradually to pulmonary emphysema.

Pulmonary emphysema, which results when the air sacs in the lungs are distended and damaged, is often found in heavy smokers. The patient suffers from shortness of breath and a cough. Treatment centers around relief of chronic bronchial obstruction by use of devices that help the emphysema patient to breathe. A variety of drugs and exercises are of value.

CANCER

Cancer (malignant neoplasm or tumor) is an uncontrolled growth of a tissue or portion of an organ that can spread (metastasize) to another part of the body. Cancer can occur in the throat, larynx, mouth, gastrointestinal tract, skin, bones, thyroid, bladder, kidney, and so forth. Because cancer symptoms in the aged are atypical, or may be ignored by the aged patient afflicted with other symptoms and often with a poor memory, comprehensive annual examinations are vital for early detection and treatment.

Cancer may be treated with surgery, radiotherapy (X-ray), chemotherapy or by any combination of the three methods. Because life expectancy is limited and the growth of many cancers is slow in the aged, there should be consideration of the value and potential side effects of potent methods before they are undertaken.

CONGESTIVE HEART FAILURE

Congestive heart failure occurs when the heart muscle has been so weakened that all pumping performance is impaired and it cannot provide sufficient circulation to body tissues. This condition may result from many years of untreated high blood pressure, heart attacks, or rheumatic heart disease. It may also be produced by diseases such as chronic lung disease, anemia, infection, and alcoholism.

Treatment for congestive heart failure is directed at improving the heart's pumping efficiency and eliminating excess fluids. Digitalis derivatives are often used to strengthen the heart muscle, and diuretics and salt restriction to remove excess fluid of the thyroid gland, or anemia, may also be necessary.

CORONARY ARTERY HEART DISEASE

This disease, which is present in almost all individuals over the age of seventy in the United States, involves atherosclerosis of the arteries that supply blood to the heart muscle. In older persons coronary heart disease is superimposed on a heart when there may be a general decrease in muscle-cell size and efficiency.

A heart attack (myocardial infarction) happens when a portion of the blood supply to the heart muscle is cut off. In the elderly it is not unusual for there to be hardly any symptoms accompanying an infarction, in contrast to the crushing most experienced by younger persons. Substitution symptoms are also common the elderly. For example, when the elderly heart fails because of a heart attack, blood may back up behind the left side of the heart into the blood vessels of the lungs causing shortness of breath, instead of chest pain. In other cases, the flow of blood from the weakened heart to the brain is diminished, with resultant dizziness or fainting rather than chest pain.

Modern treatment of the complications of acute myocardial infarction (which include irregular heartbeat and heart failure) with drugs, oxygen and clocking equipment is saving many lives and enabling the period of bed rest to be shortened. Patients with uncomplicated cases now get up out of bed and into a chair much earlier than before, and cardiac rehabilitation is begun early with good results. Cardiac shock (intractable heart failure), however, remains a difficult problem with a high mortality rate.

Common in individuals with coronary heart disease is angina pectoris. This condition results from a temporary inadequacy in the blood supply to the heart muscle due to coronary heart disease. Angina is characterized by severe but brief pain near the mid-chest region; the pain may radiate to either or both arms, the back, neck, or jaw. Angina is treated commonly and safely with nitroglycerin.

DIABETES MELLITUS

The common form of diabetes in the aged is Type II diabetes, a chronic inherited disease in which a relative deficiency of insulin or a disturbance in the action of insulin interferes with the body's ability to metabolize carbohydrates. The elderly diabetic may present few or no clinical symptoms of that disease. In fact, complications arising from diabetes may be the first signs of this disease in the elderly.

HYPERTENSION

Hypertension, otherwise known as high blood pressure, when present over long periods of time can lead to arterial disease and eventually to heart failure, stroke and kidney failure. In the elderly, high blood pressure is unlikely to be of recent origin and much of the damage to the arterial system has already been done.

Hypertension in the aged should be treated by moderate dietary salt restriction and, if necessary, by drugs. Only the milder drugs should be used with the aged, since the more powerful ones can cause sudden and severe lowering of blood pressure which may lead to fainting spells or even strokes or heart attacks—the very complications such drugs are used to prevent.

NEURITIS

Neuritis is a disease of the peripheral and cranial nerves characterized by inflammation and degeneration of the nerve fibers. It can lead to loss of conduction of nerve fibers. It can lead to loss of conduction of nerve impulses and consequently to varying degrees of paralysis, loss of feeling, and loss of reflexes. Although the term neuritis implies inflammation, this is not invariably present. Neuritis may affect a single nerve or involve several nerve trunks. Diagnostic work-up by a neurologist is indicated. Treatment of specific causes such as diabetes, pernicious anemia, or alcoholism, may be helpful.

OSTEOPOROSIS

This is a condition of porous bones where bone density and mineral content occurs when new bone is not created as quickly as old bone is lost. Osteoporosis is caused by an acceleration of normal changes that occur with age. Bone tissue and density are lost—brittleness and higher risks of fracture ensue. More women than men are affected. Risk factors include estrogen loss, low calcium and Vitamin D intake as well as body type, heredity, race, smoking and inactivity.

PERIPHERAL NEUROPATHY

This disease involved damage to the peripheral nerves the extensive network of nerves that connect the brain and spinal cord to the rest of the body. The causes of this problem range from alcoholism, diabetes, malignant tumors, Vitamin B_1, B_6, B_{12} deficiency lead poisoning, hypothyroidism, Guillian-Barré syndrome and others. Autoneuropathy affects nerves leading to the central part of the body, i.e., the heart, lungs, etc. and its affects can be cataclysmic.

SYMPTOMS AND COMPLAINTS

The following are some of the more common symptoms and complaints of the elderly. Wrongly regarded by many older patients as being the natural consequences of aging and, therefore, not worth mentioning to a busy doctor, these symptoms—and indeed, all others—should be reported to a physician by the older person or his family.

BREATHLESSNESS

Breathlessness, known as dyspnea, is common in the aged and may reflect heart failure, disease of the lungs, or anemia. It is exaggerated by obesity.

CONSTIPATION

Perhaps no part of the body is as misunderstood as the lower digestive tract, which is involved in absorption of nutrients and elimination of solid waste matter. Many people still believe that a daily bowel movement is needed for good health. This belief is false. Not everyone functions on a once-a-day schedule or needs to. It is common to find people in perfect health who defecate regularly twice a day and others who have a bowel movement once every two or three days with the slightest ill effects. There are some people who have regular bowel movements at still longer intervals, without any health problems.

CHAPTER FIVE

RECREATION AND LEISURE

"What's Most Fun"

In America there is more conversation about recreation and leisure than any other country in the world. Americans spends the most money on leisure but at the same time takes fewer vacations. This will impact on Boomers. As the U.S. Census Bureau has foretold 77 million Boomers are those born between 1946 and 1964, the largest generation in today's workforce is beginning to retire. In the next decade millions will retire. Faced with the daunting task of maintaining their pre-retirement life style—leisure and recreation will be even more crucial to them.

The United States is one of the only modern countries without vacation-time minimums mandated by law. Clearly, we are taking less vacations and leisure time each year. The reasons are numerous and complex, but the negative results of this trend are becoming clearer.

The Shrinking-American-Vacation-and-Leisure-Time syndrome results in workplace stress, absenteeism and excess overtime. So, one solution to this negative now is to maximize our creativity when it comes to vacation, leisure or play!

Leisure is defined as free, unoccupied time during which a person may indulge in rest, recreation and the like. On the other hand, recreation means refreshment in body or mind as after work by some form of play amusement, or relaxation used for this purpose as games, sports, hobbies, reading, walking, etc. Perhaps in no country in the world is there more money, time and energy spent in search of recreation and leisure with less success than in America. And it is no wonder, for in the United States there is no other people put under the strain from the constant radical change which occurs with increasing rapidity than here. Alvin Toffler (author of *Future Shock*) called this the "orientation response," the inexorable interaction between organism and environment. So it follows that we make the horrendous rush to socialize, travel, play, rest, isolate, or whatever it takes to settle the nerves, reduce the tension and relax the jaded self. Despite the use of the word "rush" more Americans take their leisure time and recreational activity in mostly sedentary ways. Suffice it to say leisure involves rest, free time and choice of recreation whereas recreation is refreshment in body and mind by some form of play, amusement or relaxation. It is obvious that they overlap.

Buzzle an affiliate of CNN published articles on their web site by Andrew Regan (2007) dealing with the overworked working world. He raises the question of whether we have reached the point where it's too stressful to relax? But when you realize that many in the working world feel overworked you wonder. The average American works over 1980 hours a year—100 more than workers in Canada, 250 more than England, and 500 more than Germany. Americans currently give back $21 billion in unused vacation time to their employers—that's 574 million days of unused vacation time. Lawrence Johnson, International Labor Organization Chief Economist states "workers in the United States are putting in more hours than anyone else in the industrialized world." The reasons for fewer vacations are need to catch up, lack of paid vacations, the profit driven mentality and to be ready for the next big project. Twenty-six percent will not take a vacation this year, fifty percent or more will barely make an effort, all will not succeed and only fourteen percent will have two weeks of vacation.

"Workplace stress can take its toll. In order to maintain a strong state of mental health, [we] need a release and a source of replenishment," said Dr. Dorothy Cantor, president of the American Psychological

Foundation. "A vacation will eliminate stress, encourage relaxation and provide opportunities for rejuvenation."

Scientific evidence has shown that people who take vacations and leisure time frequently are less likely to develop serious heart problems in the future. Vacation and leisure time greatly reduce pressures of everyday life, and eliminate stress. Stress threatens people's wellness, affecting the function of the immune system, cardiovascular health, emotional well being and overall quality of life.

In addition, the vacation offers these benefits:

1. Vacations and leisure time stimulates the imagination, and makes us have something to look forward to. It's a chance to take off the work hat and go out to play.
2. The benefits of taking vacations and leisure time for us are many. Our "Social and Psychological aspects of our lives are directly related to our physical health which vacation contributed to sufficiently.
3. No matter how active or inactive a vacation or leisure time may be, the mind should be at rest and body should feel relaxed. Taking a leave is the primary way to prevent burnout by breaking the routine once in a while can help improve physical and mental health.

Vacation is part of finding time to relax to find recreation, to find leisure, to find the child in ourselves again and relieve the stress we have and renew our spirit. Boomers if they go on vacations worry about messages and a massive to-do list is enough to keep some people from never leaving their offices. Others worry about if they're out of sight, they're also out of mind. This is typical of boomers because they place a heavy value on office face-time. They're more likely to forgo the vacation days they're entitled to rather than younger generations. With cell phones and Blackberries and WiFi everywhere, we're still linked to the office—even if we do go away. About a quarter of all vacationers in this country say they check voicemail or e-mail while on vacation. It's a combination of being expected to keep in touch, as well as a desire to be warned and to be in the know. Many Boomers raised by depression parents are workaholics and have never learned how to play and take recreation.

How to Get Started With Play

It is never easy to break away from the demands of life and guilt involved in leaving a task undone; fortunately there are some ways of handling this. Check this list.

1. Face our boredom—a certain amount of boredom, is inevitable in everyone's life. The routine job we have to do and other tasks must be done. What if we are bored during our free time? If so, we should change some things and do something about the situation.

2. Dream a little!—we lose our ability to fantasize as adult all too quickly—the real world doesn't allow dreams. Children daydream a lot and so should we. Faraway places with strange sounding names! Piccadilly Circus..... rue de la plais or Siam! The dreaming helps to sort out our lives; dreams reveal our inner selves and they give us a break from the ordinary.

3. Let the child loose—the child part of the adult may appear silly to some—like the old man who wishes to have an electric toy train and the middle-aged father who enjoys playing marbles or rolling in the grass. Let's make ourselves more flexible and emotionally responsive learning to play again.

4. Listen to yourself—be assertive. All too frequently we turn aside from what we want to do during our free time. We say yes to people who decide we will volunteer our Saturdays to help carry a group on the church picnic when we had something else in mind. We confuse virtue with good-natured willingness when we haven't been fair with ourselves because we have been afraid to assert our feelings. To say no on occasions helps our self-respect and allows that life just doesn't "slip by" without our ever doing what we really wish to do.

5. Keep active—the person that engaged in a variety of physical activities is constantly sending the pleasure center messages through sensory impressions. When alerted the pleasure center region shakes us out of the

doldrums that boredom brings. Badminton, or tag, is the type of things we can do. The time is now and to get started is half the battle.

There are a number of good reasons for participating in recreational leisure and play. Janet MacLean in *Recreation in Modern Society* listed these. Of course she emphasized the importance of building leisure skills early in life. Appetites should be whetted for play in a new recreation, not shoved down the throats of youngsters by organizations at breakneck speed.

The key is balance of both in kinds of choices as to recreation and depth of pursuit. Some of the benefits are:

1. Recreation outlets provide a chance to find meaning and self-expression.
2. Recreation is a means to restore balance—social, mental and physical—the thing that keeps you on even keel.
3. Recreation is an opportunity for involvement in life's issues, particularly for those whose age (teens and aged) narrows their choices identity in meaningful roles.
4. Recreation is the chance for self-realization—a chance to be me!
5. Recreation is a basic human need as real as food or shelter.
6. Recreation is an opportunity for voluntary experiences.
7. Recreation in the real sense is therapeutic.
8. Recreation serves as a watchdog on our natural resources for the demand of outdoor pursuits of recreating serves to protect our land. We are equipped with great neuromuscular memories so the skating done in youth and riding a bicycle come quickly back to us. Kinesthetic memory enables us to resume a game at almost any age. So, at age 35, 45 or 55 it is not too late for golf or tennis!

Recreation Types and Opportunities

It is not true that those who have failed to learn to play in childhood cannot learn to play in adulthood. There is little correlation between childhood and adult leisure. Possibly early introduction and pleasure in outdoor activities has more carry-over than the general type of recreational activity. But for most individuals the scope of opportunity is unlimited even at forty, fifty or sixty. Winston Churchill said that "to reach the age of forty without ever handling a brush, to have regarded the painting of pictures as a mystery, and then suddenly find oneself plunged in the middle of a new interest with paints and palettes and canvases, and not to be discouraged by results, is an astonishing and enriching experience." I hope it may be shared by others! Like Churchill, many baby boomers in their fifties and sixties are discovering areas of interest in which they have become passionate.

Local Provision for Recreation

A city of 100,000 population with a low per capita income offers a wide variety of programs for all ages, particularly focused on children and youth. Many more special events are offered from March to August. After school recreation programs are held at all centers Monday through Friday. This includes karate, cheerleading, open recreation period, field hockey, volleyball, flag football, badminton, sports for girls, physical fitness, "just for the fun of it," learn a new game, creative dance, youth basketball, tag and relay races, computer classes, board games, homework assistance, little artists, kids in the kitchen, crafty afternoon, atrium II afternoons, 4-H, kick ball, Girl Scouts and brain teasers. supervised overnight camping trips and other special trips have fun attached to them. GED classes, investing, the ABC's of Inventing all cost small fees. Adult therapeutic recreation programs are available, also adult basic educational programs, adult arts and crafts, therapeutic leisure field trips, bowling and many other events.

A town of 5,000 Appling County, Georgia serving their county also has a youth basketball, an instructional league 8-9 co-ed, midget girls age 10-12, midget boys 10-12 but with teams, junior boys 13-14 with teams and all star teams. They all have adult men's basketball with church teams and open division and district adult teams. In the spring they have men and women's softball, track for youth with track meets. In summer they offer T-ball, youth baseball with mini mite ages 7-8 and mites 9-10, midgets 11-12, juniors 13-14 and All-Star teams. Also youth softball in various categories, swim teams and classes for 3 years old and up beginning, intermediate, etc. They have tennis teams. Fall they provide football flag for second levels, soccer and cheerleading. Many special events are arranged—the City Festival Softball Tournament, Volunteers Banquet, Midget Football, contests, hopscotch contest, and District II Basketball and softball have girls' and women's teams. Also during the year they offer tap, ballet, and baton classes 3-18 years of age and have a recital.

Besides recreational activities organized in most communities, there are YMCA's in over twenty-six hundred towns across the country that offer sports instruction to child care and in fact several years ago they served in nearly ten million children non-school hours. Many schools have programs, for after school for working parents providing free time, games and fun things under trained supervision. Some other things that have been done by the YMCA are:

1. Serves all incomes, all ages and all abilities. Serves 20+ million people, raise nearly 600 million for scholarships, subsides and community services.
2. Reaches 10 million children in non-school hours with gang prevention programs, literacy tutoring, kid clubs and sports leagues, community service projects and including values of honesty, respect, caring and responsibility.
3. Provides childcare nationwide YMCA's are collectively the largest childcare provider in the nation. Approximately half the children in their childcare come from households with less than $25,000 yearly. The cost is very affordable.
4. Partner's with neighborhood organizations—400 YMCA's work with juvenile courts, 300 with public housing, 1550 with elementary schools, 1033 with high schools and 700 with college.
5. YMCA's encourage volunteers. YMCA is volunteer founded and volunteer led. Nearly 600,000 volunteers ask to help or are recruited.
6. YMCA's live their mission every day. Founded 150 years ago. Together is the largest not-for-profit community organization in America. All 2,283 independent YMCA's

are guided by the common mission, putting Christian principles into practice that build healthy spirit, mind and body for all. For more information call 1-312-977-0031.

It should be mentioned that many public school systems along with some churches offer programs for children after school hours as a help to parents. These programs kept many children from becoming latch key boys and girls and provide a guard against idle hands and minds. Call the Superintendent of Schools' office and they will give you information on their after school programs. Virginia Beach, VA (Population 400,000+) was selected by the National Recreation and Park Association as their first Magnet City. The purpose of the Association is to develop an outreach model to support parks and recreation agencies to set new standards of community service. It spotlights the critical role played by parks and recreation in delivery programs, which insure the quality of life and lead to healthier communities. The Magnet initiative will focus on four areas—health, sports, technology and youth. What follows is only a sample of their programs which range from water therapy, for people with arthritis, M.S. and other such problems, to ceramics, crafts, dancing, and swimming lessons. A registration form has to be filled out and a fee given. Special classes such as Karate demand a fee. Scholarships are available for many programs so upon an application some children may participate free of charge. The following table provides an example of the fee schedule for a recreation program in the Virginia Beach, VA School System (2008):

Programs & Registration Information	Bettie F. Williams Elem. Sch. School year only.	Bayside Recreation Center	Seatack Elem. School	Seatack Recreation Center
Before School Fees Hours	$12/$14 per week 6:30 am 8:00 am	No program	$14/$12 per week 6:30 am- 8:00 am	No program
After School Fees Hours	$27/$25 per week 2:30 pm-6:00 pm	*$140 per month 3:00 pm- 6:00 pm	$27/25 per week 2:30 pm- 6:00 pm	$35 per week 2:30 pm- 6:00 pm

Intersession Break Fees/Hours	$55/$45 per week 7:00 am-6:00 pm	$90 per week 7:00 am-6:00 pm	No program	$70 per week 7:00 am-6:00 pm
Day Camp Fees Hours	$20 per day 7:00 am-6:00 pm	Various options available	No program	$20 per day 7:00 am-6:00 pm
Licensed programs	Before	After School/ Intersession Break/Day Camp	Before	After/Inter-session Break/Day Camp
Membership Card Fees	No	Required Adults $55; Child $22 per year	No	Required Adults $55; Child $22 per year
Fee Waiver Available	Yes 50%	No	Yes 50%	No
Meals or Snacks Provided	No	Intersession: Breakfast & Lunch (USDA Program)	No	Afternoon Snack
Transportation	No	*Limited, Call Bayside for calls	No	To Recreation Center after Intersession
Registration Day Dates Hours	**Registration** Thursday, June 21 6:30 pm-8:30 pm	Registration Thursday, June 28 5:30 pm-8:30 pm	Registration Thursday, June 21 6:30 pm-8:30 pm	Information at Seatack Elementary Registration night
For additional information contact	Community Recreation Services 471-5884	Bayside Community Recreation Center 460-7540	Community Recreation Services 471-5884	Seatack Community Recreation Center 437-4858

Many activities are available for those interested, towns and City Parks and Recreation Commissions (the telephone directory will provide access to activities they have available from their offices) sponsor some for no cost, a large number. Some of the activities are offered by YMCA and YWCA without a fee. Go to info@ywca.org to find a location near you.

Church groups have hymn festivals, choir singing and competition and music camps. These activities are largely volunteer and sponsored by organizations that solicit individuals to join. Community theatre and drama groups invite tryouts frequently persons who never participated find an interest in acting or a related activity. Dance groups provide free community dances and sometimes instruction for some. Civic clubs often sponsor special events that are of interest. Look at the list below to see what variety of arts and crafts, dance, drama and music may be offered.

Arts and Crafts	Dance	Drama	Music
Basket Making	Ballet	Adult Theatre	Singing
Beadwork	Creative rhythms	Ceremonials	Informal groups
Block Printing	Dance mixers	Charades	Quartets
Candle making	Folk dance	Children's theatre	Choirs
Carving	Hawaiian dances	Choral speaking	Choruses
Christmas cards	Tap and Clog	Community theatre	Community sings
Decorations	Latin American	Creative dramatics	
			Playing
Clay modeling	Rock dance	Festivals	Rhythm instruments
Collage	Modern dance	Grand operas	Bands
Etching	Jazz	Light operas	Orchestras
Weaving	Social dance	Operettas	Simple melody
Furniture refinishing	Ballroom	Pageants	instruments
Knitting	Square dancing	Plays	Combos
Sketching	Foxtrot	Puppetry	Chamber music

Flower Arrangement	Waltz	Scenery making	One-man bands
Leatherwork	Disco	Story reading	<u>Listening</u>
Needlework	Charleston	Story telling	Concerts
Paper craft	Samba	Variety Shows	Home music
Model-making,	Rumba	Musical comedies	Radio, T.V.
clay & metal work	Two step	Monologues	Tape recorders
Photography	Cha-Cha	One-act plays	<u>Combined Activity</u>
Picture Framing		Skits	Festivals
Pottery		Stunts	Folk dancing
Printing		Water pageants	Holiday programs
Sculpture			Caroling

For a listing of the 2007 activities provided by your local YMCA use the Computer search engine under www.local.com, complete the city and state blocks and enter YMCA. Outdoor recreation is an area of American life that has taken on great significance in the past decade. Increased leisure time and mobility have doubled the numbers of persons involved in outdoor recreation. Most people prefer simple pleasures of leisure. According to the U.S. Department of Interior (2008), pleasure driving, walking, and hiking accounts for 40% of the total outdoor participation annually. Other activities that require little specialized equipment are playing games, swimming, sightseeing, fishing, bicycling, viewing sporting events, and picnicking. Fewer, though in increasing numbers, are participating in skin diving, mountain climbing, sailing, requiring outlay of money for equipment, are being explored.

A partial list of outdoor recreational opportunity is given here.

Astronomy	Flower shows	Nature trails
Backpacking	Gardening	Nature study
Bird walks	Glider soaring	Outdoor cooking
Boating	Hiking	Outdoor games
Camping	Horseback riding	Picnicking
Cave exploration	Hunting	Sailing
Coasting	Ice boating	Snowmobiling
Cycling	Ice skating	Snowshoeing
Driving for pleasure	Indian lore	Surfing
Family camping	Kite flying	Swimming
Fishing	Mountaineering	Target shooting
Conservation sessions	Nature Clubs	Travel

Many of these types of recreation are afforded under the sponsorship of the YMCA and YWCA and under various community organizations as follows. Generally there are four types of organizations. We will give what you may expect to be offered by these groups, their facilities, and something about the personnel that staff these programs.

Public	Voluntary	Private	Commercial
(City, Town or County) To meet public needs. Provide public facilities.	(Quasi-public, non-profit, providing varied services, often for specific neighborhoods)	Organizations with closed membership designed to meet needs of its members.	Profit-related, privately owned. Provides one or more type of recreation to the public.

Recreation programs through Agencies, Parks and Recreation. Maybe School District, etc.	Youth-serving organization (Boys clubs, Girl Scouts, YMCA, YWCA, Catholic Youth, etc. Settlement houses, Jewish Community Centers	Country Clubs, Tennis, Yacht, Golf, athletic groups or fraternal or industrial associations with close membership procedures.	Miniature golf, bowling alleys, movies, bars, night clubs, pool rooms, game machines, skating rinks, amusement centers.
Usually provide wide range of indoor sports and outdoor—have facilities—pools, gyms, golf, tennis, beaches, stadiums, parks, trails, museums, nature paths, etc. Have special events, Parades, Celebrations.	Operates chiefly indoors, may have camps, and tennis courts and swimming pools. Organizations like the scouts depend on other agency for facilities— churches, etc.	They operate their own buildings and outdoor recreation areas usually for a specific purpose like hunting, fishing, etc. Some have club buildings with facilities for sauna, dining and dancing.	Chief concern here is usually on single activity, some sports centers like Tennis Centers have amusement area—table tennis, etc. Water slides, swimming pools. Large Recreational Complexes— King's Dominion, Busch Gardens, Disney World, Disneyland, Six Flags over Texas, Georgia, Carowinds.

The staffs of public agencies are usually certified and under Civil Service requirement.	Usually people here have college backgrounds, some have social work college degrees.	Not college degree oriented, people are employed for a specific reason—tennis pro, dance and swimming instruction, etc.	Persons here are hired to do a particular type of job. In the large complexes many high school and college youth are employed.

YMCA of America 2008

Vacations

Everyone needs a vacation at least once a year away from their regular work and living place. If possible, besides the longer vacation people who constantly deal with people in their work need other shorter times away, that is, weekends and holidays spaced in between the longer late spring, summer, or fall vacation. Vacations are designed to be fun and something different, change of pace to provide new scenery and to be restful. For many people simply a good rest is the principal goal they have in mind for a vacation, one, which is away from the cares of the everyday routine. For many people going to the seashore or mountains, look for smaller places and towns if possible, other than those known as tourist centers, for this may be in many cases the most economical. Good clean beaches in the south like Rehoboth Beach, Delaware, Virginia Beach, Virginia; Wrightsville Beach, North Carolina (Family Beach); Myrtle Beach, South Carolina, and Daytona Beach, Florida, provide varied accommodations ranging from very expensive to relatively inexpensive. You will pay more the closer you get to the water. Many from New York, Pennsylvania and New Jersey go to Atlantic City, New Jersey. With gambling, rates of many rooms are sky high. Travel agencies organize weekend tours to there from several states away. There are good sources for organizing trips anywhere without paying also AAA members get trip suggestions, mileage, etc.

Average Number of Vacation Days
In World Countries

Italy	42 Days
France	37 Days
Germany	35 days
Brazil	34 days
United Kingdom	28 days
Canada	26 days
Korea	25 days
Japan	25 days
U.S.	13 days

Information Please, 2007

BEST VACATION SPOTS
Top 12 Family Vacation Spots

- Fripp Island, South Carolina
- Walt Disney World - Orlando Florida
- High Hampton Country Inn - Cashiers, North Carolina
- Palm Island Florida Resort - Fort Myers, Florida
- Bass Pro's Big Cedar Lodge - Near Branson, Missouri
- Internet Guide to Catalina Island – Los Angeles, CA
- Wild Mountain – One hour from the Twin Cities, MN
- Dave Helfrich river Outfitter – Vida, Oregon
- Roseland Ranch NY Duderanch – Stanfordville, New York
- Tarryall River Ranch – Lake George, CO
- St. George Island Index – St. George, Florida
- Mission Bay Getaway – San Diego, CA

Ten Most Visited Sites in the National Park System

Blue Ridge Parkway (NC-VA)
Golden Gate National Recreation Area (CA)
Great Smoky Mountains National Park (NC-TN)
Gateway National Recreation Area (NJ-NY)
Lake Mead National Recreation Area (AZ-NV)

188

George Washington Memorial Parkway (VA-MD-DC)
Natchez Trace Parkway (MS-AL-TN)
Delaware Water Gap National Recreation Area (NJ-PA)
National World War II Memorial Area (DC)
Grand Canyon National Park (AZ)

Our Kid Magazine's Top 7 National Parks

1. Glacier National Park, Montana
2. Carlsbad Caverns National Park, New Mexico
3. Yellowstone, Wyoming
4. Sequoia/Kings Canyon National Park, California
5. Hawaii Volcanoes National Park
6. Grand Canyon National Park, Arizona
7. Everglades National Park, Florida

America's Best Beaches, 2007

	Name	Location
1.	Ocracoke Lifeguarded Beach	Outer Banks, North Carolina
2.	Caladesi Island State Park	Dunedin, Florida
3.	Coopers Beach	Southampton, New York
4.	Hanalei Bay	Kauai, Hawaii
5.	Coast Guard Beach	Cape Cod, Massachusetts
6.	Hamoa Beach	Maui, Hawaii
7.	Main Beach	East Hampton, New York
8.	Coronado Beach	San Diego, California
9.	Lighthouse Point Park	Daytona Beach, Florida
10.	Siesta Beach	Sarasota, Florida

Top Ten Places for 2007 Abroad
Travel Industry Association of America (2007)

Bhutan

Bhutan, nestling in the heart of the great Himalayas, has for centuries remained aloof from the rest of the world. Since its doors were cautiously opened in 1974, visitors have been mesmerized: the environment is pristine, the scenery and architecture awesome, and the people hospitable and charming.

Bulgaria

The country has changed swiftly over the past decade, though in the villages you can still find folk who ride donkeys to work, eat homegrown potatoes and make their own cheese. The difference now is they wash it all down in front of a satellite TV.

China

The world's spotlight was pointed at China during its stunning hosting of the 2008 Olympics. For the visitor it's important to remember that China is a different world. From shop-till-you-drop metropolises to the desert landscapes of Xinjiang.

Costa Rica

Costa Rica is Central America's jewel. It's an oasis of calm among its turbulent neighbors and an ecotourism haven, making it one of the best places to experience the tropics with minimal impact. It's also mostly coastline, which means great surfing, beaches galore and a climate built for laziness.

Costa Rica's enlightened approach to conservation has ensured that lush jungles are home to playful monkeys, languid sloths, crocodiles, countless lizards, poison-dart frogs and a mind-boggling assortment of exotic birds, insects and butterflies.

France

Rugby fans will be kicking around France in their thousands when the country hosts the Rugby World Cup in its 20th year. The country that wrote the book on and gave the world champagne and Camembert, de Beauvoir and Debussy, the Tour de France and the Eiffel Tower will have the world watching during September and October.

Ireland

It's said that Ireland, once visited, is never forgotten, and for once the blarney rings true. The Irish landscape has a mythic resonance, the country's history is almost tangible, and its people seem put on earth expressly to restore faith in humanity.

Maldives

'The last paradise on earth' has bounced back from the Tsunami and is simply beaming with new and refreshed resorts. If a traveler's idea of paradise is a pristine, tranquil tropical island with swaying palm trees, pure white beaches and brilliant turquoise lagoons, then the Maldives won't disappoint.

Namibia

Brad Pitt and Angelina Jolie have made Namibia Africa's hottest getaway. Wedged between the Kalahari and the chilly South Atlantic, Namibia has deserts, seascapes, bushwalking and boundlessness. Blessed with rich natural resources, a solid modern infrastructure and diverse traditional cultures, it is a beautiful country of vast potential.

Oman

Oman has broken the seal and emerged into the world. The country has shed its hermit shell, revealing a land of friendly people and dramatic landscapes peppered with forts. Although it remains, in many ways, the most traditional country in the region, it's often more outward looking than it's given credit for.

Zanzibar

Low in political coups and high in bliss-charged activities, the Zanzibar Archipelago is a mere hop, skip and a jump from the Tanzanian mainland. Its heady lure has tempted travelers, traders, slave-traders and colonists for centuries, and the archipelago continues to reflect this tumultuous past.

191

World's Top 10 Tourism Destinations Based On Number of Arrivals (in Millions)	
France	76.5
Spain	49.5
United States	45.5
Italy	39.0
China	33.2
United Kingdom	23.4
Russian Federation	n/a
Mexico	19.8
Canada	19.7
Austria	18.2

Office of Travel & Tourism, U.S. Chamber of Commerce World Tourist Organization 2006

Top Activities and Destinations for Travelers

According to the Travel Industry Association of America (2008), activities participated in by U.S. resident travelers included the following:

- Shopping (33%)

- Outdoor (Camping, hiking, biking, etc.)(17%)

- Historical Sites/Museums (14%)

- Beaches (10%)

- Cultural Events/Festivals (10%)

- National/State Parks (10%)

- Theme/Amusement Parks (8%)

- Nightlife/Dancing (7%)

- Gambling (7%)

- Sports Event (6%)

- Golf/Tennis/Skiing (4%)

Additionally, TIA reports that visitors planned the following activities after arriving at their destination:

- Restaurant (48%)

- Shopping area (45%)

- Museum or Exhibit (26%)

- Sightseeing Tour (24%)

- Movie (16%)

- Theme Park (15%)

- Religious Service (14%)

- Live Theatre or Other Performance (14%)

- Festival or Parade (13%)

- Other Activities/Attractions (24%)

We remind you. People need vacations to bolster their health, reduce stress, provide relaxation and normalize mental health. Why they take vacations that they do?

There are many reasons why anyone might want to think about why you want to go somewhere in terms of (a) what sort of mood or emotion you want to emphasize; (b) nature and scenery and related outdoor activities; (c) the sorts of cultural and historical experiences which interest you. Vacations provide recreation and leisure which has innumerable benefits as Bev Driver of the Academy of Leisure Sciences states in her essay The Benefits of Leisure, "The benefits of leisure—physical and mental health, economic development, family bonding, environmental awareness, and so on—are now well-documented scientifically." In fact, some of our favorite activities like playing sports, reading a book, or just sitting in a hammock are actually leisure activities. Unfortunately, we often fail to realize that we gain more from these activities than simply having a good time. Leisure provides physical, psychological, economic, and spiritual benefits that play a major role in the overall welfare of society in general.

While often overlooked, leisure provides many physical benefits. By using our leisure time for exercise, we are able to strengthen our bodies, making them more resilient to injury. As Thomas L. Goodale from the Department of Health, Sports and Leisure Studies states in his essay *Leisure's Relationship to Health,* "Recreation and leisure activities may be one of our best methods for curbing our rising medical costs... in an era in which medical costs continue to escalate and our ability to provide medical care for all segments of the population has lessened, maintaining good health pays dividends." From this statement, we can observe that leisure provides not only physical exercise but also other medical benefits as well.

Why People Vacation

- **To build and strengthen relationships.** The number one reason for going on vacation is to be together as a family. Families find they have little time to be alone together. They want to get away from the stress of home and work. They look to travel as an opportunity to rekindle relationships. Many also seek social interactions on trips, and view vacations as a time for making new friends.
- **To improve health and wellbeing.** The vast majority of adults say that a vacation is vital to their family's physical and mental well being. Most travelers who visit California want to refresh and renew themselves by actively participating in outdoor activities.
- **To rest and relax.** Getting away from work, worry, and effort enables vacationers to refresh and renew. This is the third most common reason why Americans vacation.
- **To have an adventure.** Many travelers look to vacations for exciting experiences that stir emotions. Adventure,

whether dangerous or romantic, provides the heightened sensation that these consumers seek.

- **To escape.** Many people travel to gain respite from routines, worry, and stress. They are looking for something different: a better climate, prettier scenery, slower pace of life, cleaner air, quieter surroundings or anything else that is missing or deficient in their lives back home.
- **For knowledge.** Learning and discovery are strong motivators for today's better-educated travelers. People travel to learn or practice a language, study a culture, explore gourmet foods or wines, investigate spirituality, discover something about themselves, or a host of other learning pursuits.
- **To mark a special occasion.** Some travelers take vacations to celebrate milestones, in their lives: new relationships, marriages, birthdays, or professional achievements. Vacations that mark special occasions are usually taken with loved ones and provide memories that last a lifetime.
- **To bring the family together**, to tighten the bonds of the family, children are strangers, think about activities that will bring the family together.
- **To get a new perspective on life and on their work and professions.** They use vacations to evaluate their success or failure and consider future change.
- **To gather with military and fraternal orders such as Veterans of Foreign Wars, Masons, Elks and etc.**
- **To save money or time.** Although going on vacation almost always costs money and time, where one goes on vacation can influence costs. Money and time constrain virtually every vacation decisions. By traveling close to home, or taking a short vacation, travelers can save time and money.
- **To reminisce.** Many people travel to relive fond memories. In the case of agritourism, some vacationers, especially older travelers, will choose a farm visit to rekindle memories of the simple, rural lifestyle they remember

from childhood. They visit their first homes, military sites, have time-shares that they feel they must go to though they are tired of them. They visit a place where something special happened in their lives.

Paying for Vacations

If you have to pay considerable for a room or two rooms, you can offset this by eating outside (Burger King, MacDonald's, etc.) of the hotel or motel where you're lodging. Bringing sandwiches and fruits prepared in advance will do. Many people eat a hamburger or hotdog for lunch and go to Bonanza, Ponderosa, or a chain restaurant with serving lines for the evening meal. Some motels, etc., have pool-side concession stands with drinks and sandwiches. One thing about staying at large hotels or motels many of them have organized programs for children and adults. A number have social activities and directors who plan something special every day. I remember one place (a hotel) I stayed in at Virginia Beach, Virginia, where each evening bingo was provided in the lobby or some game suitable for the entire family to enjoy. Another thing to remember is that often a chain motel like Day's Inn, Ramada Inns and Holiday Inns give special rates for children under certain ages or provide the lodging free with reductions in meals or give them free. Many better hotels have cheaper rooms, so ask, and also what is included in the price of a room a continental breakfast may be a plus! It would be wise if going to a recreation area or seashore to choose one even ten or fifteen miles away and save twenty-five dollars a day on the lodging for four nearer the ocean, etc., then paying $80.00 to $150.00 a day to be right on the site. The people who have trailers and campers can save most all this outlay and reserve it for other expenses. In the southeast United States, less well-known places are fine for visitation in Florida—Melbourne, Ormond Beach, Del Ray Beach, Boynton Beach, Pompano Beach, Deerfield Beach, Boca Raton—all in south Florida north of Miami. Incidentally, these places have Dog Racing, Harness Racing and Jai Alai in the area. The 'Moon may be over Miami' but often the traffic, the cost tab and impact of numbers make other places the recommended place to stay. This may not save much with gas prices as high as they are. From a more distant home base, you can drive in to special places for boat cruises, the Orange Bowl, Disney World (Orlando), Key West, Hialeah and the Everglades. Write to the Chamber of Commerce in cities to get an idea of accommodations and cost. Southern California and Mexico for people living in the west provides many fine beaches at reasonable prices such as Cardiff-by-the-Sea, Hermosa Beach, Luguna Beach, etc. Those nearby California and in California and in the west can make a wonderful trip beginning in Sonoma and going south over a four or five day trip stopping along the way giving a day or two to San Francisco (the cable cars) and Los Angeles—Rodeo Drive and

Hollywood, also San Diego with its wonderful zoo. Also on the way there, the birds fly at Capistrano.

People who are members of the AAA (American Automobile Association) can receive trips planned for them with suggestions on many other things besides road conditions and state police traps. In planning a vacation or when looking for a place to go, write or call a travel agency or two and ask them to send you some literature; they may place you on the mailing lists for periodic trips and excursions they have available. Most of these agencies will handle a number of things for you; and in case you are planning overseas trips, they can be indispensable in arranging for transportation, lodging and tours. Their services are usually without cost to you as they receive their support from the hotels and transportation systems you patronize through them. Whether or not you utilize their services, the free information you may receive is valuable.

There are a number of great parks, government reservations, etc., which are worth seeing. North Carolina Outer Banks has a Federal Park that boasts beautiful beaches and wild undisturbed land. At Ocracoke, on the southern tip of the Outer Banks, you'll find a historical lighthouse built in 1823. To the south of Nags Head there is Cape Hatteras Lighthouse built in 1870; it has been moved 3 times to protect it from the encroaching sea and is the tallest lighthouse in America. At Kill Devil Hills where the Wright Brothers' first air flight took place and where the recent celebration of the 100th anniversary took place, the first English Colony of Sir Walter Raleigh was located, also where the first white child was born. The Lost Colony, an outdoor drama, is played there during the summer and is a popular visiting place. Innumerable good camping sites are found in the area. To the north a hundred or so miles is Williamsburg, Colonial capital of early America. This is a good family vacation place for Busch Gardens (a major amusement complex—The Old Country) with the Loch Ness Monster and the Budweiser Brewing Company is nearby, plus Jamestown, founded in 1607, 13 years before the Pilgrims came to Plymouth. One could take in Washington, DC (150 miles) or Virginia Beach (60 miles) and Norfolk (Douglas MacArthur Memorial, the Monitor-Merrimac Battle, Chesapeake Bay Bridge [longest in the world], also the largest U.S. Naval base, the Wisconsin battle ship, Naval shipyards), a beautiful new city with reasonable costs. The birthplace of Washington at Wakefield is a beautiful place to visit within several hours of driving and near the birthplace of Robert E. Lee. The entire original layout has been reconstructed plus real simulation of the early manufacturing, raising of livestock and gardening. For persons coming from the west a vacation centering around Washington or Williamsburg gives you the benefit of the beautiful Shenandoah Valley, the beaches, a heavy concentration of historical sites, and still only four or five hours drive to New York (approximately 225 miles). A vacation to New York besides the experiences of the "Big Apple" one can take in the magnificent landscape of western Massachusetts in the Berkshire Mountains, Bar Harbor, Martha's Vineyard, Hyannis Port, and Boston are all in the general vicinity. Vermont, New Hampshire and Maine are also in close proximity. In southern New Hampshire, one can visit the famous Lake Winnipesaukee and nearby Wolfeboro. I spent the night, on one occasion, there at the "oldest resort hotel in America"—the General Wolfe Inn. The food and atmosphere were superb at that time.

If one uses Philadelphia as a base of operation, side visits to New York, Washington, or the Gettysburg battlefield are convenient. On the other hand, you can stay in between these cities and enjoy the mountainous terrain—the Poconos (Pennsylvania). Middle age couples getting married for the second time can find fabulous quarters in hotels catering principally to honeymoon couples (Mt. Airy Lodge to name one is for couples only). Great sports and entertainment is afforded everywhere with generally reasonable prices. Lake Wallenpaupeck, just a ways beyond are the Catskill Mountains, New York, is noted for its beautiful clear water. A trip from Stroudsburg, Pennsylvania up Route 209 to I-84 provides all sorts of crafts, trails, wild animal life, waterfalls and forests. A trip up Route 402 by Magic Valley (an amusement park) to the big lake.

In 2007, the all-inclusive vacations were widely recognized as one of the best travel options for families, couples, and singles. All-inclusive vacations combine airfare, lodging, activities, meals and drinks, and transportation all into one price that's lower than the total cost of the individual components. Six out of ten people look for an all-inclusive vacation when shopping around, according to Gary Sain of Yesawich, Pepperdine, Brown & Russell (YPB&R), an Orlando, Florida-based marketing company. "This is a trend we've been tracking for some time, and we've seen a huge rise in it and expect it to continue," says Sain. The two main reasons for the popularity of all-inclusive resorts are time and value. "Customers don't want to spend a lot of time figuring out how much a vacation is going to cost them," says Sain. "And for the most part, these packages are a great value." For a list of all-inclusive vacation sites, try the following websites:

www.expedia.com
www.priceline.com
www.cheapcaribbean.com
www.vacationexpress.com
www.travelocity.com
www.orbitz.com

Recreation and leisure are too important to be left to chance. They should be planned for mainly in terms of having them. Having them regularly on whatever basis we can. A visit at good friends, even our children, can be fun. Even a work convention can be fun for the family. We shouldn't plan every bit of our time and if it's over planned, then it may become work with the planner calling for us constantly to get and keep on the schedule. And we shouldn't decide we want to go the Grand Canyon 2000 miles away when we really want to play a little tennis or golf down at the seashore or up in the mountains. We believe the amount of time spent on vacation is not the most important thing, but how it is spent. Don't go somewhere just to have a topic of conversation or as a status stripe on your sleeve—go because you want to go to see or do something that's not possible at home. Don't make it a rat race and plan more than you can do!

Learning to have leisure has kept many a person from the sanatorium or emergency ward. Middle age people have tough times taking time out, for we're the people who because times were bad in our youth and since only the rich could play, we weren't conditioned to leisure. We need to learn to take our turn at play—all of us—the taxi driver, the store clerk, the bank clerk, the teacher, the physician and whether poor or not so poor, there is something we can do to give ourselves a time of relaxation and quiet. For every hour of work there should be an offsetting hour of rest and play so that our days should be divided by thirds—one-third for work, one-third for rest, one-third to play and for time to be alone—to worship and for reverie.

Boomers have the greatest stress upon us at this time than any other. For many who cannot find ways to cope with the constant drain of energy and responsibility, the prospect for survival is dark. Knowing about opportunities for our children to find recreation that is wholesome and directed by responsible agencies or groups will provide us with a period of relief and time for leisure for ourselves. Opportunity is needed for us to have time to ourselves to recharge our batteries. For some assistance, see what is available in your community, call or write agencies about their programs for our children or ourselves. For a current listing of activities, use the search engine www.local.com, then for your city and state type in Parks and Recreation.

Everyone needs recreation and leisure and there should be several activities in which we are involved, regardless of our economic circumstance. A good hobby—stamp or coin collection, sewing, wood working, gardening, or whatever—should be balanced by the addition of some recreation activity or two. Preferably one indoor activity and an outdoor activity—square dancing or bowling and swimming, running, walking or tennis. Of all the people in the world you're the most important so treat yourself that way—take vacations—have fun, relax, take leisure—re-create and renew yourself!

For those who can take a trip to Europe this can be the ultimate. We went by boat (the Queen Elizabeth II) from New York to Cherbourg, France, and then visited fifteen countries via the Eurarail pass (Express train transportation at a reduced rate, purchased from two weeks or for longer periods) and finally after a week in London flew back to New York. Through the Cunard Lines, my daughter and I got a reduced rate for flying British Airways on the return trip. Her rate was reduced initially because of age. Even greater reductions are presently being advertised. But for the five to six days at sea, there is everything to do, movies, games, swimming, dancing, bridge, live entertainment, discos, gambling, a library, and time to relax. Eurail travel is first class and fast (three hours from Paris to Amsterdam) and dining on the train is a treat. Families can book excellent accommodations at reasonable rates or even better when special rates are offered tourists. The trains in Europe typically go to the heart of the city like in Paris, Frankfurt, Stockholm, Rome, unlike the airports that are usually 15 to 20 miles out. The Queen Elizabeth II food I found was not as good (variety and amounts) as that on the Greek and Italian lines, which may be expected as these and many other cruise ships project this as their principal forte. Hotels in Europe are there in quantity that cater to every pocketbook—even the less expensive are clean. One striking out to Europe on his own should be well advised to research his trip carefully. I don't mean every detail, time should be left to do nothing or to explore unfettered by a schedule. Tours can be found in the principal cities that run close by your lodging and the local concierge will assist you at a hotel.

Winter Vacations are at Lower Rates

If you like it cold then Iceland offers sledding, skiing, glaciers, geysers and night life in Reykjavik. There are plenty of clubs—dance ones, jazz clubs, bars and food places. The exchange rate favors the dollar meaning low hotel rates and air fares. Some hotels include breakfast (call 800-223-5500). Now if you want a warm climate how about Jamaica, Montego Bay and Ocho Rios? On the southwest coast there are old fishing villages and quiet beach towns. Seafood is cheap at the beaches, spicy shrimp is highlighted. According to AARP resorts in Jamaica are cutting rates for the winter season 65%. Beachside villas in the southwest are available at $45 a night (call 876-965-0152).

Cruises to the Mediterranean or Caribbean offer generous reductions between Thanksgiving and New Years. You can find good deals all winter long. Contact on-line brokers such as Cruise Brothers. Com or call the cruise line directly.

Other places in America that offer recreation opportunities once the weather turns colder and are less damaging on the pocket book are listed here.

Cape Cod, Massachusetts
>The majority of tourists leave when the weather goes south. Some stores, eateries and hotels close, but some reduce their lodging rates and offer third-night free deals. You can visit light houses, dunes and snow dusted beaches (call 888-332-2732).

Myrtle Beach, South Carolina
>This city has 100 public golf courses discounts up to 35%. Winter daytime temperatures in the 50's and room rates in the mid 50's. Visit Huntington State Park at Murrells Inlet (call 888-697-8531).

Tofino, British Columbia
>If you want to see winter storms of the Vancouver Island Hamlet. Watch the soaring waves and intense lighting. 50% off regular cost (call 888-720-3414).

Remember you need recreation and leisure as much as work so let's go!

CHAPTER SIX

GETTING A JOB AND SECOND CAREERS

"Bringing home the bacon"

In America most men and women work or have careers outside the home during their Boomer years. In the age bracket 35-65 a large majority of women and men hold down regular jobs some of them working at several jobs. Women who hold jobs are closing the gap with men in the work force, in 2005 only 8 million fewer than men. On the other hand many women are bosses of small and large enterprises. Recently, more women are applying to medical school in American than men. Interesting in Russia seventy-five percent of the physicians are women, their medicine is considered a technology rather than a profession.

The fact is that one third of all wives with children under three and up to school age shows fifty percent or more work outside the home. The rate of women working outside the home drops from twenty-four to thirty-five year olds (the childbearing years) then rises again.

Often people find it essential to change jobs, careers and for the first time secure a job, some because of changing technologies, competition from abroad, the downsizing of manufacturing, shifts in consumer interest and obsolescence. In short, the nature of work is in flux—smaller families, new fields of work, general change in a major way through the information, service and communication sectors. These economies are features in the new environment of work. One third of all women 30 years of age will divorce (NY Times Almanac 2010). Add this to the fact that less than two-thirds of the children will live with two parents. The divorced women 35 to 45 hardly get enough money to raise two children. Even with support they can't cover their needs so work is essential, which means for most work on the outside, is imperative. To begin a new career or start a second career makes planning essential. Even this can be nerve wracking. Retraining is difficult for it entails (1) some loss of status, (2) loss of security, (3) the competitive market.

Boomers face a struggle for jobs in many instances as they will be in competition with the young who have been more recently schooled. Hence, looking for a job other than employment in basic labor, clerking, sales, care taking, or industry (frequently they have their own training programs) will find a need to go back to school! Certainly they need to have more money than the minimum wage. Women, especially those who have worked in the home for years will have many fears associated with entering work on the outside or enrolling in courses in a community college or business school to prepare themselves for employment. There is some good news some business concerns allow work to be done at home and one can start their own business at home but this requires some finances. More about this later giving details.

Those considering or preparing to enter the work force needs to have confidence in their abilities. The middle age employee is really the "cream of the crop" of the job market. As I have pointed out earlier the middle aged person is not hobbled by the immaturity of youth nor the infirmity of many older persons. Their chief assets are: maturity, experience, stability and wisdom, also their outlook is generally more purposeful because they are playing for keeps and have more at stake. In a study a few years ago the National Association of Manufacturing rated 23% of older workers superior, 70% equal to the younger worker and only 7% poor. Somewhat like this study was one done at the University of Illinois utilizing data from 3,000 employees found 69% of the older workers had fewer absences only 9% had more than younger workers. Some 34% turned out better work, 59% turned out the same quality of work with 9% producing poorer work. Even though this is true getting a job won't be easy unless you will be working in a fast food place or a super market.

There are some special problems, particularly for women who are in their middle years and seeking jobs for the first time outside of the home. There is the bias against those fifty or over although Federal Law since 1968 forbids discrimination of those 40-65 years of age.

Some things to consider according to *Christian Life Style* pamphlet for women working outside the home includes:

1. Does the need for money justify the extra effort? Having to work outside may bring unhappiness with working when considering its affects–hurried life style, less time for self and children, strain–relationships with husband particularly where he doesn't take part of the home work load from the wife. Studies show little changes for the women who with a job rather two jobs, one for which she gets money and the other a no pay job–home care.
2. Family support and appreciation may off the necessary encouragement for a woman to find fulfillment in work outside the home.
3. A woman may go to work outside the home when she receives family support. Studies show that when the wife works she gets some additional help form the husband at home but not much in most cases.
4. Obviously a more demanding routine must be ordered when the wife works outside.
5. Work outside the home should be suited to her aptitude and be meaningful.
6. A major consideration is whether or not satisfactory arrangements for the care of children can be made. Inadequate care for children can be brutalizing.
7. A final concern involves the woman recognizing her limitations as well as strengths. If the work leaves a woman exhausted with no reserve remaining for home and family then the returns will cancel the positive effects.

If you absolutely have to have a job and you will take any that provides above the minimum wage, it should not be as hard as it was several years ago now that state after state have mandated higher minimum pay and the federal government is acting to raise pay. Nevertheless in the last decade millions of jobs have been lost, two million in manufacturing alone. New high school and college graduates, thousands more coming off rehabilitation from prison, armed forces, immigration add to the grab for employment making even the seven and eight dollar an hour jobs more difficult in many cases to secure. But there are thousands of jobs you can get as a stop gap measure and in the mean time you can decide what you want in a job, career—location, salary, skills to meet needs, etc.

Unemployment rates are high for Hispanics with approximately 7.6% out of work but still considerably below Blacks with 10.1% and all higher than Whites with 5.2% (Department of Labor 2008). The most readily available jobs are those requiring little skills mainly physical work—using a shovel or hoe or ax, or arranging boxes, goods, repetitive work—simple assembly line operations, clerking, stockers in chain stores, security jobs, adult caretakers, delivery service, helpers in carpeting, roofing, plumbing, etc., garbage and street cleaning, school cross walkers and others. The U.S. Census (2006) lists the following as the median lowest paid jobs and this suggests possible opportunities. Also, persons holding these jobs frequently change when better ones appear.

This data on jobs must be held with caution for since 2007 the nation has seen a roaring recession hit most elements of the economy. So much so that the Federal government is considering more billions of dollars of bailout money for industry, banking, and state governments to bolster the economy to avoid a complete financial collapse. To emphasize the situation just reported in early 2009 by the Associated Press, 50,000 workers cut from an already strained job market to wit 20,000 jobs from Caterpillar Inc., 8,000 from Pfizer 8,000 from Sprint, 12,000 from several other firms and 2,000 from General Motors. Some of these types of jobs had been listed as jobs available. There are jobs—most will be low paid jobs, routine-type, clerking, cleaning, fast food, delivery, hospital aides, road work, helpers, maids, etc. In any event you must try and keep pursuing. Better jobs will be available for those who qualify for there are always persons retiring, leaving for one reason or another, and expansion by some companies. If your mind is set on a particular type of work don't give up. Find out all you can about what is required and stay focused on your goal. Education is the answer for many. Certainly the bail outs going to industry, education, the environment, state government, the environment will provide thousands of jobs. You need to be aware of these openings. Many will be available in the next six or eight months, some a year from now. They will not meet the needs of all the unemployed but will help. Take a part-time job as a stop gap job while you seek full-time work.

Rank	Occupation
1.	Dishwashers
2.	Counter attendants, food concession
3.	Child-care workers
4.	Maids and housekeepers
5.	Dining room, cafeteria attendants, bartender helpers
6.	Food preparation workers
7.	Teacher assistants
8.	Restaurant hosts, hostesses
9.	Food prep and serving workers
10.	Waiters and waitresses

Source: U.S. Census Bureau. 2006

Some of these types of jobs had been listed as jobs available. This is only the tip of the iceberg as the U.S. unemployment rate is greater than 10% in early 2010.

Caution

Being unemployed, particularly those of you who have worked for years, you might be tempted to grab any job that appears. Specifically, bad times in the economy herald the arrival of many job recruitment and work at home schemes. The Better Business Bureau in West Palm Beach reported by *The Wall Street Journal*, 2009, reported a rip off scam that requires $40 to $200 up front for advice on how to place an ad on the internet, give you fake employers to call on, then try to elicit your social security number and bank account information for the purpose of stealing your identity. Be careful. Never enroll or give money or information until you:

1. Check their authenticity—use the Better Business Bureau.
2. Never give out your social security number.
3. Don't fall for a job where you have to pay for a background check, fees or other expenses.
4. Check out the company offering the job. Check with the Secretary of State, Chamber of Commerce.

Women Set To Have The Most Employed

By 2010 women who in late 2009 have lost only 18% of the total unemployed whereas men have lost 82% in the economic downturn occurring in the past two years. Women have been employed in sectors more immune to losses such as health services and education whereas men have in employment had been related to manufacturing and heavy industry—steel, auto, shipping, etc. An influx of former housewives into the job market is occurring because husbands have lost their jobs and many of them can find work even thought it may be part-time.

What To Do

To begin to find out what I want to do, one must examine those aptitudes you have, talents, gifts and skills. I'm not gifted or talented you claim. I may have skills but I'm not sure! What to "do" is tied to skills that you possess that relate to people, places and things. Skills are found in people that sometimes they do not recognize. People think of skill like the doctor's use of a scalpel used in an operation or the precise cutting of a stone by the diamond cutter. Examine the often used diagram (that follows) to see and ordering of skills of people examining what to do–those categories listed are connected with the job you want. For the essential skills in the three categories are required or prescribed and those at the top a discretionary nature that is to be used at your liking or wanting. For dealing with data the higher level is synthesizing; for people advising and for objects is putting it all together. These like lower level skills are called transferable skills. They are functional skills. The ones you use to accomplish a task. The simpler skills are those at the bottom and those more complex skills at the top, it is assumed one has the higher skills. They also have the lower ones below.

<u>Categories of Skills</u>

Lower
Order
Skills

↓

Dealing with Information	**People**	**Objects**
	Advising	Putting it all
Seeing trends in data		Together
	Settling Arguments	Precision
Finding new uses of Data		with hands
	Teaching	and tools
		Operating
Collecting Information	Managing	equipment facilitator
	Selling	Driving
		vehicle
	Assisting	
Separating data into like		Looking after
categories		

↑

Upper

Order

Skills

These skills are not traits, that is like energy, ability to get along with people, gives attention to detail, dynamic, good personality, is persistent and dependable. Traits are important in choosing a job for instance if you are shy and the projected job requires meeting and dealing with people. You may need to reconsider foregoing those types of jobs. If you have a trait of being persistent then that would subserve the skill of problem solving. With use of the computer there are tests that will give you a clue about your traits or "type" one is the Personality Questionnaire (http://meyers-briggs.com/info.html) costs three dollars. Another is the Keirsey Temperament Sorter (http://www.keirsey.com/) and it is free.

On the basis of your experience you can always claim the highest skills you can rightly have. The greater the skills you can transfer the more leverage you will have in seeking and on the job. You will also have less competition than otherwise. Along with searching for a job there are accompanying fears that because of some minuses you possess or biases that exist for you to secure even lower level positions like the racial bias, foreigner bias, physical handicap, prisoner, possess no degree, or I'm too young, too old and I'm shy.

You must, even if doubts about looking for a certain niche trouble you, make wheels of your difficult and ride on to success–in short mustering up your courage–remember faint heart never won fair lady! I remember the French phrase "Fortune favors the brave"!

The following elements will help you decide what you seek in a job—location, salary, requirements, etc. Your first question is will you live in the place the job is located? Is the salary sufficient, is the responsibility equal to your ability? Are the job situation ideal and workers on the job compatible? Having answers these questions examine your skills isolating them will help you find your ideal job and put into perspective the employment picture for you. This will help you highlight your abilities, your desired working place and provide a clue for searching for a position. Some compromise will be made often through tradeoffs, i.e., the salary is great for a job but the location is not good or the skills you have don't match the requirements entirely but the organization is very supportive.

If these elements are utilized, it will help in a definitive way get to the result of locating your ideal job and at the very least help identify your skills and put into perspective the entire employment picture for you, that is your abilities, your ideal working place and the way in which you should organize your search for a position. Many times people have the ideal job in mind but unfortunately it is in an ungodly place or too far away from your comfort and family responsibility. Only you can decide where you will work, at what you'll do and the conditions necessary for your employment.

It is important to note that the Federal Government Employment Agency provides consultation for those without jobs (who are citizens) about available job openings, vocational training and general guidance. Also there are over 2,000 State Employment agencies affiliated with the U.S. Department of Labor, which provides the following services without charge. One or both agencies (federal and state) provide these seven features:

1. Intensive review of qualifications to discover new skills or refurbish old ones.
2. Careful appraisal of interests and aptitude.
3. Evaluation of physical capacities and activities with the help of the family physician.
4. Informs the applicant about career opportunities and job requirements.
5. Counseling to assist the person in choosing new fields of work or retraining to broaden skills in old fields.
6. Consultation with workers having common problems in job seeking to help them plan and conduct a job search.
7. Selective placement, whenever there is evidence of physical disabilities or slowing down, to protect the worker and the employer for health and safety hazards.

Hunting for a Job

How Employers Like to Fill a Vacant Position

Employers seek to fill vacancy in their business by going with the tried and true. That means hiring someone known to them to be effective workers.

1. Hiring from within the firm, a part-timer, or person whose track record is a proven one or if it's a promotion pick from those already employed.

2. Using the evidence of work from an unknown person who brings proof from their record that they have the skills necessary to the job.
3. Using the word of a trusted colleague or best friend who has firsthand knowledge of a candidate having employed them or seen their work.
4. Using an agency they trust. This may be a recruiter or search firm or regular job agency. It represents a way to save time and eliminate biases they might have in advance and it keeps them from hiring via a neutral source the best person.
5. Using an ad published in a newspaper or on-line, etc. They then pick from those who respond who are the best suited or whose background fits to come for an interview.
6. Using a resume even if it were unsolicited but only if the employer has to have someone now, in other words the job must be filled pronto!
7. A trusted employee recommends a candidate for the company that works for another company.

The way the usual job hunter seeks employment. (According to *What Color is Your Parachute* by Bolles, 2010.)

1. Send many resumes to employers even if they aren't requested. It is generally thought 4% gets jobs this way.
2. Put a job wanted ad in the newspaper, on-line, etc. Employers are wary of these kinds, having recognized the overblown, the untruthful and exaggerated hype sometimes used.
3. Use an agency, this will cost you a fee. Some agencies will allow you to pay them over a few months when they get you a job. This is not perfect but if you are a teacher, technologist, researcher, etc. this may be the only way to find a job in an area you want to locate and you know no one there. Many state and federal agencies are required by law to advertise positions. These ads elicit many responses but unless you know that many are foreclosed

you will be disappointed for all too often jobs are given to the insider.

4. Use your network of friends or co-workers. These people sometimes know of positions available and have information of their accessibility.

5. Submit to a business concern in writing or in person their ability to do the job they think you need usually illustrating with examples their expertise.

6. Finally many people think last of the company they work for or want to work for. They may try to get a position as a part-time worker, consultant or maybe they have had experience with a similar company, with this parlay it into getting an interview. The known quality of a worker is the chief factor but without a contact unless you're on their payroll or have a like work record you'll be out of luck. Employers hiring within their organization look around to see you they don't have to take a chance on failing

The Use of a Resume

Most employers begin with a resume in filling some slot to working. Most job seekers recognize this, the question is what kind of a resume? The answers here are difficult because you are trying to guess what type of vita, in this case a succinct note of what you want, your qualifications (education, experience, special expertise, etc.), how you would fit their job description and perhaps what would you bring as intangibles to the firm and facts of your personal life (information about your family–wife and children if any, health, something about your desire to work in a certain field). Then maybe a brief summary relating your persona–work style, effectiveness and willingness to learn. This may not do it, some people put a picture on or with their resume. Of course you run the risk of someone not liking that personal introduction to you. Some will probably like it. Some employers do not like résumés but most employers use it to screen out those they are not interested in hiring. One thing is sure do not submit a long resume, this is a cul de sac! Check the spelling for accuracy and the sheet for mistakes is crucial. However if you are an educator, writers, management at a high level, more detail is desirable so to include what you did when pointing out accomplishments and experience and in general knowledge you have about the position sought is important. The résumé is usually used by those looking for work and the most by all odds as the entree to a job by most employment seekers. Unfortunately only about 4%, as mentioned earlier achieve success this way. One problem is that you do not know whether the bosses or the person they report to wants a man or woman employee, a brown, black or white person, older or younger that you, male or female or even religion and don't overlook nation of origin. In sales work employers usually want a diverse group hence they would look at all the attributes possible such as mentioned above. In other positions where cooperation in paramount, how the prospective employee fits in is moot. This is very important.

According to Ann Mann at Lee Heck Harrison in Overland Park, Kansas (2009), who collected resumes from job recruiters, these were the things hated by employers in a resume.

1. Long resumes—those over two pages.
2. Several applications for jobs in the same company.
3. Jargon abbreviations or titles. They don't mean anything to outside eyes.
4. Misspelling and bad grammar.
5. Confusing summary statement at the top of the resume.
6. Stalkers—those who continually call about the job.

Sample Resume

Name

Address $ City, State Zip Code

OBJECTIVE

EMPLOYMENT

JOB TITLE   YEARS EMPLOYED (EX: 2004 - 2008)
Organization Name   *City and State of Organization*

Describe responsibilities and accomplishments here.

JOB TITLE   YEARS EMPLOYED (EX: 1992 -2004)
Organization Name   *City and State of Organization*

Describe responsibilities and accomplishments here.

EDUCATION

DEGREE EARNED OR   YEARS ATTENDED (EX: 1988 - 1992)
MAJOR
Institution Name   *City and State of Institution*

Describe honors, related activities and accomplishments here.

SKILLS

• Bullets may be used here to create an attractive list of
  skills

The Interview

If you get an interview there are several aspects upon which
you will be judged for the job. The aspects are: skills you possess,
initiative, your knowledge, your persistence, experience, who you
know (or about whom) and the persuasiveness you exhibit. Being
too aggressive will turn off many hirers as will too much talk on
each of the items discussed. Your résumé should be in their hands if
not bring a single page one and hand it to the interviewer. Who you
know is not generally important but if your field is in editing, writing,
a book agent, a marketing director, or consultant then don't be shy
about dropping a name. Suffice it to say you need to be prepared to
discuss, and talk about these topics.

We should talk more about first impressions. Joyce Brothers,
famous psychologist, says that the first 30 seconds of the interview
is the most important and she says most decisions on hiring are
made then. Dr. Brothers calls this the "halo" effect–it is the what
we radiate from ourselves–it can be positive or negative. God forbid

you stumble on the rug upon entrance to the interviewer's office. The "halo" effect is the first impression we have of a person when we meet them. To demonstrate the psychologists affirmation of this Dr. Brothers asked a friend of hers (owner of an electronic firm) to interview several people on the effect of first impressions or the "halo" effect. What he didn't know was she fooled him by sending the same man to interview with him twice. For each interview he changed himself–once unshaven, hippie look, sloven, wore sneakers, tennis shoes and had shaggy hair. He did however speak intelligently about his interest in the field. Also though rumpled he was clean! On the second interview the plant was clean-shaven, had a standard haircut, had a dark business suit on, looked the electronic chief in the eye, had a firm hand shake and spoke intelligently about the prospective field of work. These visits were on subsequent days. The interviewer didn't recognize the men were the same individual, if he had the plant was prepared to say the other man was my cousin. Later Dr. Brothers' friend reported to her that the gentlemen he interviewed last would be hired by him for his company but the first man never. The electronic chief couldn't believe he had validated her principle of first impressions. Psychologists had isolated two facets of the interview for a job, first, the "halo" effect and secondly the interview itself. This latter aspect is composed of three factors–these are questions from the interviewer; assuming usually he has seen and read your resume. (1) So you're interested in our opening? (2) Why do you want this job? and (3) What can you tell me about yourself?

Regarding the first query the answer is not just "yes" but yes plus like I'm very much interested in this position for it's the kind I've been looking for quite a while. Response of the second question cannot be that I think it would be interesting or because I like working with people–most personnel executives would write you off on that answer for they would assume you didn't really know what you wanted to do. You should be able to tell something involving the nature of the work in which you would reveal you are fit for the job offered by the firm. The final questions about yourself–your life history won't cut it! The interviewer would think "oh hum." What he or she is looking for is a clue to your motivation, character and ambition. One might say, if cars were his interest, I've liked to sell or repair cars ever since I tore one apart and put it back together. Or ever since I was a little girl selling lemonade, I've wanted to sell things, to display things, to organize things, etc. Your replies cannot be simply yes or no but something also but not too long, keep your answers to two minutes or less. If they want more information they'll ask. If you've had some activity or lost a job because of being fired don't bring it up—you deserve another try. If you are asked directly about a certain job, which didn't turn out so well, be truthful but put the best light you can on the experience. There was a man I knew who was a principal of a small high school from which he was fired. The Superintendent interviewing him in another school district asked him, why are you leaving the job you have? The principal simply said he was fired and gave briefly the situation he was in at his school. The Superintendent was impressed with his honesty and hired him. He also knew something about the setting unstableness in the other district before he met his new principal. Nevertheless one should accentuate the positive, eliminate the negative and stay away from Mr. In-between!

It is well known by psychologists that there are certain features of the first impression and interview, which is understood, will help you get the job. Dress for success not overly, conspicuously nor too casually, for men wear a white shirt and tie and for women a nice fitting dress with pleasant colors and design but no high heels, glamour is not what they are looking for on most jobs. Now if the job is for acting maybe creativity and some outlandish outfit is suitable to demonstrate a part or dialog you'll present, or other effect. When you arrive for the interview be sure your hands are not sweaty, dry them if they are before you meet the hiring person. Also when you shake hands make sure your shake is firm—many a person lost a possible job because of a weak handshake. Upon entrance to the office make sure your head is raised and look the person in the eye and continue that throughout the meeting. You may not be able to choose the sitting location but if you are to the left of the interviewer you're in luck! People, studies show, pay more attention to you if you are to their left. But even on the right there should be no barrier between you and personnel, interview. In general the closer (not right upon them) you are to the speaker the more equalized is the relationship. When entering the room for your talk about the job hold you head up high, smile and stand straight. Check your clothes before the interview for dandruff, wrinkles, slip showing, hose sagging or hair out of place. Remember you need to have everything going for you that you can and that also means being on time! One final note be sure to rehearse the presentation you will make ahead of time–even go over it several times for practice makes perfect!

Getting an Interview and Enhancing Your Prospects

There are several things you need to keep in mind in finding a job:

1. Seek a position with a small organization (25 people or less). Two-thirds of the new jobs are there.
2. Get help for finding interviews from friends and other people you know. You need many people to help for it increases your chances.
3. Get information on a company after you have looked the company over, using the library–their encyclopedias on Careers, Dictionary on Careers (5 vols.) and Informational Interviews. The library has hundreds of occupation sketches, which are detailed and have <u>crucial</u> information.
4. Find out who will in fact hire you for the company. Lean on your friends and contacts to see that you get to see that person.
5. Request twenty minutes of their time when you get an appointment and if arranged keep your word.
6. Alert them of your potential and knowledge of their organization. After the meeting write them a note or call them to thank them for their time.

On the other hand, six factors that you should recognize which militate against you getting employed are:

1. Forget large organizations, they typically hire within go beyond the NASDAQ group of companies.

2. Find by yourself places to interview using ads, resumes and career notices.
3. Do your homework before going there to apply for the job.
4. Allowing Personnel Department usually in a Human Resources Department to interview you. Their job is to screen you out, theirs is a negative approach so avoid this if possible.
5. Set a time limit on the appointment you make with a company. Do not beg for a job or say any time suits you to visit them.
6. Send a thank you note or make a call to the reviewer.

A mature worker should never hesitate to take further training in refresher courses or in a new occupation. Further training is greatly appreciated by personnel managers or employers, because they realize that such a person has the stamina necessary to fight and not let age (middle) become a problem in making a living. For those of you who have never completed their education evening schools can prove a big second chance. Vocational Education through Public School Systems offers wide varieties of opportunity. Evening college and programs like those at community colleges, Teletechnic courses from universities like Old Dominion University, Southern Florida University, California University system, which provide a variety of programs the M.S., continuing education programs and workshops. City school systems have special vocational programs available. A chance to complete high school work and begin a college degree is clearly there. Counseling is available and tailored to the needs of older people. There is research which shows intelligence doesn't evaporate at forty or fifty. Even gains are reported. So you want to go to work, make your plans and start. America's labor force will require nearly 200 million people by 2020–you could be one! These figures are assuming a turnabout by 2012 of the economy. Here are some among many jobs you can get with training or college credits.

Associate Degree (AA Degree) Community College	Bachelor's Degree (B.S. or A.B.) College or University
Paralegal	Data base administrator
Dental hygienists	Computer resource
Registered nurse	Computer engineer
Health information technician	System analyst
Respiratory therapist	Physical therapist
Cardiology technologist	Occupational therapist
Radiologist technology	Special Education teacher
Child care	High School teacher
Sales	Elementary School teacher
	Records in schools, hospitals and businesses
Law enforcement	Communications
	Marketing
Adult Education Training Often receive a Certificate	**Trade School** Award a Diploma with Study Completion
Dental assistant	Auto mechanic
Hair dresser	Data processor
Auto mechanic	Dental assistant
Realtor	Desktop publisher
Nurses assistant	Food service
Opening a small business as	Hair stylist, cosmetologist
Home cleaning	L.P. nurse
Child care and baby sitting	Air conditioning and heating
Sell goods made in the	Secretary
home[quilts,	Telephone repair
Baskets, afghans, etc.	Electrician

To review and to supplement the best ways to secure a job:
1. Through friends, family, community contacts, career centers, community college and college or high school where you graduated. Has a 1 in 3 success.
2. Going to the employer's place (factory or office) where you want to work even if there is no vacancy. Unbelievable nearly 50% success rate. Again remember "fortune favors the brave"!
3. Using the yellow pages you locate the position or job you like in a town or city where you are. Call them and ask if

there is an opening in the type of job you are interested. Nearly 70% percent success!

4. With a group repeat the advice given above using the Yellow Pages to isolate the jobs the group is interested. The success rate is out sight—80+%!

5. Do a life-rearranging job change, this is by far the most difficult method to seek a job and get one. It entails additional education frequently moving, cost schooling, franchising, starting a business of your own, etc. Besides being perhaps disruptive to the family.

You may not get a job using any of these tactics. But if you use the Internet successful rate is going mainly to medical technician or computer people. Mailing at random is hardly better as is answering advertised ads in trade and professional magazines for they have thousands of applicants in their thirties and forties applying. A number of local newspaper ads could be better if the job is a lower level pay, however, little chance of a good job. Signing with an employment agency has a 5 or 6% rate of success up to 30 or 50 percent with women. The fee is higher for better jobs to get a teaching job. It may be the only way although some schools secure a teacher or principal through an agency so they offer contracts to those who come with proper credentials. Recruiters are mostly in technical fields as geologists, chemists, or physicists. The recruiter usually gets his fee from the company or industry hiring.

Another Reminder of Places To Seek Work
Here are four places you might find work:

1. The location of the company hiring often place signs identifying the jobs available, interview time, when to come and where, and also what to bring by way of information.

2. Take the Civil Service Exam. At least 12% pass and a good score helps with a job usually 1 of 8 or 9.

3. Visit a former teacher or professor about some job they may know about if you were in their class. They often have a job in mind or two!

4. Take a trip to the State or Federal Service office. Often the effect of this is to get information of what is out there in terms of employment, job requirements, and pay.

Occupations with the Largest Job Growth, 2004-2014.

The following assumptions are dependent on the economy turnabout in the next 2-3 years.

(by number of new jobs; numbers in thousands of jobs)

	Employment		Change	
Occupation	2004	2014[1]	Number	Percent
Retail Salesperson	4,256	4,992	736	17.3
Registered nurses	2,394	3,096	703	29.4
Postsecondary teachers	1,628	2,153	524	32.2
Customer service representatives	2,063	2,534	471	22.8
Janitors and cleaners, except maids and housekeeping cleaners	2,374	2,813	440	18.5
Waiters and waitresses	2,252	2,627	376	16.7
Combined food preparation and service workers, including fast food	2,150	2,516	367	17.1
Home health aides	624	974	350	56.0
Nursing aides, orderlies, and attendants	1,455	1,781	325	22.3
General and operations managers	1,807	2,115	308	17.0

1. Projected.

Information Please® Database, © 2007 Pearson Education, Inc. All rights reserved.

Industries with the Fastest Wage and Salary Employment Growth, 2004-2014

Industry description	Thousand of jobs		Change, 2004-2014	Average annual rate of change
	2004	2014[1]		
Home health-care services	773.20	1,310.3	537.1	5.4%
Software publishers	238.7	400.0	161.3	5.3
Management, scientific, and technical consulting services	779.0	1,250.2	471.2	4.8
Residential care facilities	1,239.6	1,840.3	600.7	4.0
Facilities support services	115.6	170.0	54.4	3.9
Employment services	3,470.3	5,050.2	1,579.9	3.8
Independent artists, writers, and performers	41.9	60.8	18.9	3.8
Office administrative services	319.4	449.9	130.5	3.5
Computer systems design and related services	1,147.4	1,600.3	452.9	3.4
Outpatient, laboratory, and other Ambulatory care services	836.1	1,160.4	324.3	3.3
Child day-care services	767.1	1,061.9	294.8	3.3

NOTE: 1. Projected. For these figures to become a reality, a huge economic comeback is required.

Information Please® Database, © 2007 Pearson Education, Inc. All rights reserved.

Metropolitan Areas with Greatest Projected Job Growth		
MOST JOBS ADDED	Number of jobs ('000s)	
Rank, Metropolitan statistical areas	2008	2030
1. Atlanta-Sandy Springs-Marietta, Ga.	3,262,320	5,829,280

2. Dallas-Fort Worth-Arlington, Texas	3,923,730	6,353,970
3. Phoenix-Mesa-Scottsdale, Ariz.	2,492,140	4,538,020
4. Los Angeles-Long Beach-Santa Ana, Calif.	7,732,930	9,592,200
5. Houston-Baytown-Sugar Land, Texas	3,321,470	5,094,390
6. Las Vegas-Paradise, Nev.	1,252,280	2,959,420
7. Washington D.C.-Arlington-Alexandria, Va.	3,955,540	5,650,980
8. Miami-Ft. Lauderdale-Pompano Beach, Fla.	3,371,940	5,038,330
9. Denver-Aurora, Colo.	1,719,990	2,992,940
10. Orlando-Kissimmee, Fla.	1,387,360	2,604,410
11. Riverside-San Bernardino-Ontario, Calif.	1,810,770	2,872,620
12. Tampa-St. Petersburg-Clearwater, Fla.	1,709,090	2,726,440
13. Austin-Round Rock, Texas	1,038,240	1,989,100
14. Seattle-Tacoma-Bellevue, Wash.	2,269,840	3,173,160
15. Minneapolis-St. Paul-Bloomington, Minn.	2,336,290	3,235,330
16. San Diego-Carlsbad-San Marcos, Calif.	1,924,550	2,767,580
17. Chicago-Naperville-Joliet, Ill.-Ind.-Wisc.	5,725,050	6,539,300
18. Sacramento-Arden-Arcade-Roseville, Calif.	1,258,400	1,973,940
19. Portland-Vancouver-Beaverton, Oreg.-Wash.	1,392,900	2,029,060
20. New York-No. New Jersey-Long Island, N.Y.	10,729,210	11,282,210

21. Baltimore-Towson, Md.	1,707,170	2,226,330
22. Nashville-Davidson-Murfreesboro, Tenn.	1,055,010	1,563,780
23. San Francisco-Oakland-Fremont, Calif.	2,747,270	3,247,320
24. Salt Lake City, Utah	811,500	1,262,200
25. Boston-Cambridge-Quincy, Mass.-N.H.	3,130,670	3,560,790
26. San Antonio, Texas	1,140,550	1,567,340
27. Kansas City, Mo.-Kans.	1,322,230	1,742,070
28. Charlotte-Gastonia-Concord, N.C.-S.C.	1,077,620	1,482,490
29. Indianapolis, Ind.	1,135,500	1,527,790
30. Raleigh-Cary, N.C.	663,390	1,044,190
Total 30 MSA's	**77,404,950**	**108,466,980**

Source: NPA Data Services, Inc.
Regional Economic Growth USA for 2008-30 (2009)

COLLEGE OR CAREER BY HIGH SCHOOL COURSES

On the positive side there are ways to help yourself if you want to go beyond the minimum wage. Many will need to obtain more education. Avenues abound for taking courses for new positions at home through the computer or by mail. Even college degrees may be obtained from Universities like Phoenix University (picked at random) who claims to be the largest private college institution in the nation. They state that you can get a degree in two and a half years. Claims of these schools make can be obtained from State Departments of Education in each state's capital. Get their literature and check out what it costs, programs, their veracity, etc. There are many of these types of schools. Business colleges abound offering one or two for diplomas in secretarial work, business bookkeeping, management and a variety of other business related jobs.

Some career schools or institutes have programs at their conclusion offer diplomas in a variety of fields. One such school is Stratford in Washington, D.C. (1-800-363-0058 or www.scitraining.com). They offer sixty-one career diplomas (see below) in fields calculated to give you chance of employment and a boost to your ego along with higher pay than the low wage hourly paid groups. Here are the forty-five categories. They also will provide free career information. In yesteryear Universities offered some of this work through their extension departments, some still do, the work is done at home via mail and computer. One note; these Colleges and Universities do require work - not just going through the motions. So be prepared to work if you undertake getting additional education in this manner.

The purpose of career institutes like Stratford are to provide career training through guided study at home upgrading existing skills, learning new ones and earning a High School Diploma through independent training at a time convenient for them. The following categories are available for study by students Business, Counseling/ Education, Creative Careers, Computer Technology, Legal, Medical, Vocational Trades, and others. Most of their students are older, therefore, serious and committed to their studies.

Alphabetical Course List (Stafford College, Washington, D.C.)

Art	English as a Second Language	PC Repair
Astrology/ Parapsychology	Fashion Merchandising & Design	Pharmacy Assistant
Auto Mechanics	Fitness & Nutrition	Photography
Bookkeeping	Florist/Floral Design	Physical Therapy
Business Management	Forensic Science	Private Investigator
Case Worker	Funeral Service Education	Psychology/ Sociology
Child Day Care Management	Gardening/ Landscaping	Radar Technician
Child Psychology	Happiness Consultant	Real Estate Appraisal
Computer Programming	High School Diploma	Relaxation Therapy
Computer Training	Home Inspector	Security & Police
Conservation/ Environmental Sciences	Hotel/Restaurant Management	Sewing/ Dressmaking

Contractor/ Construction Management	Interior Decorating	Small Engine Repair
Cooking & Catering	Internet Specialist	Start Your Own Business
Cosmetology/ Esthetics	Legal Assistant/ Paralegal	Teacher Aide
Creative Writing	Locksmith	Travel & Tourism
Criminal Assistant	Medical Bill Collector	Veterinary Assistant
Dental Assistant	Medical Billing Specialist-Online	Wedding Consultant
Desktop Publishing & Design	Medical Office Assistant	Writing Stories for RNC
Drafting with AutoCAD ®	Medical Transcriptionist	X-Ray Technician
Drug and Alcohol Counseling	Motorcycle/ATV Repair	Zoo Maintenance

According to *Time Magazine,* 2004, these categories of jobs will grow larger than others. This is projected from 2000 to 2010.

Food preparation-Starbuck's, Fast Foods, etc.	673,000
Customer Service Representatives	621,000
Registered Nurses, biggest gain of all health related	561,000
Retail sales persons, the largest of all occupations with part-time workers	510,000
Computer Support Specialists	491,000
Cashiers, those that have retail and restaurant experience	474,000
Office clerks-general	430,000
Security guards, low pay around $17,900 per year	391,000
Computer software engineers	380,000
Waiters and waitresses-has high turnover but with tips okay	304,000

General Operations Manager	364,000
Truck drivers-heavy and tractor-trailers	340,000
Nurses Aids, Orderlies	323,000
Janitors and Cleaners	317,000
Post Secondary Teachers and College Instructors	315,000

STARTING A HOME-BASED BUSINESS

Many people that are unsuccessful in the hunt for a job they wanted attempt to start a business at home. Only a few get rich this way and what is typically realized is about three-fourths of what regular outside pay provides in the same kind of work. There are other drawbacks mainly in managing time, that is a balance between the needs of your family. Because each success generates more motivation to work harder and longer time for the family might become less and less. Another thing an individual has a job but they keep hunting for customers, better ideas of how to do their work and publicize it, etc. So, in fact they continue hunting for a job to be successful.

If you have thought about doing a business at home but don't know what kind, search the Amazon categories at http://www.amazon.com/ or Monster. Libraries and bookstores will have information you need. *Working from Home: Everything You Need to Know About Living and Working Under the Same Roof* by Paul and Sarah Edwards (1999) in paperback is considered by many to be the bible of information on home businesses. Imagine what you'd like to do, even dream of something, but remember you need to study and have considerable information before you get under way. Some people go about this too slowly and inadequately then lose out to someone who beats them to the idea. I knew a friend who talked to me about an invention or an adaptation of an idea he wanted to market. He researched the idea, what would you do to get a patent, how to market and unfortunately numerous other questions consumed his time. The idea was to design a cover for the backs of trucks, which would keep debris from falling out incurring damage to cars or people. After making slow progress he was beaten by someone else who got there first. If you have an idea for an invention there may be funds available for helping to make it a reality through the U.S. Patent and Trademark Office (Dept. of Commerce).

Look in your own community for an opportunity. Consider what is needed, what is missing, how to save time and energy for people. Some such ideas are home delivery of groceries, drugs, food from restaurants, cleaning service, home repairs, yard care, baby sitting in your home even for the elderly.

A franchise may be a good investment. One could start at home in a small way and could begin a catalog, which could be sent anywhere advertising a service, product or help. So if your community is small you could reach out by mail or computer. A man I know started a business newsletter providing information about local businesses, how to do things and where to get various sorts of things and assistance in general. It prospered hence expansion occurred and he began to take ads in his letter which now has grown to be a magazine. I visited him in St. Thomas, though he wasn't getting rich he was living well and enjoying it. Nearly everyone on the island knows him also! Working for others in telecommunication is a thought for many have used this to be successful. You can do this along with your regular job. Teach your spouse or children to help and even ask your boss if he could use your services. Ask him if this is possible, also search the following Web Site http://www.workoptions. com/telecom.htm Chances are high for failure with these businesses when started from scratch: restaurants, dry cleaners, machine shops, baking companies, trucking, car washing, clothing, infant wear and grocery stores.

Ferguson's Encyclopedia of Careers and Vocational Guidance, 14th Edition, 2007

FRANCHISES

Many franchises are part of a chain of establishments so you get help from a well-known name and likely to be successful if an unknown business may not get the kind of support you thought or advertisement you would need. Naturally the famous names of big businesses like a motel, hotel or even good-sized eating places will cost considerable up in the six (smaller motel) and seven figure bracket and therefore is beyond most everyone's reach. But if you have some money or can borrow some go for it. Caution, only after you have investigated it thoroughly, I mean talk to people who know something about it, that is those in the business with a franchise (see people out of your community, they will likely give you straight answers). Research through libraries, consultants and Internet such as the Better Business Bureau. If you put a lot of money in an enterprise and you fail to get it back that may lead to bankruptcy, certainly a quandary and perhaps misery. Franchises have a low failure rate of only about 5%.

These are the things you must consider when buying a franchise also the same for starting your own business. The three major factors are and you must answer these questions truthfully (for home business franchises, etc.). What knowledge and skills are required to run you business, what do you know about doing this work and what skills will I have to employ to make this work. Answers to the questions are the first step.

When you need to search for an occupation a good start will be to examine the *Encyclopedia of Careers and Vocational Guidance,* 14th Edition in four volumes published by Ferguson. All the volumes II through IV are devoted to occupations as many as several hundred are given. Each occupation presents some history, information about the job, its earnings, requirements, the work environment are prospects! Also other sources are provided and the Web Site given. Some selected occupations appear here as adapted from the Ferguson publications mentioned above are illustrated here.

BED AND BREAKFAST OWNERS

Twenty to twenty-five thousand such businesses exist in the United States also known as an Inn or small Hotel ranging in size from four rooms to ten. Today they may be found in a large city but more frequently they are found in small towns, in the country along rivers, in the mountains and near the ocean. The owners interact with the guests, provide information about noted places to visit, museums, tours, recreational areas and landmarks of interest. Typically these establishments serve one meal a day–breakfast although some serve two meals.

History

Cottages for rent found in America along its highways in the 1930's were the precursors of the modern tourist motel. In the last fifty or so years the B & B business developed. The idea was an extension of the tourist home or motel business only on a generally smaller scale. Many people who had large homes from the Victorian age 1880 to 1900, some were historic or were located in recreational areas began opening their homes to guests and most added breakfast. Those people traveling found breakfast non-existent in rural settings so homes gave breakfast recognizing the guests via auto could make it to the next destination by the next meal. The hallmark of these places became clean and comfortable rooms, friendly hosts, tasty meal(s) and conversation. Usually these establishments are well furnished and many have special decor and period furniture. I remember going to Montreal on an occasion nearly forty years ago and stopping in St. Albans, Vermont after seeing an advertisement about a Bed and Breakfast home. They furnished a large room with a double bed and provided two cots for the small children we had. It was a beautiful old Victorian home with a special tone of its own. I found out that St. Albans was involved in the American Civil War. Confederates raiding from a Canada site robbed the bank there and fled back to north of the border. I visited the bank, still standing, and read the memorials, historical signs, etc., that I found.

The Job

Many bed and breakfast homes have well-documented backgrounds as the former home of a famous general or politician. In Cape May, NJ you see them in Victorian homes, brownstones in Brooklyn or a home designed by Frank Lloyd Wright. Many of these are furnished with antiques or special decorations with a theme such as an oriental setting, western motif, southern, puritan or the theme of a well-known book or story or historical incident, like the Civil War or space exploration in Cape Canaveral. They often reek with individuality.

Taking care of business means getting up early in the morning to prepare breakfast, assuming you have gotten the groceries you need the day before, noting special requests of the visitors. Some places cater to wide differential dietary needs. This, however, is not standard. By early afternoon, 2 p.m., the rooms and bath facilities must be ready as many visitors will start their trips very early in the morning and, therefore, wish to light for the night early avoiding also a last minute look for a place to stay. Keeping a register–their names, addresses, any phone numbers–thought a small part of the work demand keeping records such as bills to be paid, cost of operation, social security accounting for those you hire or maybe even yourself. Tax records for paying the local township, etc., state and federal and for adding to the bill of the overnighters. Purchase of new for replacement, etc., or different furniture, linens, toilet paper, soap, etc. Make available business cards with salient features of your home-business. Unobtrusive signs about smoking or no signs. You get the idea. Your schedule would involve the following areas or work–up at five or six at the latest for breakfast and clean up following it; then begin cleaning the rooms and making the beds, etc., at ten or eleven. Save time for bookkeeping in the early afternoon one hour say 1:00 p.m. then at two or three o'clock shop for groceries and other needs–light bulbs, soap, new towel rack and whatever. Have house ready for occupancy at 4:30 p.m. Be sure vehicles are cleared from the driveway or parking place and have yard tidied and manicured. Managing a place is more than meets the eye. One has to decide what to charge, that is no small task. One needs in summary to be a manager, an organizer, likes people and has some time to interact with the guests.

Earnings

The money to be made is dependent on several things (1) the size of your inn, (2) the amount of funds you charge, (3) your location and (4) the reputation you achieve. Small homes that can accommodate only three or four people–two bedrooms with a charge of $30.00 per night for a couple–children extra and filled three nights a week will probably accrue 8 to 10 thousand a year. A large bed and breakfast home (eight to ten rooms) could make a substantial amount near $100,000 upward if they charged $75 or $85 a night and were filled five nights a week at $75 per night, you could take in $144,000 per year. Many families do this using older children to assist in serving meals, cleaning or caring for the lawn. They usually are paid by allowances. A frequent pattern of ownership is a man and his wife, two old or young maid sisters, or a mother and daughter/son. The reward that comes to this business is meeting people, knowing about them and being stimulated by their conversation.

The growth of these businesses will be as fast as many other kinds of businesses–a projection is fifteen to twenty (perhaps somewhat less during this slowdown) percent growth a year. There are too many in some locations but not enough in other places where they could flourish.

Ferguson's Encyclopedia of Careers and Vocational Guidance, Vol. 14, 2007

FOOD SERVICE WORKERS

This work includes the following jobs: waiters (men and women), counter attendants, dining room helpers, fast food workers, dining room helpers, and to other work around food, you may, for instance prepare salads or drinks. Today's food service industry is one of the largest and most active in the nation's economy. In the nineteenth century particularly in European cities many large eating places existed mainly in hotels where food was served in elegant style utilizing many employees to handle the lavish setting and food. In earlier times, the American inns dotted the major roadways and usually had lodging and food available for travelers, some states had laws requiring towns and cities to have such establishments. Mobile societies today like in the USA have many varieties in food offerings from Chinese to Sinn Wang, Western cuisine to Italian lasagna and pizza and available almost any place you travel. Increasingly people eat out, even entertain friends by going to a private club or fine restaurant. Many thousands of jobs are available providing an opportunity to interact with people and sometimes be offered a job at higher pay than they have through the contacts they make.

The Job

There are many variety of jobs in food service, the environment may be a small restaurant, a fast food place, a cafeteria, coffee shop, grills, diners, sandwich shops and even stands seen on street corners or in ballparks. In indoor facilities working means more than just waiting on the customers, in slack time they may be required to clean food equipment, mop floors, take out the trash and polish the serving silver, etc. If they add up the cost of meals they may also be asked if the worker doubled as a cashier to sell a variety of goods at the counter such as mints, chewing gum, candies, pencils, chap sticks, crackers, etc. You may be able to eat a meal or two at no expense to you at the establishment. In formal and expensive restaurants the main jobs in serving food goes to the experienced personnel. These establishments follow formal and correct procedures in serving dinners, etc. The Captain or Headwaiter in large eating places usually greet the customers and seat them although they may turn them over to an assistant to seat them.

BUS DRIVERS

Drive bus intercity or local regular route or charter, assist passengers with baggage, collect fees or tickets. Check vehicle for adequate running condition—examine oil, gas, and water levels along with tire air before departure. Drive bus over predetermined route, keep order on the bus, comply with traffic regulations, park vehicle so passengers can load and unload easily. Provide information on transfer connections and time arrivals. Report any problems or accidents that occur. Regulate lighting, heating and air conditioning for passenger comfort. Keep records of cash receipts and tickets. Make minor repairs, which may involve changing tires.

Skills Needed

Truck and Bus Driver (Commercial) Vehicle operation. Care and maintenance of large vehicle knowledge. Information on highway or road routes relative to speed limits and restrictions or detours, if any. Needs to be courteous and helpful to passengers and in recognizable control. On the job training is usually available.

Prospects for Work and Pay

Typical annual earnings $30,000-$32,000 a year. The growth rate running 20-25% making the yearly job openings close to 35,000. Self-employed represent only 5% of the total of these employed each year with part-time nearly 40% of the total.

Ferguson's Encyclopedia of Careers and Vocational Guidance, Vol. 14, 2007

CUSTOMER SERVICE REPPRESENTATIVES

This job is one where the employee interacts with the customer providing information about products and services or to take orders for goods. Many times the job is to handle complaints. It may relate to billing, checking accounts, look into the provisions of contracts also review insurance policies. Could order tests to verify the causes of product malfunction. Recommend improvement in products, packaging, shipping, service or billing methods or other aspects of relations with customers.

Skills Needed

Be able to deal with various types of people, to be able to communicate with customers and to understand what they are trying to find out from you about the company, its products services and facilities. Employee needs to completely understand the company and its operation to best serve the interest of the customer. Can be hired with high school diploma.

Prospects for Employment and Pay for Work

Typical pay ranges from $27,000 to $30,000 a year. The growth in this field runs as high as 25% with the annual job openings each year of 500,000. In the self-employment area around 3% for part-time work around 18%.

PAYROLL AND TIMEKEEPING CLERKS

These clerks compile employee time and payroll data as the main requirement. Involved also may need to compute employees' time worked, production and commission. May post wages and deductions. Will need to keep informed about tax and past workers obligations, etc., to pay related retroactive increases. Handle information on pension plans, report payroll, special programs (United Way, etc.) to management and whatever involved payroll deductions.

Skills Needed

One needs mathematics skills, accounting ability, needs to be able to communicate with employees, have social skills, be consistent and steady. Needs to be able to follow directions. A High School diploma might be sufficient, many of them have business, typing, etc., included in their curriculum.

Prospects for Employment and Pay

The typical yearly earning for these clerks currently is $31,000 to $32,000. The growth annually is around 17% per year with some 35 to 37,000 new jobs a year available. Of these, 15-16% are part-time whereas the self-employed represent slightly more than 1%.

Ferguson's Encyclopedia of Careers and Vocational Guidance, Vol. 14, 2007

PERSONAL AND HOME CARE AIDES

These aids assist elderly or handicapped adults with daily living at their home or a center catering to group care for these needy adults. Their work in the home includes a variety of things like keeping house—doing laundry, washing dishes, preparing meals, cleaning, etc. also, generally have health-care related duties monitor vital signs, give medication under nurse or doctor direction. May help dress the adult, drive the adult to visit the physician's office or visit kin or friends. Inform kin of the status of their client.

Skills Needed

Foremost is ability to get along with people, to have social skill and to like older people. Having beginning nursing training courses or two dealing with care of the elderly would help. These courses or workshops are often offered by hospitals, community colleges, or social services. Call local service group or agencies to inquire usually found in the yellow pages. Some knowledge of medicine which can be received from these training courses. Candidates for this work would be those who are involved with helping or providing services to others—teacher, social workers, nannies, child care worker, funeral attendance, and church workers.

Prospects for Employment and Pay

Typical pay for annual work between $17,000-$18,000. The annual job openings 230,000-240,000 a year with a growth rate of 41%. Of the positions available 4.5% are self-employed whereas around 40% are part-time, many persons utilize these as second jobs to boast their income.

REAL ESTATE SALES AGENTS

Sells property, buys property or rents property for clients. Has to have knowledge of property, property listings, interviewing prospective customers, discuss condition of sale, drawing up contracts. Confers with escrow companies, lenders, home inspectors, pest control inspectors to make sure requirements are met before the closing date. Be able to determine what customer wants in housing, property, etc. Arrange to view property occupied, advise clients of market conditions, mortgage rates and evaluation of loans available, legal requirements and be aware of latest information provided by Real Estate Associations and literature on real estate matters and current concerns.

Skills Needed

A person to be successful in real estate needs to be very good in communication ability. Sociability is very important for selling property is crucial that one have this aspect of salesmanship. Certainly knowledge of mathematical skills, business law management, salesmanship are essential. These elements would be found in a business degree (B.A. or B.S.) but one could get these in an Associate Degree (two year) community college program or even by taking piecemeal course to cover these subject areas. There are courses on Real Estate offered as a single course but it would not cover wheat the courses covering the areas mentioned above would. There are Real Estate agents who have no degree that are successful.

Prospects for Employment and Pay

Michael Fair's proclaimed America's career expert says the annual earnings should be around $40,000. We think this may be true in a rural or small town setting but generally the earnings will be much higher than that in the urban setting where cost of housing is higher and commissions higher. Job openings will run from 40,000-45,000 yearly. With 60% self-employed and around 20% part-time with many of these using this as a second source of income. The growth of jobs is about 15% annually. The severe down turn in housing construction, manufacturing and mortgage cost will affect the job market greatly!

SALES REPRESENTATIVES - WHOLESALE AND MANUFACTURING

Sell goods for wholesales or manufacturers to business or to groups of individuals. One needs considerable knowledge of the material, items and things sold. Must be able to answer customers' questions about products, prices, uses of items and terms of credit, guarantee, arranging for delivery, installations and follow-up on the effectiveness on equipment.

Skills Needed

Prime skills are social ones—communication, be able to talk intelligently about the product, equipment, etc. offered—its use, price, guarantee, support offered in start-up of equipment. Understand how to promote sale of products and train people to assist work in knowing how to use equipment sold by manufacturers. On the job training is available in many manufacturing settings.

Prospects for Employment and Pay

A large number of jobs annually are available, estimated to be 170,000 or more each year, with pay close to $50,000. The job growth will run at 15% with part-time employed at 8%.

A Final Word:

There's a job out there for you, it may be less than you desired or more than you expected. In any case you need to invest time and energy into researching the job you want and the kind you can reasonably fill adequately. To repeat what we have said in this chapter related to job finding I will recite some of the salient features you should use to locate a position.

1. Use a placement office–one that's organized both for profit and those for non-profit. Use the college placement office and their career centers. Use also state and federal guidance and career agencies. One of these may not land you employment but it will give you tips and an understanding of the job market and how to find out about kinds of occupations, etc.

2. Use job fairs and workshops that are offered by your local Chamber of Commerce. Attend college and school career days and employment opportunity sessions frequently advertised in your local newspaper. Some are sponsored by businesses who are searching for employees. The Tampa Tribune (Feb 2010) announced a Job Fair for construction development ($425 million) needing 2000 - 3000 workers of all kinds - even in hard times.

3. Network and Explore References. Many jobs are not publicized and must be found, in some instances businesses have not sought help. Use a business card that indicates your expertise and qualifications (briefly told) name, address and email and telephone numbers. Use cards and letters to discover jobs or to learn more about a particular opportunity. You availability of your kind of work to prospective employers through email or to get information on the parameters of work which interests you!

4. Search the Web, which is the user-friendly part of the Internet for jobs. Use Monster.com or some other clearinghouse for careers and job searches. Be selective, considering the source of information, know the field and protect your privacy.

5. See classified ads and use them. Think about what they are saying about the work, that is, the requirements and the pay. Find out who the employer is–reputation, etc.

6. There are several career manuals and books covering job-hunting and career changes worth reading at reasonable cost. *What Color is Your Parachute?* 2010 by Bolles, *150 Best Jobs for Your Skills*, 2008 by Farr. Also by Farr, *300 Best Jobs Without a College Degree*, 2006.
7. Read the fine print. If you consider taking a position requiring a contract, go over it carefully. Check the benefits, part-time jobs rarely pay or provide any! Note vacations, sick leave, hours of work (does overtime get extra pay?), total emoluments, etc. and work conditions. Find out who is to be your supervisor, the chain of command and ask about anything else that you are concerned with related to your work.

GOOD HUNTING

CHAPTER SEVEN

LOVE, SEX AND MARRIAGE

"Do You Like To Kiss?"

If you read books on or about love, you rarely ever see an attempt to fashion a discrete definition of love. This is due in part to the fact that it interfaces with so many other aspects of our lives–marriage, sex, family, loss of spouse, view of self, attachments, and death. Even divorce is not exempt, for in the process of separation one is frequently called upon, at least to himself, to redefine the meaning of love or evaluate what it is not. There are other components–intimacy, passion, and commitment as suggested by noted Psychologist Robert Sternberg. Liking to kiss may have reference to love in that we usually like to kiss the love object or express our satisfaction in this way. For many this is motivated by the physical but probably more because in the long run a lot of other harmonies exist between two persons–view of life in general, goals, compatibility and complementary needs projected for each into the other, etc. The kiss, liking or not liking it, comes to be a gauge or mark of how a marriage is making out. When the author visited the honeymoon cottage (where the newlywed daughter and husband live), he checked to see if the "kissing machine" was still working. Little kissing usually indicates that perhaps little pleasure exists in marriage, a lot of kissing then a great amount of pleasure in marriage! We recognize it can be perfunctory, also. When the kissing stops, whether at twenty-five or fifty-five, for most the party is over. This could be a crisis point of whether or not to try anew with someone else who likes to kiss or tough it out because there are offsetting advantages to staying with a union. Intimacy and passion may be gone but commitment remains.

Love is one thing in childhood and adolescence; it is something else for Boomers and this will be the principal reference to love here. In the meantime, there are some things concerning love in general that need to be discussed briefly.

THEORIES ABOUT LOVE

According to Rollo May, the Psychiatrist, there are four kinds of love in Western tradition, via Greek literature. One is sex or lust–libido. The second is eros (God of Love), the drive of love to procreate or to create–the urge toward higher forms of being and relationship. A third type is philia (friend), brotherly love - like the name and meaning of the city Philadelphia or love in friendship. The fourth is agape, the love devoted to others, the prototype of this love is God's love for man. Certainly there is another kind of love–stergo which means patriotic love, the love of one's country which I presume in our time may not mean the same thing as it did for instance when Richard Lovelace wrote the lines in *To Alcastra on Going to War* – "I could not love thee half so much, loved I not honor more."

On the other hand, Dr. William Kroger, the Human Developmentalist, suggests there are, from the standpoint of the developmental, four types of love–the first one "I love I" is seen in the child who loves only those who contribute to his well being and comfort and egocentricity. The second type of love is projected self-love (I love me as seen in you). This type is frequently found in immature people who see qualities of others that rightly or wrongly they attribute to themselves. Romantic love is a third type and it is the basis of marriage for most persons for they have been conditioned to believe it is the highest form of love. The principal element of this love is passion and idealism. Unfortunately, when sexual drives fade the partners often become strangers to each other with little commitment or intimacy. The final type of love is mature love identified as the condition where each partner thinks only in terms of the other person's happiness–their chief enjoyment is in giving, not getting or possessing. The sexual impetus does not drive them into marriage and those couples with this base to their marriage usually remain married for a long time. Unfortunately, this is a rare type of love, although it is usually taken to distinguish love apart from mere attachments, likings, desiring, wanting, etc., as Freud used the term, although he said, that love is the attachment and not the feeling. There may be feelings associated with attachment but they are not always pleasant. Love can be romantic and lofty, on the other hand, it can be selfish and highly ego-centered. Some of our loves make us happy and provide a great sense of fulfillment; others keep us constantly striving, feeling inadequate and full of anguish. Therefore, feelings associated with love are not dependable as the sole basis of love for they vary too much, as Fromm, the Psychiatrist, says, as much as the ways we express love.

Robert Sternberg, IBM Professor of Psychology and Education at Yale University, has formulated a theory of love (1986) in which he suggests there are three faces of love. The authors believe these ideas are as compelling even today. The three faces are commitment, intimacy and passion. Sternberg visualizes love as a triangle, the more commitment and intimacy and passion you have, the larger the triangle and the greater the love! Intimacy is emotional closeness, sharing, communication and support. Passion is motivational, physiological arousal, intense desire, it develops quickly and involves kissing, touching, hugging, making love. Commitment is cognitive, it starts at zero and grows. At first it is a short-term commitment to love another person and then it becomes a long-term commitment to maintain that love as expressed by fidelity.

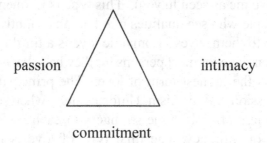

The shape of love based upon this theory says commitment is the cognitive component of love and is all that some couples seem to have left after the intimacy and closeness have been lost and the passion has died down. Intimacy is the emotional component of love. Some people can bare their souls to each other but have little in the way of commitment or passion. This is the characteristic of high-grade friendship. Passion, on the other hand, is the motivational component of love, it calls the tune in some love triangles. This might be an affair or a fling in which there is little intimacy and even less commitment.

Triangles may be used to define various loves beginning with non-love. In this triangle there is no intimacy, commitment or passion. In liking another person, you have intimacy—we can talk to a person, tell them about our life and dreams, there is closeness and warmth but not passion or commitment. With infatuation there is only passion—it is adolescent instant love upon seeing his dream girl or her dream boy.

Empty love is frequently called cold love; there's no passion or intimacy, whereas, romantic love has passion and intimacy but not commitment (Romeo and Juliet type). These are like summer affairs which die when autumn comes and vacations are over—she goes one way, he another. Passion plus commitment is what Sternberg calls "fatuous love" (lacking reality). It's the Hollywood type of love—boy meets girl and marries next week—the commitment is to the passion that's aroused them but the emotional core necessary to sustain a commitment is not there.

Finally, there is compassionate love, which is constructed of commitment and intimacy but not passion. This is long-term friendship—the kind of committed love and intimacy seen in marriages in which the physical attraction has died. Consummate love is where the three forces are all there—passion, intimacy and commitment. Sternberg says this achievement is nearly impossible— like keeping off weight after you have lost it. This love is possible only in very special relationships.

To sum up the kinds of Triangles of love there are eight running from non-love with no aspects or components of love to consummate love which involves all parts of complete love—passion, intimacy and commitment.

Since Dr. Sternberg's original theory the Triangle theory of love he added an additional element; a sub-theory of love recognizing another aspect fundamental to the nature of love and the Triangular notion of defining love. This suggests love as a story meaning that each individual is exposed to a great number of a variety of stories to give us different ideas of how love can be internalized and understood. The stories come from watching other people in varied relationships, in watching television, seeing movies or reading or even through their own juvenile experiences. Such experiences help to mold our view of what love is or what it should be in a large measure.

There are many kinds of stories according to Sternberg, i.e., addition, art, business, collection, history, mystery, game, police, religion, etc. For example

> Addition – strong anxious attachment, anxiety or thought of losing a partner
> Art – love of or for physical attractiveness
> Game – love as a game or sport
> Police – you have to keep close tabs on your partner
> Travel – love is a journey

Twenty-six love stories were given to 105 study participants that were almost evenly divided between men and women aged 17-26. They were asked to rate the stories as related to their lives and feelings of their connection and relevance to them. The most popular stories for men were art, pornography, sacrifice, and science fiction. For women, travel was the overwhelming choice.

An analysis showed the three components of triangular theory of love—passion, intimacy and commitment positively predicted satisfaction. These stories that showed significant correlation with satisfaction all negatively predicted the satisfaction ratings. The theory predicts that the couples that are more similar are more likely to be attracted to one another and to be satisfied with their close relationship.

The stories generate different types of triangles. Maybe more than 26 stories. The stories involve two aspects which may or may not be alike. The stories arise as one interaction between person and experiences—though not associated with happiness they are associated with dissatisfaction. Couples tend to be happier if their story patterns are more or less preferred ones, based on a conversation with Dr. Robert Sternberg, Dean, Arts & Letters, Tufts University, February, 2009.

Many theorists believe women are better achieving intimacy than men and they value it more than men. If they fail to get intimacy they desire from a man, they try to find it with women or another man. They establish close friendships and are able to say things to women they can't say to a man. This may account for the fact that women have a much more extensive network of support than does the average man—principally from women.

Passion though initially may be the positive force, which drives people together and though quick to develop is also quick to level off. This negative motivational force, the one that works against the attraction, is slow to develop and slow to fade. The result is first an explosion of passion that is followed by habituation when the more slowly developing negative force kicks in. Like coffee, cigarettes or alcohol addiction that can be rapid once however habituation sets in, increasing the amount needed it no longer stimulates the arousal that occurred earlier. When a person is duped, they end up more worse off than before—depressed, withdrawal symptoms, irritable, loss of appetite—the negative force is still there after the person or substance is gone. One thing is true, according to Sternberg, the consummate love involves couples who love each other more than anyone else. Among many loves there remain a "lost love" or "parent love" which may never be eradicated.

A Triangular Theory of Love, Psychological Review 93, pp. 119-135. 1986.

Love and Sex

One thing should be said, love and sex are not the same. Sex is a way of expressing love to be sure. We should say that love and sex are not necessarily mutually exclusive of each other. In the first place, sex is a basic drive—an appetite like hunger or thirst. Nature made this appetite pleasurable in order to insure the continuation of the race. Sex is physical—it can be identified and measured. Love, unlike sex, is a state of mind and it is much more elusive. Love and sex often occur together, so are mistaken for one another.

Love, according to Allan Kaufman in his work *Interview with Sex*, is choosy—"It insists on one particular person. . .sex on the other hand is a passionate interest in another's body." Love may be just as passionate, but its interest is in the whole personality. Love is a deep and constant feeling for another person. The other person's happiness is as important as yours. A person who loves another wants that person to be happy forever—it involves faith in that you allow yourself to be vulnerable to hurt—it involves giving love with conditions—only those imposed by yourself. Like it is written in the Bible, Corinthians I. 13; Love suffereth long and is kind, is not puffed up, does not act unseemly. . .

Love gives sex its other satisfactory meaning. There are sinister uses to which sex is put—to achieve power, to trap someone into marriage, to punish oneself or someone else, or to make one feel important. The word itself has become a catchword for advertising. It has come to mean fulfillment, freedom, doing your own thing—the ultimate. Sex is as natural to living as love is to self-actualization, this is the making of one's potential into his best possible self.

When love and sex are intertwined, life is greatly enhanced. The stages through which we develop love start with the child when he discovers his body and becomes attached to it, stroking his genitals and learning to masturbate. It also happens in girls. These attachments are extended to people who care for him and make him happy. The next significant period comes sometime between 5 and 11 or 12 when manipulating his own body is taboo. Attachments are generally reserved for like-sex playmates although this period does not mean everything in the social-sexual area is latent. Many girls and boys in the early part of this period experiment with sex by playing house and doctor-nurse. It is also true that the like-sex attachments are often the source of homosexual contacts. Toward the end of this period, many girls form crushes on uncles, older persons not only their own cross-sexed parent. The adolescent has already experienced many lovers. But when maturity of the sex glands is accomplished, boys and girls begin to notice each other and finally most of them prefer the company of the other sex than their own. This attachment is strong, often called "puppy love." It may not relate directly to strong sex feelings although certainly the physical stirrings are there. Like many attachments of adolescents to objects, ideas, etc., this one too may be idealized. Much like the Victorian Age attempt to express love without sex, some adolescents are not overwhelmed with the idea to initiate sex. A girl may have many puppy loves without participating in direct sex activity or giving up her virginity, and the boy likewise. Most youth will have experienced heterosexual activity by the time they are eighteen. The sense of curiosity and wonderment is woven around the love object and becomes a drive to incorporate the other person as oneself. Aiding in this maturity is the desire, strong in the adolescent, to divest part of his family heritage and try a new attachment—this time in values with another person. The love object partly makes the girl or boy a new personality. When attachments become very special and childhood attachments are gone, then a longer lasting stable love eventually leads to marriage or cohabitation.

AS BOOMER MARRIAGES AGE DO THEY GO STALE?

The typical marriage does change over the years. It need not necessarily grow colder as it grows older for among the healthy the ardor of sexuality may diminish very little. Most husbands by the middle of life have mellowed, become thoughtful and tender human beings. Wives have become more understanding though less passive helping to increasingly bear the burden of life. The earlier years have served to iron out many difficulties between husband and wife. Of course, there are many marriages that did not survive to this point. Complete love, according to Dr. Rose Franzblau, a middle years expert, is made up of two components, romantic love and tender love. Both must always be present. There is no doubt that with aging, certain physiological changes take place that affect sexual activity. At that point, tender love is more predominant, but romantic love is still there. This is now expressed in the mindfulness and consideration that each shows for the other.

No matter what can happen, the statistics tell us the sad tale of nearly 1,126,000 divorces per year in America with a rate of 3.5 per 1,000 in 2008 (National Center for Health Statistics, 2009). The heaviest incidence of divorce occurs from 20-35 for both men and women. Most divorces occur in the first seven years of marriage.

World Almanac 2008 shows marriage and divorce have dropped to 3.5 with the marriage rate at 7.1, however, many divorces or separations never appear in statistics for one or the other partner just walks and the divorce is never formalized legally. The rate of divorce is questionable* based on the data from the U.S. Department of Health and Human Services, 2008. The marriage rate per 1,000 is 7.1 and the divorce rate 3.5, 7.3 and 3.6 in 2006. The reason for this trend is probably accounted for *Divorce rates excludes six states including California, the most popular state.

Data from the University Chicago's National Social Life, Health and Aging Project (NSHAP) 2007 showed that many men and women remain sexually active—participating in vaginal intercourse, oral sex and masturbation—well into their 70's and 80's. The early boomers those born in the late forties 1946-48 are now in their early sixties. Many more to follow. Those in the later boomer cohort born in the early 1960's are in their 40's entering middle age. Most studies show the highest incidence of sexual activity among women and men to be in their forties and among healthy couples gradually dropped. This is in keeping with the earliest scientific study of men and women's sexuality of the Kinsey's 1948 and 1953. This study had mostly middle class women in the women's study and overall too few minorities.

Dr. Edward O. Laumann (noted sociologist) of the University of Chicago and his team interviewed 27,500 men and women between the ages of 40-80 about sexual habits and problems reporting their findings in *The Journal of Urology*. The global study reported in depth in the Archives of Sexual Behavior, Vol. 35, 2006. Their survey included a two-hour face to face interview with 3005 men and women around the country, also took blood samples, saliva and other samples that would tell about hormone levels, sex related infections and other health issues. Some of the findings are as follows:

1. Sex with a partner the previous year by 73% of people age 57-64. Fifty-three percent of those 64-75 and 28% of those 75-85. Those active said they had sex three or more times a month.
2. Women of all ages were less likely to be more sexually active than men. But many more widowed.

3. Research done by Trojan (the condom manufacturer) in 2005 surveyed 1600 American women ages 18-59 about sexuality. They found 83% of female boomers are somewhat to very confident sexually. Sixty-two percent have a good sense of what satisfies their sexual desires—a greater percentage than among younger women!

4. Half of the people having reported at least one related problem most common in men—erection trouble (37%). In women low desire (43%), vaginal dryness (39%) and inability of having an orgasm (34%).

5. One out of seven men used Viagra or some other similar product.

6. Only 22 percent of women and 38% of men have discovered sex with a doctor since age 50.

7. Sexual problems can be a warning sign of diabetes, cancer or other problems, untreated sex issues can lead to depression and social withdrawal, and people may stop taking medications because of sexual side effects.

A number of myths have been vanished by Laumann's research. The first myth, perpetrated by young people, is that sex doesn't exist for people over fifty. Of the thousands of participants in his study, 4500 were 40 to 80 years old, were non-European westerners, 81% were men and 70% were women, who reported they were sexually active. 46% of the men and 43% of the women had regular sex at least five times a month.

A second myth is that sex for over the fifty-year mark is boring. Not so, as 73% of Americans said sex was considered very, extremely or moderately important in their life.

A third myth is that women don't want sex. In the global study by Laumann only 32% of American women reported a lack of interest in sex. This implies that the other 68% love the urge. Remember those who are not sexually active do not necessarily lack desire. Little interest may be tied to lack of a partner—divorcees, widows, etc.

Myth number four is older men can't perform. True, some men can't pop a rod or have difficulty getting an erection, but, in his study, some 18% of non-European western men ages 50-59 reported erectile dysfunction. Another survey of 2100 Minnesota men ages 40-70 indicated that 51% of those in their 70's could achieve an erection firm enough to have intercourse. The problem for most men relates to health issues such as the impact of diabetes, heart condition, or daily medications, not desire. In a conversation with Dr. Laumann (in February 2009) he told me his research reveals that the sexual problems of the elderly are not the inevitable result of aging but in response to stressors. This was reported in International Society for Sexual Medical (2009).

The single boomer is having sex regularly but only 39% invariably use protection (many women may have passed menopause so they figure no pregnancy looms as a consequent) from HIV according to a AARP study of several years ago. Linda Fisher AARP's Research Director says "many boomers don't have a sense of danger about sex. They came of age before the HIV epidemic and never learned how to negotiate condom or testing with their partners." By 2000 women's share of AIDS cases among those 50 and older doubled from 8.8 percent to 15 percent. According to the 2008 NY Times World Almanac the figure is now 7.8 percent for ages 50-59. Although a drop still represents thousands of women. Boomers should be cautious of their new lovers before they engage in intercourse. It's a sensitive matter certainly, but with tact it can be discussed openly.

Sexual functioning is a problem for some men particularly related to ejaculation and impotence. On the other hand females are plagued with frigidity, inability to be sexually stimulated, difficulty in reaching an orgasm, or vaginismus. Those problems requiring surgery are very expensive and available only in large hospitals or specialized clinics.

SPECIFIC SEX PROBLEMS

Male: Premature Ejaculation

Men who are plagued with this problem are unable to control their ejaculations. Once they become aroused, they reach an orgasm quickly. They feel guilty because they have been unable to satisfy their partner. The causative factors are debated: some say it is anxiety, others that it comes from hostility between the partners. Masters and

Johnson believe that stressful conditions happen during a young man's initial sex experience brings on premature ejaculation.

Therapy

This procedure is to slow down the orgasmic reflex. This is done by having the wife stimulate her husband's erect penis until he is about to have an orgasm, then she would take the thumb and two fingers and squeeze a little below the penis head stopping the ejaculation and reducing the erection then resume the foreplay. This stop-and-go method is practiced over a period of several weeks until the husband can tolerate being stimulated without ejaculating. When this point is reached, a cure has been effected. This approach has been found helpful in many cases. Sometimes distracting one's mind from the coital act will allow a man to gain control—thinking of some non-sexual content like work, etc., sometimes effects a cure. The frustrations of the woman in this situation must be considered for, in the absence of coital orgasm, manual stimulation to orgasm by the man is recommended to provide some fulfillment for her.

Male: Retarded Ejaculation – Difficulty in Controlling Orgasm

The man suffering from this malady cannot control orgasm, the retarded ejaculator cannot trigger it. Some with this difficulty have never had an orgasm. For most men, ejaculatory inhibition is confined to specific anxiety-provoking situations such as guilt feelings about the sexual situation. It may be tied to religious upbringing and some clinicians relate it to an unresolved oedipal complex (in the case failure to attach significance to any woman besides mother) and/or an ambivalence toward one's partner.

Therapy

The best approach is usually found in the clinical situation where psychotherapy is also being administered. This is important and for this reason home-made therapy may not be successful. Usually some kind of stimulation is required whereby the woman eventually brings the man to orgasm with the penis near the vagina. Finally, the woman is told to stimulate the man almost to orgasm at which point he is to enter the vagina with pelvic thrusting. This type of problem is difficult to solve, but patience and outside assistance is usually required to relive this circumstance. Your physician can direct you to a urologist or sex therapist to help you.

Male: Impotence – Inability to Have Erection

Men who are in this category are usually constantly anxious and frustrated. It has been estimated that at one time or another half of all men have been impotent. Even though they are able to be aroused, they cannot have an erection (also called erectile dysfunction). Most men seek help from their physician when the problem becomes a chronic one. For men, it is of signal importance that they be able to perform. In the climate existing today, especially for young men, where women are now often being very assertive and initiating sexual relations, have already, by some accounts, been a factor in the rise of impotence. To perform on demand is sometimes threatening and inhibiting to masculinity.

Therapy – Aid for Impotence

Those with an impotency condition should have a physical examination. Stress, fatigue, undiagnosed hepatitis, high sugar levels, alcoholism, smoking, drugs, low levels of testosterone and other problems (heart disease, diabetes, surgery) may lie at the root of the difficulty. Many therapists think that impotence has at its roots some pathology, that is, Parkinson, neurological problems, etc. Obviously, psychological problems bear on this—fear of failure, conflict, excessive demands by a wife or lover all may be involved. Frequently depression or marital troubles relate to impotence so need treatment. The practice for remedy usually suggests that a couple caress each other in sexual play at home, under quiet conditions, but not to engage in coitus. The middlescent woman is encouraged to accept clitoris stimulation to orgasm if the sexual tension becomes too great. This routine usually builds up excitement in both partners. Eventually, erection and intercourse can be accomplished. Sometimes a period away from attempts at intercourse is desirable. One thing is sure, tension, stress, conflict and hatred are cul de sac where male erection is concerned. The climate for lovemaking must also be unhurried and protected from interruptions and noises—relaxation is an important ingredient.

It's only an estimate, but it is believed that 10 to 20 million American men are sometimes affected by impotence. Normally when a man is sexually aroused, nerves affecting the penis triggers a chemical reaction that causes two slender areas of spongy muscle tissue in the penis to relax, then to fill with blood. The engorged tissues press against veins that drain blood from the penis trapping the blood and producing an erection. Failure of the system is often the fault of nerves or blood vessels that have been damaged by disease or injury. Urologists have found that cells lining blood vessels release nitric oxide, which causes surrounding muscle to relax. It is known that cigarette smoking, high blood pressure, and/or diabetes damage these nitric-oxide-producing cells. They are suspects in any investigation of the causes of impotence. Many doctors are recommending the use of Viagra or Levitra for thousands of their male patients.

Medication itself may be a cause of impotence. Drugs for high blood pressure may affect a drop low enough in blood flow to the penis to preclude an erection. These sympathetic blockers as Aldomet, Ismelin, Catapres, Tagamet (anti-ulcer agent), Nexium, and Zantac used widely to neutralize acid may lower testosterone levels. This hormone is responsible for sexual desire in men. Sometimes a change in the drug to alternative ones by the physician can solve the problem.

Drug therapy can be used for men with nerve or blood vessel damage caused by diabetes, multiple sclerosis or a spinal cord or pelvic injury. A major advance in treatment is the use of Sildenafil, which increases blood flow to the penis. It does not help those with diabetes or alcoholics and for side effects—headaches, gastrointestinal upsets. Fatal interactions have occurred in men taking Sildenafil with nitrate medicine. Another drug is Alprostadil that increases blood flow to the penis. It is not absorbed in the blood flow hence has fewer side effects as Sildenafil. It can produce erection in men not excited. The Alprostadil is injected into the base of the penis or placed inside in the form of a pellet. If used 20 minutes before sexual intercourse 90% of men get an erection. In some men it can cause priapism (cause an uncomfortable prolonged erection). This problem can be neutralized with a shot of epinephrine thus preventing damage to the spongy tissue of the penis.

Some 20 to 30 percent of older males with impotence have hormone deficiencies. For this group, testosterone injections, give by a doctor, may make achieving an erection easier. Spanish Fly, Zinc, Yohimbine, and vitamins (high potency) have not been proved by clinical investigation to be effective.

Surgery

About 10 percent of impotent men can have damaged blood vessels repaired, if the damage is caused by injury to the pelvis. Localized blockages are much easier to fix than those caused by fat buildup, which affects vessels throughout the penis. In bypass surgery, the surgeon grafts sections of an abdominal artery around narrowed branches of the main artery leading to the penis. Where the major veins draining the penis leak blood too quickly, the veins are sewn shut so that smaller veins take over the draining. These vascular procedures are still considered experimental and are performed at only a few medical centers nationwide.

Psychological reasons are often the cause of the inability to have an erection. A single failure to get an erection according to Dr. Helen Kaplan of the New York Hospital (Cornell Medical Center) or alcohol or stress over the ability to perform sexually may cause impotence. Fear and stress all to create more adrenaline, which constricts the blood vessels leading to the penis and results in relaxing it. If a man can have erections while sleeping his problem is likely to be psychological.

There are four major types of approaches to aiding men in obtaining an erection. One by a mechanism and three by surgery. The first mentioned is by use of a suction device. In this case a man inserts his penis in a acrylic tube which is attached to a pump which is operated by your hand. Air is pumped out of the chamber creating a suction causing the blood to flow into the penis. A less complex device—a condom like device lets the man create the needed suction by drawing air by mouth through a tube into the device.

The second method for achieving erection is via bypassing clogged parts of the arteries leading to the penis. The abdominal artery is snaked through a surgically made tunnel beneath the skin to a new site just above the penis, where it is spliced into two arteries which increase the blood flow therefore erection.

In the third instance known as an inflatable implant the surgeon implants a three-part prosthesis through an incision in the abdomen or below the base of the penis. When the man squeezes the pump in the scrotum, fluid is forced from the reservoir into thin tubes causing an erection. To deflate the tubes he presses a release valve on the side of the pump and the erection automatically down.

The final type is known as a semi-rigid implant. This is the simplest penile prosthesis of all. It involves two firm but bendable silicone rubber rods which are inserted into spongy muscle tissue on each side of the penis. Usually the rods are in a bent position so that the penis lies close to the body. To stimulate an erection the man can simply push the rods or extend them straight out. Each of these surgical methods are expensive with the inflatable and the semi-rigid implant being the least expensive but with these the success rate is reported to be very high. The least expensive is the non-surgical suction device. The importance of one's sex life which bears on a happy marriage and life in general will send some men to use these approaches to improve their erection ability!

<u>Female: Inability to be Sexually Stimulated</u>

Women who have this problem receive little or no pleasure of a sexual nature from attempts at erotic stimulation. Like impotent men who are chronic cases, these women so handicapped view sex with disdain and alarm usually because of lack of sex education and inhibition. In the worst cases, some have never experienced sexual pleasure or have an orgasm.

Of course, as mentioned earlier, some 8 to 10 percent of all women never experience orgasm. One approach to the solution of this situation is a sex therapist technique called sensate focus which consists of having a couple forego sexual intercourse and orgasm while the woman caresses her husband's body, after which he stimulates her by stroking. By having the wife act first, we help counteract the guilt she may have from previous failures and the fear that her husband will reject her. The attempt here is to eliminate the pressure to have an orgasm. When this is done, the woman often can feel sensuous and sexual excitement. The sensate exercise is expanded to light, genital play. The husband strokes the woman's body, touching her breasts, nipples, the clitoral area and the vaginal entrance. The woman guides his fingers and hands by telling him and moving herself to receive the maximum feeling. If the man becomes excited, then the woman is usually told to bring him to orgasm manually or orally after she had had a chance to experience non-pressured and comforting genital play. Manipulating the penis usually creates a sexual response in the woman. When the woman reaches a high peak of excitement, the couple moves to have intercourse. The woman usually takes the top position initiating coitus slowly and tentatively thrusting at first but focusing on the sensation in her vagina. In this way she controls the intensity and exact location of her clitoral and vaginal stimulation. The man does not allow himself to have an orgasm until the woman is ready. Considerable emotion is frequently generated by these encounters due to their long problematic duration. But, this type of treatment allows a therapist to observe the point of blockage of sensuous feeling. Usually good prognosis is indicated where the husband has patience and genuine care, and pathological conditions are not present.

Female: Difficulty in Reaching Orgasm

Dr. Helen Kaplan, Sexual Therapist, suggests that there are two facets to this problem: On one hand the problem is primary orgasmic dysfunction if she has never experienced an orgasm and from secondary orgasmic dysfunction if the disorder developed after a period of being able to reach a climax. The problem of inorgasmic disability is said to be absolute if a woman can't achieve an orgasm under any circumstance (10% never achieve orgasm under any circumstances) and a situational one if under any circumstances can she have an orgasm. Women who suffer only from orgasmic problems often have strong sex drives. They fall in love, enjoy sex play, lubricate sufficiently and love the feeling of intromission by the penis. Nevertheless, they can't have an orgasm, stopping short, only reaching the plateau stage and no further. In the situational case, women can achieve orgasm by self-stimulation, vibrators or by their husbands' manual dexterity or orally. In therapy, the search for conflicts, inhibitions, use of drugs or medicines, also fears are sought as a clue to the problem's cure.

Therapy

In solving the problem indicated here, an attempt is made to eliminate the inhibiting factors of the sexual environment in order to achieve the first climax. Since women are least threatened when at home, they are counseled (the inorgasmic woman) to masturbate at home in a situation where they will not be intruded upon. If their own attempts fail, then generally a vibrator is recommended which can be applied on her genitals, the labia and the sides of the clitoris. Some become hooked on this method so usually after the experience of several orgasms by the manual method—hands/fingers, and she is able to stimulate herself, the husband is brought into the picture to make love with the wife and told not to make any effort to have an orgasm. After he has climaxed and there is no pressure for her to perform, quickly he uses the vibrator or manually stimulates her to orgasm. Usually after a few of these sessions, women climax during intercourse after stimulation.

Female: Vaginismus – Inability to Control Vagina Muscles

This circumstance is seen in the woman whose body is normal but whenever the male attempts penetration, the vaginal muscles involuntarily close off the entrance making intercourse impossible. This is relatively rare. The problem arises as fear of intercourse and its association with pregnancy, disease, lack of experience and pain or abuse. Most women who seek help in this regard are usually sexually responsive and orgasmic. The basis of this problem may be a rigid hymen, pelvic diseases (arthritis) and tumors, childbirth diseases, and hemorrhoids; also guilt, rape and a husband's impotency.

Therapy

After assurance that there are no pain-producing circumstances surrounding the vaginismus, an attempt is made to understand the nature of the fear of vagina entry. A re-conditioning of the involuntary spasm of the muscles is undertaken through having the husband and wife examine in a well-lighted bedroom the opening of the vagina. The woman is then told to put her finger in the vagina. When this is done without pain or discomfort, she is told to move the finger around inside until she can tolerate the touching without pain. The woman is always allowed to control the situation. Following this, the husband inserts his finger or two fingers into the vagina, rotating them carefully and stretching the sides of the vagina. When the woman can tolerate this, a move is made for intercourse. Entry is made tentatively and gentle thrusting proceeds until desire for full vigorous copulation is desired by the woman. If pain is involved, the procedure is slowed or repeated until the woman wishes for penetration. Very good results have been achieved through this procedure which is used by many sex therapists. The process above may require more practice with the woman alone using her finger(s) to rotate in the vagina or a tampon when she feels comfortable with this invites her partner to try it.

It is true that many knowledgeable couples work through their own problems by being patient. Many will have to have help from their physician or therapist specializing in remedial methodology. We should mention that most couples who have sexual problems practice poor, abrasive and non-effective methods. Some poor lovemaking results merely from a couple's ignorance about sex. For instance, it has been observed that many couples do not know where the clitoris is or seem to know that it is the seat of ecstatic pleasure. The author has observed that some graduate students in Human Development courses cannot place in the proper position the endocrine glands (including testes and ovaries) when asked to on an outline of the body. Many couples have intercourse as soon as the man has an erection and he climaxes without considering his partner. Then they wonder why the woman is unable to have a climax. Women typically are slower than men in achieving an orgasm but once stimulated are usually capable of multiple orgasms. The circulation of blood to the woman's vagina and the pelvic regions takes more time than it does to engorge a man's penis and women are slower after tumescence has been accomplished in return to normal. The rule for both partners in the sex act is to attend to the enjoyment of the other but at the same time make sure that you receive what you would like out of the lovemaking. Sure it will vary: sometimes an orgasm isn't necessary, but the communion, nearness, stroking or satisfaction of one or the other is usually sufficient.

Women need to understand their needs sexually and many need the help of their husbands and/or partners. Talking and patience is needed. A too-aggressive woman often repels many men as many women are turned off by cave-man treatment. Many people need (both men and women) to rid themselves of some prudish beliefs about sexual morality. Some would like to try activities that to them are arousing and erotic but are stymied by puritan partners or their own inhibitions. Couples should invest in a good sex manual like Alex Comfort's *The New Joy of Sex*, if for no other reason than to see what is considered normal and the range of possibilities. A few years ago Psychiatrist David Reuben said he and his wife tried a lot of positions and situations found in a sex manual but that he was not overwhelmed by their effect. This is what most people find, but many may find one or two variations, which they come to enjoy. Good sexual morality between man and woman demands they be supportive of each other; when reinforcement takes place, this motivates the other partner to strive to please and improve his or her performance.

DESIRABILITY OF SEX AND FREQUENCY

The *Redbook* report on "Female Sexuality" a decade or so ago mentioned earlier still involved one of the largest number of women (100,000) ever included in a survey on sex. In this study, some 23,000 women who responded were over 35 or in their Boomer years. The desire for sex in healthy women reaches its peak in the late thirties and forties. Many men and women do not have a partner to engage in sex and they may be inhibited in doing so because of religion, physical condition, or fear of disease. For healthy men, the desire for sex maintains a plateau from the early twenties onward to the fifties, even then some will not slow down much until their sixties. The frequency of intercourse per month for women is indicated below.

Times per month

0	1-5	6-10	11-15	16-20	21
2%	26%	32%	21%	11%	8%

The New York Times Almanac 2010 reported the mean incident of sexual intercourse in 2006 was 57 times. Divided by twelve months equals 5 times a month. The survey by the National Opinion Rearch Center shows a drop from 2002 63.9 and 2004 59.6 in those years.

It was found that ten percent of the women in the survey reported earlier agreed with the statement that no sex was about right in terms of satisfaction per month. Of those having sex 16-20 times per month, 90% said this was about right. Those having intercourse over 21 times, 11% felt this to be too much. But 6% of the women felt that 16-20 times was too little and 5% thought that over 21 times too little. Most significant was that of those in the 1-5 frequency category, 74% thought this was too little; of the 6-10 frequency group, 41% thought this too little.

It is generally thought men are desirous of more sex from their 20's to the 40's than women and from the 40's to the 60's more evenly with women more active in initiating intercourse. Lack of partners and sexual dysfunction in upper ages effect women's sexual outlet than as it does some men.

Views about motivation to have sex among the genders has been challenged recently by research done by Texas University Clinical Psychologist Cindy Meston and her associates forget about thinking men are from Mars and women are from Venus. Their five-year study (2007) identified 10 reasons from men and women from 237 distinct reasons people have sex. It has been assumed that men have sex for physical pleasure and women have sex want love. The Director of Sexual Medicine at Alvarado Hospital in San Diego (2007) validates the Texas University research by stating the motivation is similar between the sexes. The Top Ten reasons for having sex are given below emphasizing lust in the body as the major reason for sex according to the Texas University Research.

REASONS FOR SEX

MEN	WOMEN
1. I was attracted to the person	1. I was attracted to the person.
2. It feels good.	2. I wanted to experience physical pleasure.
3. I wanted to experience physical pleasure.	3. It feels good.
4. It's fun.	4. I wanted to show my affection to the person.
5. I wanted to show my affection to the person.	5. I wanted to express my love for the person.
6. I was sexually aroused and wanted the release.	6. I was sexually aroused and wanted the release.
7. I was "horny."	7. I was "horny."
8. I wanted to express my love for the person.	8. It's fun.
9. I wanted to achieve an orgasm.	9. I realized I was in love.
10. I wanted to please my partner	10. It was in the heat of the moment."

Seth Bornstein *The Associated Press*

The only time love is mentioned is number nine by women otherwise you see they mention attracted and five "wanted to express love," experience pleasure, feels good, sexually aroused, was horny, it's fun, wanted to experience physical pleasure and in the heat of the moment—overwhelmingly lustful and excited bodily. Many women in their fifties gave the same reasons for having sex. Beyond the thrill of sex certainly there are the comforting aspect of it, the bringing together of a couple of closeness, belonging and togetherness also a sense of love beyond the physical of oneness which is the ultimate between a couple as they express extreme sensuality.

The incidence of sex among Boomers has not changed much since the Kinsey studies of the 1950's! Some thought there were flaws in the samples of his studies for instance too many middle class women, lack of minorities, and mainly college educated women. The following is close to what Boomers are experiencing or will look forward to as they enter their sixties. Sociologist Laumann, in his University of Chicago study, found people whose health was very good to excellent were twice as likely to be sexually active as those with poor or fair health. One of seven men need Viagra or other similar aid to improve sex. Twenty-two percent of women and 38% of men had discussed sex with a doctor since age 50. According to Dr. Allison Moore, geriatric specialist at the University of California, L.A., many doctors are embarrassed to bring it up and some may not how to treat sexual dysfunction.

Boomer's Sexual Intercourse by in Mid Life

Group	Number	None	Once a month	Once a week	2-3 times a week	More than 3 times a week
Men						
46-50	43	0%	5%	62%	26%	7%
51-55	41	5	29	49	17	0
56-60	61	4	38	44	11	0
61-65	54	20	43	30	7	0
66-71	62	24	48	26	2	0
Total	261	12	34	41	12	1
Women						
46-50	43	14%	26%	39%	21%	0%
51-55	41	20	41	32	5	2
56-60	48	42	27	25	4	2
61-65	44	61	29	5	5	0
66-71	5	73	16	11	0	0
Total	231	44	27	22	6	1

SEXUAL ACTIVITY

An interest of sex researchers concerns sexual practices or what people do when they are sexually intimate with each other was reported by Pamela Regan (2003). A national survey revealed that although there are a number of sexual activities from which to choose, the most commonly practiced is vaginal intercourse, with more than 95% of the heterosexual respondents stating that they had vaginal intercourse the last time they had sex. Oral sex, although less common than vaginal intercourse, was also reported by a sizable percentage of respondents. Specifically, about one third of cohabiting men, and one fifth of cohabiting women, reported either giving or receiving oral sex during their last sexual interaction. The numbers were slightly lower for married individuals, with approximately 24% of married men and 17% of married women reporting having participated in this activity during their last sexual event. Other forms of sexual expression occurred far less frequently. For example, only 2% of cohabiting men and women (and even fewer married respondents) reported have engaged in anal intercourse during their last encounter.

Homosexual couples practice many of the same sexual activities as do heterosexual couples but report higher frequencies of particular behaviors. For example, lesbian couples engage in more kissing, caressing, holding, and breast stimulation during sex than do cohabiting or married heterosexual couples. In addition, oral sex and anal sex are more commonly used by homosexual couples than by heterosexual ones. Approximately 40% to 50% of gay male and lesbian couples report usually or always engaging in oral sex during lovemaking, compared with 20% to 30% of heterosexual couples, and gay men are more likely to have anal sex than are heterosexual couples (Lever, 1995; Michael et al., 1994). Research in depth on both homosexual and heterosexual activities is difficult due to limited sample and time or its bias directions for its subject matter.

The results of two national surveys conducted by sociologist Janet Lever (1994, 1995) suggest that homosexual couples may also be more experimental than their heterosexual counterparts. For example, many of the lesbian respondents—particularly those in their teens, 20s, and early 30s—had incorporated dildos (43%) or food (35%) into their sexual activities, had engaged in bondage or discipline (25%), or had participated in three-way sex (14%). Similarly, 55% of the gay male respondents had used dildos (in anal sex) during sex, 48% had engaged in three-way sex, 24% had participated in group sex, and 10% had experienced sadomasochistic sexual encounters. It is important to note that Lever's question concerned activities during the past 5 years; hence, we do not know how often participants engaged in these activities.

SATISFACTION IN SEX

Boomers report better sexual activities—more often, more pleasurable with more lasting effects when the following things occur:

- Verbalize your thoughts about love making.
- When there is equality between the couples.
- When the emotional levels are high and connected.
- Reading material that provides sexual messages; like different types of foreplay and sexual variety.
- Spending more intimate time with your partner.
- When the partners are in good health.

These facts are reported (2008) by Janice Swanson of Mayo Clinic a specialist in Human Sexuality and Edward Laumann of the University of Chicago, Sociologist well-known for his sex research. The connection between sex and emotion and sex to satisfaction is still a question since Kinsey's time and seems to leave us groping in the dark as to how much we enjoy it. To illustrate, one survey including 26,000 people found that 52% of Americans are not fully satisfied with their sex lives. Harris Interactive Poll conducted the survey; who is a reputable firm sponsored by the makers of Durex condoms (manufactured by SSL International). They hired scientists to go over the results and publish the findings. Last year Pfizer (pharmaceutical company) had Laumann report responses from 27,000 persons on their sexual well being with better experience. He found sex problems less prevalent than the Durex study.

A survey by the American Council on Aging claimed the over 60 population were having sex yet and that 40% wanted more. Certainly general health in the wider population is improving the situation but the many studies show disparities and are hard to agree on figures that harmonize all the variances. Probably some rise from Kinsey studies and earlier Duke studies but not dramatically. Medical schools give little instruction to their students other than that which relations to disease and accident connected to the sexual so seem hesitant to talk or advise about sexual matters. The general public has little understanding of the work of urologists, sex therapists and others who could assist in sexual counseling such as psychologists. Sex education may assist in some ways but that's not its purpose. Popular sex books are suggesting avenues for improving satisfaction provided enough people read them and apply their ideas they say!

Studies (Lawrence and Byers, 1995) have shown that married couples have often considered factors in their satisfaction as including:

(1) reaching an orgasms
(2) engaging in frequent sex
(3) reaching an orgasm at the same time
(4) receiving more sexual rewards than costs

SEXUAL PREFERENCES

The results of Michael's 1994 study show that despite the wide variety of acts from which to choose, both sexes found only a small number appealing. Some 96% of younger women and 95% of younger men (18-44 years of age) rated vaginal intercourse as very appealing or somewhat appealing; similarly, 93% of older women and 95% of older men (45-59 years of age) found this particular act to be somewhat appealing. In fact, vaginal intercourse was the clear favorite. Watching a partner undress was the second most preferred activity, although this was rated very appealing by more men than women in both the younger (50% vs. 30%) and older (40% vs. 18%) age groups. This was followed by receiving and giving oral sex, with both men and women indicating that it was more appealing to receive than to give. Other behaviors or events seemed to appeal to only a very small percentage of people, for less than 5% of women and men said that they found using a dildo or vibrator, watching other people have sex, having sex with a stranger, or engaging in passive anal intercourse to be very appealing. No respondents thought being forced to do something sexual was very appealing, and none of the women and younger men (and only 1% of the older men) rated this as highly appealing.

Much less is known about the sexual preferences of homosexual men and women, Lever's (1994, 1995) national surveys yield some insight as follows. For example, her male respondents said that their favorite bedroom acts included hugging, caressing, and snuggling (endorsed by 85%); deep kissing (74%); receiving oral sex (72%); giving oral sex (71%); masturbating a partner (52%); and being masturbated by a partner (51%). Their biggest sexual turn-offs were engaging in insertive anilingus (disliked by 26%) and engaging in receptive anal intercourse (disliked by 14%). Many men selected these two particular sex acts as turn-ons; fully 29% said that they preferred insertive anilingus, and 43% endorsed receptive anal intercourse. Lever (1994) concluded, when it comes to anal play, it appears [that gay] men either love it or hate it.

Homosexual women expressed similar sexual preferences. For example, most participants said that they "loved" hugging, caressing, and cuddling (91%); French kissing (82%); caressing a partner's breasts (82%); and sucking a partner's nipples (80%). About 75% identified holding hands, touching a partner's genitals, and having their own genitals touched as appealing practices. Like homosexual men (and like the heterosexual men and women in Michael et al.'s [1994] study), more lesbians prefer receiving oral sex (75%) than giving it (70%). Women reported that their least favorite activity is anal stimulation, with more than half expressing a dislike for anilingus (both giving and receiving) and anal penetration.

Prostate

Around age forty-five to fifty men might expect prostate problems, cardiovascular difficulties, diabetes and variety of maladies—declining levels of 17-ketosteroids associated with testicular fibrosis and tubular atrophy. For those over 50, about 60% of all men suffer from an enlarged prostate gland; this is no problem unless it blocks urination or has a malignant growth associated with it. Even if it has to be removed, approximately 30% find they have increased potency as a result after an operation removing the prostate. It has been found that at least half of these impotencies are psychological. Many men claim to be impotent when it has been found that they are regularly masturbating or have a mistress. Prostate problems are a serious prospect and can lead to death. Screening by the PSA exam and manual check by a physician is urged for all adult males. Some help from a therapist would probably aid the situation although some men are looking for an excuse not to perform with their wives. Menopause has the same effect on some women what with the hot flashes, weight increases, dry skin, etc., many women think their sex life is over. They do have their difficulties and it should be mentioned that prostate problems for the man may be no laughing matter; before removal if he has sex, it may mean not being able to urinate for the next six to eight hours. He may, therefore, after a couple of bouts with this, decline to engage in sexual activity.

Except in the most severe cases, heart problems should not mean the end of sex. Exercise nowadays is advised for heart patients and sexual encounter is frequently a good muscle-toner; in addition, it is worth about 150 calories loss for each engagement. As for vaginal shrinkage, lack of lubricants, and penis flaccidity due to lack of estrogen or testosterone, Viagra, Cialis and Levitra, steroid substitutes can be administered to reduce losses and dramatic sexual changes. There is no reason for the majority of people not to have sex regularly though, unfortunately, many are affected by cultural taboos as: after menopause you don't have sex any more, or our children or kin to say you're too old to be doing that stuff and when a spouse dies in the middle years, many think their sex life is over, so dismiss it. Young adults who suggest this kind of advice should try giving up their own sex lives. Undoubtedly, the best evidence we have at the present time tells us that to sustain more fully and increase the length of life, the best guarantee is a regular effective sex life. The lack of partners, though little research has been done on this, doesn't keep most people from sex, be it by masturbation, a close friend, or by some other manner (vibrator, dildo). Various avenues open to women are discussed in *Our Bodies, Ourselves Pregnancy and Birth* by the Boston Women Collective 2008. Many sensitive matters related to sex are discussed here that will be of interest to most women.

SUMMARY ON SEX

Men and women cannot share equally in the privilege of a mature sexual relationship until each understands that sexual function is truly the birthright of both—something that a man and woman are privileged to do with each other and for themselves, not something a man does to or for a woman. It should be remembered that sexual response is solely the function of the individual—it evolves from within from the mind. It starts with a proper mental outlook. The physical processes begin in the mind, which then relates the message to the pituitary, hence to ovary and testes. What the partners do share is responsibility for their emotional environment, which in turn is an expression of the emotional bond of the marriage itself.

Without mutual consideration based firmly on each individual's assumption of sole responsibility for his or her sexual function, there rarely is sexual security in a marriage. When male or female fears for sexual performance intrude upon or even dominate a marital relationship, the partners are denied the incredible value of confident sexual expression, which is the essence of interpersonal communication. Without a secure opportunity for sexual expression in marriage, tensions that the partners can accumulate from every complexity of contemporary living rarely have sufficient outlet. Without full sexual accord, couples contending with marked personality differences or handicapped by dissimilar social backgrounds generally can find no common denominator through which to mediate their social tensions, their personal differences, or their natural sexual demands.

The transition years are usually designated as the decade between 35 to 55 years of age. This is a period when women and men become their own person. Obviously, some men and women transit from 35 to 45, others from 45 to 55, and some refuse to be pigeon-holed. What changes are to be expected in the quality of life when and if we do transit? How does aging affect sexual interaction and, therefore, affect communication between men and women committed to each other.

As we age, there are only two factors necessary for continuation of effective sexual functioning; first, a reasonably good state of general health and, second, an interested and interesting partner. It must be remembered, experts tell us, that as every man ages he may notice some combination of (1) delayed erection time, (2) reduced ejaculatory volume, (3) reduced ejaculatory pressure, (4) reduced ejaculatory demand, and (5) some degree of penis flaccidity.

As woman ages, she may be aware of (1) slowed production of vaginal lubrication, (2) reduction in volume of lubrication, (3) thinning and loss of elasticity of vaginal walls, (4) shortened orgasmic experience, and (5) some shrinkage of the vagina. Knowledge that these changes in sexual functioning are to be anticipated during the transitional years is only important in that such knowledge is real protection against the fears for performance that develop when uninformed men and women are naturally concerned or disturbed by the onset of any alteration in established sexual response patterns.

MARRIAGE

The elements of remarriage in the Boomer years are not the same as they were the first time, for usually the first marriage involved a high degree of intense physical attraction and the projecting of one's self image upon the desired person. Both of these may be involved in the second marriage but also of prime importance is communication, companionship, good mother or father-ship to children, economic status, and the provision of an added dimension to life. There will not be many persons who, having been single all their lives, marry after forty. It is a fact that women who are thirty and divorced have a better chance to remarry than those who have never married. There are also those who never try to marry and they succeed!

The Boomer cohort marriage group will end in 45% to 50% divorced. The second marriage will have a 60% to 67% of its marriages end in divorces. Besides 23% have never married by the time they are forty. A majority will get married a second time. Most Boomers with an experience behind them in a first marriage (males 30.5, females 29). Their median age is male 34 and female 32. Marriages can be more than numbers with forethought nothing in the life of man is as important as those aspects of human aspects it embraces. What makes for happiness in marriage and important elements are considered next.

Sound Fulfilling Marriages

Embedded in marriage is the source of these aspects and factors that can lead to a strong, harmonious, loving partnership. Dr. David Olson, one of America's foremost marriage researchers, has focused on aspects in the lives of married people that provide them the power to be the happiest couples. This is predicted—with 93% accuracy whether happy or unhappy. Involved in this study were 21,501 married couples from 50 states utilizing a comprehensive assessment tool called ENRICH which focuses on 20 major areas in marital relationships. The ten top list follows:

1. I am very satisfied with how we talk to each other. Happy Couples, 70%; Unhappy Couples, 15%.
   Talking – it's essential in everyday living—and if you only grunt at each other you are still communicating. This isn't saying much for being intimate for without communication there is little or no closeness. Contrary unhappy couples cite 15% as happy with the talking we do to each other.
2. We are creative in how we handle our differences. Happy Couples, 78%; Unhappy Couples, 15%.
   Openness to change is important because often difficult things occur that require new approaches, new answers— crises arise demanding innovation, adjustment. Ability to rearrange during stress and troubled period will help the couples maintain its normal bearing sooner and stronger.
3. We feel very close to each other. Happy Couples, 98%; Unhappy Couples, 27%.
   Closeness is the space between a couple and that no one else is allowed to enter—this is private territory. This is their heart of hearts—the most emotional tie between the man and wife—the bind of love. Ninety-eight percent gave this as most important of all the timbers of their house of marriage.
4. My partner is respectful of my views and not too controlling. Happy Couples, 78%; Unhappy Couples, 20%.
   Argument will occur they are inevitable, it is the way they are handled that is important. Knock down drag out affairs

are another thing. Difference of opinion will exist but resolves issues in reasonable constructive manner marks the strong marriage where recognition of respect and each feels understood by the other partner.

5. When discussing problems, my partner understands my opinions and ideas. Happy Couples; 87%, Unhappy Couples, 19%.

In happy marriages the man and woman are well aware of the views on a variety of subjects held by their spouse. They are close to each other so that they understand the position take on many subjects. If differences arises at times straight forward discussion occurs, compromises follows or agreement ending in a harmonious situation.

6. I am completely satisfied with the amount of affection from my partner. Happy Couples, 72%; Unhappy Couples, 28%.

A lot of affection suggests emotion is strong. Where emotion is strong between a marriage couple it foretells usually good sexual relationships. Dr. Olson reported from his sample 85% agreed that their sexual relationship is satisfying and fulfilling and 90% said their partner did not refuse sex in an unfair way. Affection between a marriage couple makes for a feeling of comfort, security and health by them which sheds its light on their children and others.

7. We have a good balance of leisure time spent together and separately. Happy Couples, 71%; Unhappy Couples, 17%.

Being married doesn't mean you own the spouse. This is contract that is to provide not a schedule for a wife or husband to follow exactly. The happy couple trust the other to be free to have time to themselves, make arrangements— trips, parties, etc., certainly consult with partner on details. But each have time to themselves, have separate friends, join clubs of their choosing, even churches, etc. You don't expect this to be a revolving door. A balance of leisure can be arrived at by a marriage counselor.

8. My partners' friends or family rarely interfere with our relationships. Happy Couples, 81%; Unhappy Couples, 38%.

   When family interferes with marriage there is usually trouble brewing. Frequently in the form of mother of the bride or groom continuing that role. The mature couple may allow this but others will soon rebel but not before the marriage is sometimes weakened. Friends over visit getting in the way of family routines and together time in the family or man and wife can be a problem. Also, giving advice to a man and wife that may be out of line and damaging to the relationship between a man and wife is possible and uncalled for.

9. We agree on how to spend money. Happy Couples, 89%; Unhappy Couples, 41%.

   Most of us spend four-fifths of our time while awake working, spending, or figuring what to do about money! That people, or couples, or groups argue about money is a fact of life. The difference between happy couples and unhappy ones on how to handle money is; (1) they agree on how to do it. (2) They agree on how much to save. (3) They agree on how much debt to allow. Happy marriages will be those that discuss financial matters and agree on relevant issues.

10. I am satisfied with how we express spiritual values and beliefs. Happy Couples, 89%; Unhappy Couples, 36%.

    Faith and spirituality held by couples becomes the basis of values and behaviors that enlarges love and closeness of a man and wife. The expression of values deeply held is an important element indicating where happy married persons differ from those unhappy ones.

Another very important area that makes for happy married life is agreement on parenting—how each partner feels about children—their care, their place in the family, child rearing practices, shared responsibility and the like. A spouse who is indifferent to children is a drawback to a happy marriage.

TEN MAJOR PROBLEMS FOR MARRIED COUPLES	% WITH PROBLEMS
We have problems sharing leadership equally.	93%
My partner is sometimes too stubborn.	87%
Having children reduces our marital satisfaction.	84%
My partner is too negative or critical.	83%
I wish my partner had more time and energy for recreation with me.	82%
I wish my partner were more willing to share feelings.	82%
I always end up feeling responsible for the problem.	81%
I go out of my way to avoid conflict with my partner.	79%
We have difficulty completing tasks or projects.	79%
Our differences never seem to get resolved.	78%

RE-MARRIAGE

Most Boomers will marry for the second time, either for reasons of the first time, divorce or death of a spouse. As mentioned earlier, Health, Education and Welfare predicted that by 1985 one of every two marriages would end in divorce. This projection has come true and is now (2004) edging upward favoring divorce. By the time middle agers reach fifty, there are many more widows than widowers. To point out the problems of women beyond forty getting a second husband, one need only think of the population differential of men to women; in the United States there are some 6 million more women. Many are in the upper age brackets but the influence of these numbers filters down to the middle age groups. Men divorcing or becoming widowers at 45 will marry again; the typical liaison being with a woman three to five years younger and often the woman is 15 to 20 years younger. Even for the 50 to 55-year-old men this holds true. One bright spot for the ladies is in England where there is a surplus among younger males in the age bracket 20-40—something like a million. A visit to central London for a few weeks might result in an opportunity to meet eligible males. Also, Australia and Alaska. Of course, if the prospective male has a reasonably good job, you may have to live there. But it's worth a try!

According to the U.S. Census Bureau, in 1972, the percentage of those with five or more years of college, 35-44, who have never married was rather astounding. Overall those that never marry, up to 44 years of age, represent about 13% in 1972 and 16% in 1985. Since then decline in married numbers have nearly doubled (U.S. Bureau of the Census, 1998). Nevertheless marriage is a common event as 9 of 10 marry at least once in their lives

Never Married: Age 35-44

	1972		1985		2008
Race	Female	Male	Female	Male	Male & Female
White	20%	8%	13.4%	18.7%	Combined
Black	11%	11%	--	--	47.9

Advanced education is also a drawback to marriage. One thing may be the self-imposed limitations that one makes or that a choice has to be made either/or have a career or marriage. The highly trained woman professional is not likely to choose a husband several educational and class levels below her—maybe one level lower. Nowhere is this more evident among black women in high salaried jobs or ones requiring master's and doctorate degrees unless they reverse the old time order of men marrying up and women down. They will experience a problem someone marrying other minorities or whites. Men see no handicap in marrying generally and may easily accept a woman from a lower socio-economic class. Men see marriage as an asset in business, social community affairs and most communities for the ministry, school administrators and teachers.

Although in 1969, 93% of all men and 95% of all women by the time they were 55 had married, this heavy trend toward marriage has reversed itself as evidenced by the above figures for the 35-44 age group.

For Boomers looking to remarry there are a number of prospects in and out of the pool. In 2007 the U.S. Census Bureau shows in the 45 to 64 age group After 65 the odds are traumatic; 3 men to 100 women. It needs to be recognized that from the general population millions have been depleted as undesirable. Note: Two million felons or their kind in Federal, State, local prisons, thousands in missions on the streets, millions unemployed, several million low intelligence and mentally disturbed and many never married some of these may but it will take some coaxing.

Interracial marriage has increased over the past ten years. The *Associated Press* in 2007 published an eye-catching article discussing the racist taboo of black women dating and marrying white men. The long-held racist disapproval of such relationships notwithstanding, the U.S. Census Bureau in 2006 revealed 117,000 black wife-white husband couples, up from 95,000 in 2000. Romance between black women and white men has become a hot topic in black geared magazines and on websites even hitting the big screen in big movies.

The syndicated article writer Dionne Walker (Tampa Tribune, 2009) points out that white men are not the answer to all the problems black women have particularly those with advanced education but they do offer a solution. Black women reflect the frustration many feel as the field of marriageable black men narrows. Nearly seven times more black men are likely to be incarcerated than white and twice as likely to be underemployed. They have a low rate of black men in college only 26% men 18-26 are enrolled in college compared to 36.5% of women according to Council of Education. U.S. Bureau of Census 2006 reported 60,000 Black-White married couples.

Many are marrying Hispanics whose population is edging over thirty-five thousand and are increasingly moving from the U.S. to other parts of Central America.

No longer does social and economic factors push people into marriage. The scorned single woman of yesterday who was relegated to an inferior position, stayed at home to do menial tasks and came in time to fill the prophecy of the neurotic spinster busy body, prim and proper "old maid" exists no longer. Their alternatives for work—teaching, secretarial or nursing transplanted the single girls successful men in business, medicine, government, the professions, engineering and the arts. A new ethos has come aboard in the land assuring women that singleness is a worthy alternative to marriage and that the single life style can in many cases expand a woman's opportunities for self fulfillment and development in a way that would be impossible were she to assume the traditional role of the wife. The single woman can have children, men friends and even live with a man or woman according to her desire.

The New York Times reported in 2007 50% of women are now living without a spouse. This is up from 35% in 1950 and up 2% since 2000. Since 2000 *The Times* report married couples are a minority for the first time. Shaping this situation is that women are marrying later or living with unmarried partners more often and for longer periods. Also women are living longer as widows and after a divorce are more likely than men to delay remarriage sometimes delighting in their new found freedom. In addition marriage rates among black women remain low. Only about 30 percent black women are living with a spouse, according to the U.S. Census Bureau, compared with about 49 percent of Hispanic women, 55 percent of non-Hispanic white women and more than 60 percent of Asian women.

Many women after marriage do not want to marry again or they may cohabitate but may hesitate. There are men who say, "once is enough for me" and that's it! The divorce rate for second marriages is 60% and for third marriages it is 73%. For those determined to get married there are many opportunities through ads in magazines which have existed for decades, now available at one's finger tips on the Internet. Over the Internet using Facebook, etc., you can meet many kinds of people, agencies abound for coupling up people and protecting them. You can hide your identity and select a neutral place to meet if it gets to that point. Ultra care must be the watchword! If you do.

Most couples looking forward to marriage plan to work outside the home. They intend to have an egalitarian marriage though it often does not work out that way particularly when children arrive. However they characterize their marriage they have certain ides to start with about the person they wished to marry. P.C. Regan and E. Berscheed, in their book The Psychology of Interpersonal Relating (2005), lists the ten most desired characteristics in a marriage partner for both sexes. Current literature suggest these are still relevant today.

Top 10 Desired Characteristics in a Marriage Partner

Men	*Women*
Good overall personality	Honesty and trustworthiness
Honesty and trustworthiness	Kindness and compassion
Attractive appearance	Good overall personality
Intelligence	Intelligence
Good health	Attentive to one's partner
Kindness and compassion	Good sense of humor
Good sense of humor	Self-confidence
Self-confidence	Good health
Attentive to one's partner	Attractive appearance
Easygoing nature	Easygoing nature

It is interesting that even in men appearance is only third in the list. Also the ten listed for both men and women are the same only the order is different. Honesty ranks first with women and second with men, is significant also intelligence is listed fourth by both sexes.

Slanted slightly different signs of non-love in people after marriage psychologists list "giving little to a partner" is similar to the characteristic of attentive to one's partner. Mistrusts the spouse parallels Honesty and Trustworthiness. Also Does not listen to the partner's discussion of problems. Other signs of non-love—no or little sex and has personality problems.

SIGNS OF NON-LOVE

Allan Fromm, noted psychiatrist, lists the following five signs of non-love.

1. The person does not have many friends. It can be rationalized that they work all the time, are committed

to the care of a mother or father hence stay close by, and after all he loves you and pours out adulation. Maybe you feel he is the victim of his or her environment. Caution suggests that the one who has great capacity for love spreads it over many people. He or she is loving in general. One who has few or no friends or only finds one person interesting is not likely to have a well-developed ability to love.

2. The person has the feeling that "nobody loves me" or "nobody understands me." The individual who feels unloved is usually one who is not loving and is not giving love. The psychological mechanism is one of the defense known as projection. We project on to other people our unpleasant selves, which we do not like to face. Often in an argument a man feels rage rising in him and shouts at his opponent, "What are you getting so mad about?" Yet this man has been doing all the talking and others cannot get any words into the conversation. A good tactic sometimes but not rational. Suffice it to say, the projection here suggests, if I feel nobody loves me, the probability is that I am not loving toward anybody.

3. Excessive ambition in a person pre-empts ability to love. The inability to love is seen in persons who are possessed by a drive to get ahead or reach some pinnacle in the world. This person has a "love" and has no room for another like the man who spends all his time with his business in the pursuit of making a million. Or the woman whose passion is wrapped up in real estate or selling of stocks and bonds has found her love. If ambition is excessive, we usually can be sure that there is little emotion left over for other people or enough to sustain a healthy marriage relationship. This is especially crucial in the middle-aged person for it smacks of neuroticism serving to blind one's inner fear of failure and providing a routine which allows one to keep from flying to pieces.

4. The inability to say no is another important sign of non-love. Genuine love grows from respecting the other

person and ourselves. Those who can't say no appear to be very loving but in truth may be just the opposite. This type of person who is driving compulsively to please everyone does it to gain favor. It is as though she has to please because she feels down deep that she is unworthy of love otherwise. This is very damaging to ability to love.

5. The person who is the perfectionist. Avoid this individual like the plague. For if you marry, you'll be uncomfortable in a very brief time. For loving by this person is conditioned upon the fact of your performance—for he says, I will love you if you will do this or do that. This person cannot tolerate our foibles, in fact, cannot abide people generally for he is perfect. Most of us are human and make many mistakes and faux pas. The female perfectionist makes an excellent secretary or research assistant because she has to do it right. When the perfect housewife can't control every situation and dirt gets on the rug all hell breaks loose. This kind of person—be it man or woman, will be extremely difficult to live with; they are usually inflexible and humorless generally.

Compromises and Swap-Offs

We must recognize that love has strings attached to it. We are brought up to understand this—"If you don't stop hitting your sister, I won't love you." So we learn in childhood under certain conditions we are loved. The brave boomer like the spirited child will risk much on occasions for adventure but the vulnerable child will watch his step. The boomer who feels insecure and the need to be loved, with an object to lay their love upon, might be inclined to risk little in fear of not finding a partner. This can be shortsighted but many women and some men think they can change their partners. This is unlikely. Although we have talked about growth and change in marriage and a person forty years of age certainly can adjust, learning new ways, but the structure of personality will not be entirely reversed.

You say to me the value of having a mate overrides other considerations. I know that there are swap-offs and that couples rarely join in marriage on equal terms, even though this is the ideal.

I remember a lady speaking to me about her possible marriage; she had four girls, the prospective man had six children. She was college educated; he was not. He did have a good income. The question of suitability, given affection and love, involved around would she be willing to undertake to care for his children in return for love and being a good provider. The answer came after the introduction of their children to each other in a short-term family-like situation. They did not get married. The lady later married a minister (Episcopal) even though she was divorced and had four children. In this instance the children may have been the catalysts in the marriage, in addition to love for he adored the children.

Most men will however steer clear of a woman with several young children. With the wealthy this may be of less concern. It seems to be difficult to make a suitable arrangement when two people also bring their children with them to a union. The children particularly when they are 10-16, in many cases they resent the intrusion of the new man and eventually this leads to friction between the couple. Some men will entertain the idea of taking a woman into marriage who has small children if there are no more than two of them. Frequently the negotiation in these cases involves a woman of relative youth with the older man's financial ability. The children get a father, the wife and children support. In most cases like this the wife stays at home. There are instances where usually the woman does not work at a career. In many cases the combining efforts by both partners working makes for greater advantages in their lives—more affluence, more clothes, vacations, larger homes and cultural advantages. One thing is true, those who marry in middle age do not have to consider pleasing families of the mates we chose or to justify our lifestyle; we take for granted that at 40 or 50 we are our own person. We are never going to be able to guarantee our love or the love of other people will be perfect. Our ability to love has been influenced by the earlier loves of our childhood. Adult love is frequently imperfect because childhood love was faulty. There are many points at which learning to love takes a wrong turn and all in the normal process of growing up. Growing up itself is an obstacle course filled with booby traps. Everything struggles to grow—young animals, tender plants and sensitive human beings. The most important thing in most of our lives is love—love with a special person or persons. That our love lives are filled with hazards is understandable for the thing that is so important we can't control—that is, another person. So we learn to adjust, to give and take, and to be hopeful. Remarriages are often superior to first ones because the illusions of youth are gone, couples try infinitely more to be successful, have fewer expectations and they understand more of the totality of life. Nevertheless the figures show that divorce rate are higher 60-67% for the second marriage as in first marriage around 50%. *Divorce*, Editors of Socrates 2006

For second wives and husbands there is some expected foreknowledge and consideration necessary before entering into marriage. In the first place, most men do remarry, usually three out of four, within a year to three year period of being divorced or widowed. Ninety percent of all remarried men who were divorced say that their second marriage is better. However the high divorce rate on second marriages rebuts this! The divorced man (age 35 to 45) marries in 2.7 years and the widowed in 3.5 years. There are many men who marry within a year but fewer women. Women who remarry do so at a smaller percentage rate. Men remarry for a variety of reasons; to escape loneliness, to forego the discomfort of eating out or fixing meals, for business purposes where wives are required, for sexual relations, to regain the status of marriage, to have children, and for older men who want to have a place for their children to visit.

Some marriages occur out of spite—on the rebound—these are soon in trouble. Also remarriage to the same partner happens in the thousands and have a fair lasting quality. There are many other reasons a lot are dubious like marrying to get a passport for immigration or some kind of admission.

There are some important items one should go over while assessing the possibility of remarriage. These apply for men and women.

1. Has the divorce or death experience been a growth experience for the prospective partner? Where depression and passivity is chronic, caution is advised.
2. Does the intention to marry relate to social and status climbing? Sometimes one will accept this as part of a negotiation.

3. In the case of the man, has he been a good provider? Or in the case of the woman, has she been a good mother?

4. Is he or she still in love with the ex-spouse? This needs to be known or it will color the life thereafter in important ways.

5. How many times have they been married? Three or four times in marriage adds up to your being the next loser. Third marriages have a 73% divorce rate.

6. Is he or she remarriageable? Sometimes the romantic notions may not correspond to your timing. He or she having survived a divorce may want time to play the field or if you are the first attraction after divorce you might receive the brunt of the sad saga of the first marriage.

Advice for the prospective second wives during courtship that should be considered seriously. Many persons marry in haste only to think about what they have done in leisure. Perhaps doubt will be the lot of all of us in the pre-marriage situation but some can be relieved by foreknowledge before we make the final step.

1. You should find out all you can about the previous marriage, why it broke up, get a three-dimensional picture, do not take the word of the man solely for many will hide important aspects of the circumstance. Remember the divorce settlements are public record and can be examined in the Register of Deeds or Document Department Offices at the County Seat. Remember also that this information covers up real problems of a marriage to facilitate a divorce. Often a false charge is admitted to such as constructive desertion that may be a cover for adultery. In no fault divorce this may not matter. Nevertheless the records about divorce are usually accurate.

2. Love him openly, warmly, constantly.

3. See as much of him as you can in a variety of situations.

4. Talk over every aspect of the financial situation—alimony, loans, taxes, obligations, wills, and insurance, etc. The matter of middlescent property, holdings of stocks and bonds and what will be the disposal made of them need

to be settled in advance. Many couples will wish their estates to go principally to their children; attendance to this removes a large hurdle.

5. Examine your basic ideas about lifestyles.
6. Make sure you are sexually compatible—you're not children, you can talk over these matters, if sex was good or bad before you should know it.
7. After a man is 35, you may get change in his life, but don't expect it. Don't carp about his leisure pursuits, be it football, fishing, or what he does in his work life, if he's 45 this is fairly well set.
8. Make life exciting for your prospective husband—be generous at the appropriate times with gifts, introduce him to new friends and places. He will think life with you is going to be exciting.
9. Remember, children of your spouse may resent you even if you have no children, and if this is the case it will complicate matters for you. The children will not wish to share their parents with a strange brood. Children, in loyalty to their absent parent, will not want you to take up with a "new" father. My brother and sister and I all resisted any special attention by a man to our mother following our father's death. We were 15, 17 and 19. This was a mistake, for mother never married although she was only 43 when widowed and was an attractive and healthy woman.

There are some pitfalls in courtship. Don't overestimate how much you care for his children and if you don't like them, forget about pursuing this courtship idea. You should be scrupulously honest about your life, your health, your life with your former spouse or friends. If you fabricate tales about yourself or ex-mate, they sometimes come back to haunt you and frequently if they chance to meet your ex-husband he may be liked by your present boyfriend. So believing horror stories about him will fall on deaf ears! Your courtship shouldn't last forever if you intend to marry, for males are frequently procrastinators and will offer a variety of excuses—wait until the children are out of school or until my former wife remarries.

Of course, if you don't wish to marry but have a steady friend, then fair enough, this is no great concern.

Remarriage can serve as a healing balm, it can also be very trying. You will have to control your desire to express differences between the former and present life. If children are involved no matter how good they appear to be, you will have some problems—the natural parents do and so will you. Try not to compete with his children for affection. You will have, in some instances, to expect irritation from an ex-wife, sometimes this comes from an ex-husband. Trust your husband even if your former one was a rat, and try to keep romance alive and when life's demands are hard on you tell your husband some adjustments are needed. Establish a pattern of talking out problems or over things from the very beginning.

PRE-NUPTUAL AGREEMENT

Whether one is remarrying or entering cohabitation it is not a matter of throwing cold water on romance to recommend each partner discuss certain financial aspects and other arrangements between themselves before they marry or move in together. Remarriage isn't decided on simply based on finances but you need to know how a change in your marital status may affect the alimony, child support, pension, health care provisions o a previous divorce. Pre-nuptial agreements are most important where couples have property retirement plans and children also wills, insurance, trusts, social security, etc. As more couples choose to cohabitate to assure equality is essential. Written agreement protect both the man and the woman from being hurt like in cases where one is wealthier and the relationship breaks p and you are a target for a law suit—your partner may sue for "palimony." You may have quit your job to make a home for your partner who in return promised to look after you only to find out all the assets you acquired together were in his name. Oral agreements don't hold water you need written one better with your own lawyer. Prior to a marriage or cohabitating the couple should discuss these terms and develop a suitable agreement. Vaugh W. Henry, an expert on Estate Planning, suggests that simple sorting out before marriage what is your and ours is important. He and many legal experts recommend prenuptial agreements to minimize potential disputes and to protect assets. The following are considered the important elements of a prenuptial agreement:

- Discuss the assets each brings to the marriage or cohabitation.
- Discuss what debt each has. Usually you aren't responsible for debts incurred before marriage, but everything needs to be on the table.
- Discuss what other financial responsibilities either of you has such as aging parents, alimony or child support.
- Talk about how you as a couple plan to handle finances.
- Discuss your current insurance policies and if these will change after you are married.
- Discuss your current tax liability and how this might shift once you are married.
- Share your respective retirement plans, including how much you are saving and in what type of investment, and decide if this needs to be adjusted or reevaluated.
- Find out state requirements for marriage contracts.
- Draw up and sign a written agreement with the help of TWO attorneys. You each need one.
- Draw up a cohabitation or property agreement if you plan to live together without marrying.
- Sign it, well in advance of your wedding, to avoid claims of coercion later.
- Revisit and revise your contract if you move to another state or want to alter the original agreement.

For the boomer love can bloom again, sparkle and bright ever anew thrilling as if one was twenty again. Sex can be stimulating and exciting as it had first been discovered. Marriage the second time itself could be as wonderful as ever before. Despite the fact that life represents a continuation of problems and solutions there remains for the boomer remarried couple the promise of the good life. It can be a time for new intimacy with children in most cases gone, a renewed interest in each other that existed in an earlier time or could occur in a second marriage.

If it's a second marriage your new maturity has taught you to understand the need to intermingle your roles, for husbands to be more nurturing, to support his wife's drive for mastery or engaging in a new enterprise. For wives to accept a husband's hobbies—sports, fishing, hunting, etc., and have time to do things for each other often forgotten in the heat of child raising. A new relationship with children that are nearly grown can occur as they began to see the wisdom of earlier parental guidance. The boomer has learned not to give advice when asked. The children approach parents as adults enhance life for them and us.

Deeper relationships with friends can become a reality with time for socialization that allowed little time before. Companionship with people we would like to seek rapport with will be available. Opportunity to devote energies to new community service, which we would like, will be available, before which we were probably "drafted" for United Fund or some such drive. The enrichment comes from to doing what you will have the leeway of picking your charity you can do what you think is needed because you want to do it! It is true, as spoken by the ancient and venerable prophet Hillel, "If you are not for yourself, who is and if only for yourself, what are you; and if not now when?

CHAPTER EIGHT

DIVORCE AND AFTERWARDS

"After the party is over"

Voltaire wrote "divorce dates from just about the same time as marriage; I think that marriage is a few weeks the more ancient." This is like saying death is present at birth. It is undoubtedly true that the seeds of divorce are present at the outset of marriage. The fact that of every two marriages one ends in divorce has been true since 1985 except in the last year or so with a slight drop. The Boomer group represents a large proportion of the population wherein many divorces occur. Even second marriages have a 65% divorce rate. The question of whether this trend will finally be reversed is when enough couples, mainly young ones, base their marriages on growth principles or will serial marriage prophesized by Toffler some years ago in his *Future Shock* mark the direction in coupling and uncoupling remains to be seen. It is easy to account for a number of uncouplings from marriage by the fact that they were mismatches in the beginning. In western society with an emphasis on material success, the sensual gratification of every need breeds unrealistic goals for people. The fact of increasing longevity also affects the divorce rates. In our mobile society the initial bonding takes place with little formality, with little background experience and family values in making choices among people and virtually no restriction as, with whom; only one question is raised, do I love him or her with love equated with the erotic.

It is a wonder that as many marriages last as long as they do for the factors which are involved are so overwhelming that the number of inappropriate marriages to begin with are astronomical. Another problem is that in a period of transition like we now find ourselves, the typical traditional marriage is being severely tested. The feminist movement, rights' movement existential philosophies and the concept of "open" marriage trend to cohabitation proclaim that marriage rests upon the assumption that the growth of partners in a marriage to their highest potential is the ideal. The shackles of suppression of women's roles have been broken—release that accounts for millions of women seeking their own identities—and for many the "new fulfilled person" demands separation from their spouse. The more divorces there are, the easier it is for others to seek them. The former taboos are nearly erased except in a few enclaves involving some religious ethnic groups, and small towns and rural communities. Today it is often possible for a Protestant minister to be divorced and maintain his pastorate or marry a divorced woman.

The reasons why almost half of all marriages will end in divorce, when in 1900 only one marriage in fourteen culminated in this fashion, can be summarized as: (1) the change from rural to urban way of life; (2) the improvement in the status of women; (3) the grounds for divorce have changed - "no fault" divorce laws make it easier; and (4) loss of those values which reinforced the principle of life-long monogamy. This has caused the erosion of economic blackmail and continuance of "dead marriages" forwarded under the old adversarial system. The nature of divorce is complex and does not occur overnight. Many factors interact as seen in what G. Levinger (Journal of Marriage and the Family, 1965, 27-1) calls those aspects, which bear upon the stability of marriage. There are two features to this scheme, on one hand, external support and internal attractions which tend to keep marriage together and external attractions which work against marriage. If the supports are indeed commanding enough in terms of the internal attraction (comfort, companionship, status, personality needs, love), then marriage will be healthy. If the internal attractions are insufficient, then the marriage may stay together based upon external supports due to such things as legal barriers, religious commitment, family ties, children or career needs. When the external attractions to escape marriage become strong enough, then the emotional tie to the marriage will be broken. The impetus - the attraction of another man or woman, growth opportunities, freedom from responsibility, then divorce is inevitable. Divorce is rarely a simple matter, the emotional and adjustment aspects are at the least very trying and energy sapping.

EFFECTS OF DIVORCE

The effects of divorce are pervasive and its impact is great upon the nuclear family and to a lesser extent the wider kinship group; in addition, it has a relationship with economics, status, adjustment in living and social arrangements and our psychological equilibrium.

The question arises, is divorce helpful or harmful? There are some basic principles upon which to draw some conclusions; however, besides these it depends upon individuals and the circumstances. In the case of adversarial (court contested) these are more likely to be the case and much less likely in a mediated or no-fault divorce.

1. Usually divorce, no matter how amiable or how much desired is like the loss of a loved-one in death. Compounding loneliness and lost status is the feeling expressed by many a divorced person of being a fifth wheel.
2. It is sometimes difficult for many women to adjust to a single status and to assume responsibility for economic matters is overwhelming to many—women may find that getting credit, banking and investing is not so easy even if they are used to holding down a job.
3. Some of these same difficulties haunt the divorcing man who usually moves out of the home to less satisfactory surroundings where he becomes responsible for his meals, laundry and countless little things unnoticed before. Even if the man is desirous of divorce he frequently finds the demands made on his finance resources limits him from launching his new freedom with anything near affluence.

4. The effect on family and children, let alone friends, brings guilt and suffering regardless of who is the alleged victim or villain beyond pre-calculation and as is frequently suggested, one can divorce a spouse but never a child.

And, most experts in marriage attribute the majority of breakups to both parties, not solely the one awarded a decree if it be via the courts. There are some positive things about divorce.

POSITIVE THINGS ABOUT DIVORCE

- Many persons bonded in marriage in unequal situations such as being immature, educational levels, mental health, social and economic backgrounds, frequently profit by divorce. The years of trauma bring no healing of the difficulties hence bring about formal separation. Divorce is often devastating on children, but it is not essential that a child have two parents certainly when they are a warring father and mother. The important thing is the quality of the one parent relationship; hopefully both parents will continue to be responsible to the children for that is crucial to their mental health.
- Divorced persons, both men and women, have higher rates of remarriage than single and widowed of similar ages. And at the present rate of 80-90 percent of men divorced marry again and 75 percent of women do.
- The divorced person is given the opportunity to reconstruct his or her life, construct a new view of self and independence, take on new responsibility of their choosing, get an education denied by early marriage and develop into a responsible self-directing person.

COUNSELING IS RECOMMENDED BEFORE DIVORCE

It is generally believed that half of the divorces could be prevented if both parties went to see a marriage counselor. According to sociologist Clyde Veder a third of divorces would be prevented if only one person of the couple went to counseling. Interesting enough is that 10,000 or more each year in America remarry their former spouses and many who divorced still cohabitate with their former spouses. Evidently the discord between them in the present was less than the destruction between them in the past. A study in South Carolina ten years ago by their Mental Health Index found that 62% of divorced couples found that they wished they had tried to keep their marriage together.

It should be mentioned that many marriages that are in difficulty could be modified without resorting to divorce. Increasingly, numbers of persons who marry have had premarital counseling service offered by some church ministries, community agencies, or through college courses as marriage and the family or related ones in psychology and these help solve problem marriages. Many divorced persons give pause to reflect, what went wrong with my marriage? The demands of marriage are so elevated and often unrealistic that the goals are impossible to reach, differential growth rates pose a problem and most people do not try to impose the discipline on themselves that is necessary for marriage to be successful. When marriages are first made, the expectancy exists that the couple will grow together; even though this may take place, they may grow in different directions or rates than the other. Some marriages can thrive on this if it is a part of agreed-upon freedom. In some cases there is simply no growth for one of the partners. Uncorrected difficulties in a marriage eventually come attached to strong emotions often developing deep hostility toward the partner who is unwilling to change when the other partner's demands grow and change has taken place in them. Before couples become deadlocked emotionally, counseling should be sought about the marriage. It may do nothing substantial to save the marriage but it will clear the air somewhat and ultimately prepare the way for a less emotional separation and divorce. It will also have the effect of softening the blow for children, and if they are older provide insight into the marriage problems. Children also know that an attempt to reconcile differences is being made and that they are not the cause of the divorce but that it is caused by problems beyond them. Being realistic, the second divorce is sometimes due to children where the families cannot intermesh and be compatible.

There are a few things that a counselor can do for the couple who has reached an impasse. If a couple is left alone, things usually go from bad to worse. Under the pressure of hurt feelings and disappointment, they lash out at each other, or withdraw from each other. This creates more injury—most people can stand some argument but not the silent treatment. As disappointment builds up, so do the barriers to communication and hopes for settling differences become almost nil. With our basic needs unfulfilled—to love, to be comforted, to be understood and have a confidante—it is only a matter of time before we turn to other sources of help and solace. The new support or interest may come from a new love and sex interest, our children, our careers, the security of our parents, or in alcohol or drugs. Dr. David Mace, founder of England's National Marriage Guidance Council, says that something that could have been good turns out bad. He suggests it is like a child who received a building kit and tries to make a model plane. In his lack of know-how, he cannot put it together. In increasing exasperation, he uses unnecessary force to place it together only to break it. With patience exhausted and control gone, he smashes the pieces that he looked forward to completing. Yet with the help of a cooperative parent, the child might have been made the model airplane which he would have been proud. Where the situation is analogous, Dr. Mace suggests the help of a marriage counselor might affect a cure for an ailing marriage.

COUNSELING CAN HELP

A certified marriage counselor can serve to mediate between a man and wife, help to clarify the issues involved; in short, he or she can serve as an interpreter. Competent counselors have training in fields of guidance and counseling, human relations, and come from professionals in psychiatry, social, work, ministry and psychology or education. Although, unfortunately, in many states marriage counselors are not required to be licensed members of a recognized professional organization as the American Association of Marriage and Family Counselors, these licensed counselors are competent to deal with problems between husband and wife; also the family in general. Counseling will not save all marriages from dissolving, but if a couple is honest in attempting to find a solution, which may finally be divorce, a certified marriage counselor can help. The counselor is most effective in working with a man and wife when they bring the marital problems to him as early as possible. When a marriage is emotionally deadlocked, the relationship falls apart rapidly. When a wife and husband are no longer working together talking it over but begin to work against each other or they inflict injuries on each other, which cools their affection and builds up hostility and resentment; under tension things are often said with the couple becoming cruel to each other in their attitudes and actions. Often the things they do to each other under stress become greater causes of conflict between them than the original disagreement that started it all. Of course, minor problems should be worked through by husband and wife, lover's irritations and tiffs are minor things. Quarrels are natural to marriage, also some shouting and ventilation of anger; these can usually be worked out by the couple. When there is no way out of a loggerhead situation, then it is time to seek help. A true story will help many by Theo Pauline Nester, "How To Sleep in a King Size Bed Alone" (2008).

The road to divorce often occurs when one partner, sometimes a year or so earlier, feels the marriage has failed. There is a sense of discontent, stored resentments and arguments. Differences are evident but unspoken. Distance becomes greater with togetherness lacking. A multitude of feelings—love, guilt, shame, fear, anger, etc. intermingle. Plans for separation develop.

Sometime about a year before the divorce movement voicing displeasure is announced to the partner. During this period counseling takes place sometimes or one last try by having a second honeymoon (one last try). Relief that the partner knows about the situation. Still there is tension, mixed feelings, depression, doubt, guilt and fear.

By six months or before divorce has been decided upon one openly speaks badly of the partner/situation in order to set the stage to leave it. The decision is set in stone because of its long time nature. It is a time when an affair is likely to occur. It is the time when the partner begins at the first time one is considering divorce. The partners feel betrayed by the other, feel resentment, guilt, sadness, anger, etc.

The next stage is the beginning of the process of divorce through legal avenues. The partners separate telling their friends of their situation. Their families already know and are giving comfort, advice and assistance. Emotional upheaval due to separation and defining self is somewhat a different way, themselves. Divided loyalties occur among friends and families. Children, when they find out particularly young ones feel responsible for their break-up and behave in ways to make their parents get together.

Finally there is a recognition during the legal activity of afterward that the marriage has ended. Adjustment to a new life—physical, emotional and social has taken place. Acceptance of a new life occurs with the realization that the marriage wasn't happy or satisfactory. One now has the opportunity to create a new future and identity suitable to them and time to discover talents and resources.

The following is some general information on the experiences of men and women in divorce (Kathleen CordoranMediste.com) 2008.

For women:
- They initiate divorce twice as often as men.
- Ninety percent of divorced mothers have custody of their children (even if they did not receive it in court).
- Sixty percent of people under poverty guidelines are divorced women and children.
- Single mothers support up to four children after tax with income of $12,200. This doesn't include food stamps, medicine, or public housing.
- After divorce women experience less stress, have better adjustment than do men because they notice marital problems and feel relief when they go away. They also rely on social support systems and help from others and experience increase in self-esteem when they divorce and for new roles to their lives.
- Working women who place their children in childcare experience greater stigma than men in the same position. Men attract more support and sympathy in the same position.

For men:

- Men have greater emotional adjustment problems than women. The reasons they have less intimacy, social connection, reduced finances and interruption of the parental role.

- Men marry more quickly than women.
- Men are initially more negative about divorce and devote more energy to attempt to save the marriage.
- When men are involved in mediation where child support is negotiated there is greater satisfaction with the amount they have to pay.

Concerns for Children in Divorce

Divorcing couples who have children must realize that they hear a great responsibility toward their progeny who are not yet mature. Their children feel guilt, often attribute the divorce to themselves and the emotions much like their parents. Therefore the parents should be certain that they make sure the following principals are carried out.

1. Let your child know that you are parents forever. Divorce is not the end of your responsibility as parents—your children need ongoing affection, interest, and concern from each parent. This is particularly true for very young children. There should be no divorce before children are six or seven, but unfortunately this is the optimal for when a marriage is broken up, the child's home is gone, he loses trust and confidence in himself. Many mothers go to work following a separation and the child senses therefore an additional loss. The age of 6-12 are no doubt crucial ones too, for children are just beginning to see, understand parental problems, but they remain only bystanders. If at all possible, it would be better to avoid abruptly uprooting the child from his accustomed pattern of life. An effort should be made, at least for a time, to keep the same house, the same school and companions for the children. Don't get rid of the playthings—old teddy bears, dog-eared books or toys. The child often feels singly alone, after a divorce, for sometimes the little girl or boy goes with mother and the older brothers and sometimes sisters go with their father and move, many times some distance away. Many younger Boomer divorcees go back for a time

to their parents' home taking children far from the spouse and possibly other children. Children desperately need stability provided by both parents and the grandparents also.

2. Consider the trauma inflicted upon the child. Divorce may be next to death in its pain, inducing grief, hate, despair and depression. Children are often left out when parents turn their anguish on themselves. Of course, in the child the hope of the re-uniting of their parents is held out as a promise. Children often feel they are unloved and will be abandoned by their parents and reason, if you loved me you would stay together—or "if you leave Daddy, you can leave me." I recently observed a little boy of five united with his stepfather after a six-months separation period (the father and mother had divorced) proclaim over and over "I love you, daddy, I love you, daddy." At five years of age he has suffered two losses of fathers, the second father (step) decided he should see the boy on a regular basis so this will take some of the fear and unhappiness out of his life. But prognosis for happiness is slight for the boy who is already nervous, fearful, talks incessantly and is hyperkinetic. Children, like this one, grow up and marry but many of them are not able to love, for they lose the sense of being loved and worthwhileness, therefore, cannot confer trust and genuine affection upon another person. Even natural separations are hard for children. Early this summer I met a small girl (6 or 7) at a beach gathering, her absent father was a naval officer stationed abroad. I picked her up and sat her on my lap. I asked her a number of questions about herself and before she left me, she kissed me. Later we went down to the water's edge, she took my hand and wanted me when we entered the ocean to hold her above the waves. Before we left the surf, she asked me if she could call me daddy. "Certainly," I said as I wondered about the life of this little girl.

3. Your ability to cope will transfer to the child or children. Children react to the difficulties involved in a divorce much

the same way we do. If we take the route of nurturing bitterness and the turning of our children against our former spouse it leads to being non-productive. Some time we need help from outsiders in making our way. Consider the case of Evelyn Porter who was deserted by her husband after thirteen years of marriage; she was the mother of three children, none old enough to hold a job. She had been, as she described it, "just a housewife," with little education and no kin people to help. She was frightened and bitter. The children were seriously affected by their mother's struggle and despair. They became rebellious and were often in trouble at school. To survive she went on welfare. Evelyn's case was referred to the courts (conciliation); she was introduced to counselors who encouraged her to enroll in an office training course; having done so she was able to land a civil service position as a clerk. She found her self-confidence increasing each step of the way in developing a new life. Her mental health improved and her children were doing better in school. Trying to hold in your spitefulness is difficult but reciting the bad things about your former spouse, particularly to your children, does not help. In any event we should try to be fair with the children about our divorce—simply tell them why we are divorcing and remember they need both parents. A number of good books written for young children are available in Waldenbooks stores or like stores which explain divorce very well in suitable language. Do not help your spouse divorce the children also. If we blast their mother or father, we aid in programming them for fear and failure in their lives—the bottom line suggests to them, who can you be sure of—mom or dad?

- The child should not be used as a pawn. Often in an attempt to get back at the former spouse, the child is used as the agent. One husband had his child spy on his former wife to confirm suspicions he had about her. In the long run the child refused to continue this activity and as a consequence felt guilty of betraying both parents. Even after our marriages have broken up, we should try to be reasonable in our treatment of our children, their desire for visitation, vacations, and in regard to gifts, that is, not overdoing giving at the expense of the other parent. Children should not be tempted to play one parent against another—they frequently do this anyway with little encouragement. Parents vying for affection of the child can get them started in this game. The sting of separation felt by children from one parent or the other can be relieved considerably by making visitation with us, if we do not have custody, a happy time. We should plan things which the child will enjoy, although visits should not just be fun and buying trips for this has the effect of setting up invidious comparisons between parents, also of spoiling the child. This tendency is difficult to suppress for we feel responsible for the child's changed world and wish to compensate for it. And we should keep appointments for visitation with the child or children for this engenders trust and love. If there are things we must do while visitation is in progress we should do it, explaining why it is necessary. For very young children this should be prevented for if they have to be left in the charge of a strange person, it can be very traumatic for them. Appointments or work at the office you need to do can be shared by taking them along. In fact, if there is work to be done at home, the yard or the store, let them assist you where possible. This has the effect of helping them understand you and what you do, and eventually they will see how it relates to them. We should make them feel that they are loved and have two homes to be welcomed into—yours and your spouse's.

There does not seem to be an appropriate time for divorce for children short of adulthood. Even then it has some effect on them. But during the early formative years most children have difficulties.

Behavior Patterns of Children and Adolescents as a Result of Divorce

Human Development Specialists generally acknowledge the following problems follow children and youth in families split by divorce.

One to Two Years of Age

Regress in terms of toilet training, mastery of new skills, have trouble sleeping, begin sucking their thumbs, difficulty leaving their parent, crying more often and temper tantrums.

Three to Five Years of Age

Less likely to regress still apt to whine, be irritable and cry. Often feel responsible for their father leaving. Afraid their worst fears were coming true.

Six to Eight Years of Age

These children show considerable sadness, some blaming their mothers for driving their fathers away. Some boys want their mothers to marry so they can have a father. Loyalty conflicts with feelings of physically being torn apart, often crying and sobbing. Children at their age have great conflicts and will take sides but after a year come to grips with the reality of the situation.

Nine to Twelve Years of Age

Usually able to see family problem clearly and try to settle things. Have fear of loneliness. Display anger at the parent who they believe is the cause of the divorce. May have one or two ways of adjustment; the first, an outward acceptance with intensified activities which serves to shield them from reality. The other response; one of extreme anger and weakness. These children, at least many of them, develop headaches, stomach problems, and many do poorly in school. The children learned to feel sympathy for their parents and often comforted them after a year or so though many still feel anger toward the parent they didn't live with usually their fathers.

Adolescence

These age youngsters feels no responsibility for the divorce of their parents but they still felt considerable pain. Many felt negative about marriage, their education, their future. To many it accelerated the process of disengagement from their parents. They starkly recognized the differences in parents in divorce, wondered about their sexual needs and were sometimes worried and sometimes had psychological problem, unhappy with your parents dating, feeling parents are no longer parents or available to them.

Some are engaged in wanton sex, drinking and drugs. Most adjusted fairly well after a year. Some see the divorce coming because of understanding of them. but many times a youth uses a parent who leaves the family and moves a considerable distance away and rarely visits them.

A way of summarizing the research the usual case takes children a year to settle the basic hurt, the conflict and anger for the typical child or adolescent. Tied to the duration of maladjustment of the child or children is the length of the continued argument, hostility, and emotion generated between the parents themselves. The final negative effect on children is still to be discovered, but we should remember that it does not turn our children into homosexuals, deviates, etc. It should be noted, one positive effect on some children is that in the case where there are many children in the family particularly the young, who are likely to receive less attention by their parents, in dividing the family they are likely to receive more. In fact they may be the only child left with a parent or one of two that are with a parent.

Many fathers do not tell their children about divorce but leave it to the mother. We believe this is a mistake. We also suggest the following things be told by the father to the child or children concerning divorce.

1. Tell the truth. Children are remarkably perceptive; telling them will help them cope with the problem.
2. Spare the grim details. Limits should be set; the bedroom problems or extra bedroom ones should be omitted.
3. Be clear in what you say and say it when the divorce is definite. Language should be appropriate to the age level and don't shock children with last-minute revelations that you're leaving. It is hard to decide the right time but in giving reaction time to the children and a chance

to question, they can better absorb the psychological jolt. Remember, do not apologize for if this was all that was needed in the first place there would be no need to separate.

4. Allow children to ventilate their feelings. Yes, even to allowing small children to hit you, curse you, or throwing tantrums with inconsolable crying, will bring a degree of calm and the beginning of acceptance.

5. Assure your child or children by telling them of your love and outline the future for them. Talk about where they will live, their schooling, expectation of your visits and care. Your children need to be reassured about their security, even older ones will worry about clothes, spending money, camp or college. Don't use this session to win loyalty to yourself either.

6. The children should know that the decision to divorce is final. Reconciliation might take place but holding out false promises continues the anguish and feeling of insecurity with the children.

The Effects of Divorce on Men

Most men experience "separation shock" and even those who felt escape from the marriage was desirable do as well. Kathleen Corcoran (mediate.com) asserts that men have greater emotional adjustment problems than women. Shock is followed by denial and then a roller coaster stage of emotions. This shock can produce intense emotional and physical reactions in men. The following scenario is true mainly of the adversarial divorcement much less true with mediated divorces although usually one spouse will suffer in these cases the marriage ending. Many feel absolutely lost, for often the children are gone and the man is faced with finding a new place to live, look after his clothes, get his meals and see to the cleaning of his new quarters. Many of your former friends and associates, with whom you previously socialized, may no longer welcome you as a singleton, and indeed many where the divorce has been pending for they have taken sides. More often than not, the wife's side for she has determined the family's social life and if she did not work out of the home, she usually has had time to be well-acquainted in the home neighborhood, whereas a man may know only a few of your neighbors. This all adds up to the feeling of anomie—not unlike death. There is, if the marriage has lasted for some time, the continuing attachment to your former life. At one time you were the king in your castle and now you're alone, remembering your former life—your wife, your children and all the wonderful memories one usually has built-up over the years. The responses of anger, jealousy, fear of the future, guilt, self-blame and sickness all well up in you. You have diarrhea, headaches, insomnia, hives, palpitations of the heart, muscle twitching, and chronic colds.

Adjustment comes sometimes after a year or two. In the denial stage they feel like their wives never loved them. They try to ferret out their past lives, make some sense of it but it defies them. For almost all men it will take something like two years to get over this though for some a longer period is required. Men get over the immediate effects, then when the final decree time comes the symptoms often recur all over again. Nevertheless a part of man's life is gone, he feels inadequate to cope with life, his ego status is nearly zero, and he feels he will be rejected by all women. For a few who have a woman they are going to live with, this is another matter.

A number of men have told me that they felt so guilty they gave much more in a divorce settlement than was necessary. And many are overwhelmed by the fact that their families frequently take the side of the daughter-in-law. Be sure you tell your side of the story for otherwise you and your children many hear how terrible you were, how you manhandled your wife, ran out with other women and were in short a Scrooge. The hypocrisy in society is much greater than the inexperienced person would ever believe. I know both men and women who eventually withdrew from their churches because of the post-divorce atmosphere toward them. There is a lot of heartache for men who have not really thought about some aspects that go along with the divorced life. In fact, some who were titillated by women before, some of them married women, will find that they flee from you when you are single—the married women consider their games of stolen moments, glances, handholding, heavy hugging at dances and tete-a-tetes safe when you were married but a no-no if you are

304

single. The single women frequently don't want to be put on the spot (are not interested in marriage) nor do they want to hear the tale of woe and will not be put on the spot if their playmate is married. Even so the bon vivant who goes out gadding about every night is a myth. For the Boomer man, a shock of another type might be experienced, the demand of some women will give him claustrophobia in the genital area.

Adjustment may be made in a year, the man will find the first three or four months the most difficult and for some normalcy won't be reached until much later according to Dr. Robert Weiss, Director of the Sexual Recovery Institute in Los Angeles.

The following advice is helpful.

1. Tell your side of the story, tell your friends and kin people. Family who will help to look after the children should know right away.

2. Be prepared for a range of responses from outright condemnation of you to withholding of comment. Some will offer help while others dig for details.

3. Be discreet about broadcasting your divorce at work for many would be put in jeopardy by this announcement. In some cases this suggests if the guy can't keep his personal life together he makes a poor representative for us. Other bosses might take the view that home entertainment for our clients is out now. In any event, many people believe that divorced persons can't be as effective as before they were divorced. You should nevertheless explain the circumstances to your immediate superior and let him know you think the effects of the divorce, at least the worst part, will be over soon. Your co-workers need know little of the details but tell them the simple facts briefly.

4. Try extra hard to keep up with your work even though you won't feel like working and will be distressed. On the other hand don't use your work as an escape; it does help to have a regular routine both at work and away. Overtime work may work against you when support payments are decided upon by the judge.

5. Don't be afraid to ask for help. Some of the best use of money may be in counseling—men usually resist this, but if it helps to set your head straight and assists you in making a better decision, it will be more than worth the time and money you invested. In selection of a counselor, get a trained person and/or one recommended by the Mental Health Agency or some other reliable group. Avoid the far-out guru type. Dr. Mel Kranzler, an authority on divorce, says that seeking professional help is one way to avoid the pain you need not suffer and it's a good sign of mental health.

6. One should not give way to believing you are a victim. Think about what you can do for yourself. A new suit, haircut, learn something about child care or how to cook several dishes; if you are out of shape, start running. Most of all we need to consider what have we learned from our divorce. Dr. Kranzler, in his work *Creative Divorce*, says we need to set realistic goals for ourselves; despite the problems that hassle us, still life presents alternative choices to us—face the unpleasant circumstances, then take stock of your credits and move positively forward. Be sure to look at yourself in terms of how you act toward others, your view of women and relationship with your children. No matter how painful this should be a beginning of a new you.

The Effect of Divorce on Women

Much of what has been said of men can be said of women. They are more likely to have the custody of children than the husband. In many cases the burden of going it alone, particularly if they are housewives only, can cause a complete emotional collapse. But women are not usually afraid to ask for help and they almost always have a network of friends they can tell their troubles to and help and advice they can expect. The traditional roles played in society by women allow them more easily to ventilate their feeling and receive attention from varied sources, than men. This can be of help, nevertheless some will undergo extreme depression and need the assistance of a counselor or psychiatrist. Many times the minister of your church has had special training in this area and will be glad to have you contact him. Frequently women feel the need to get a person (of the opposite sex) that they do not know to listen to them as an aid in talking out their difficulties. Expressing one's feelings to an empathetic listener works wonders!! If the husband has initiated the divorce, the woman in all probability reacts in anger, and if she asked for the divorce, the likelihood of feeling guilty is there. Usually there is an ambivalence about divorce which shifts from euphoria to depression—many women greet divorce with elation then give way to despair, feelings of regret and inadequacy develop in time. As a woman has to fit herself into a new role—that of a divorced woman— there is no clear, generally accepted model for such a woman in our society.

Since 90% of women seek divorce fewer have emotional problems and the series of stages that most men go through do not affect them. However some are left by men, many in the most dire of straits. This latter group suffer shock following denial and disbelief that this could be happening to you—you try to find a solution to your marital problem, you are convinced divorce is not the answer but it's beyond your control. Shock takes over—panic, anger, you're numb, you're losing your mind, you are fearful of the future. Following the roller coaster takes over you can't settle your thoughts and feelings you sway them feeling hopeful to feeling hopeless. You try to sort out in your mind what's going on thinking if you understand it the pain will go away. Then you bargain thinking you will do anything to bring your spouse back. You learn that you rarely can and that you can't control another person's mind and behavior. Finally one lets go and give up realizing the marriage is over. This may take a year even longer and it will be painful. For the women who sought the divorce other problems await. The decisions, if she doesn't plan to stay with the home, are legion. Does she move to another town, go home to mother? What name should she use, what work do you do, and how to use your time? All of these call for answers! And if you are a woman trying to look after three young children, you have real difficulty. Remarriage as a prospect is virtually nil, and unless general financial help is coming, your immediate life prospects are grim indeed!

The role of the divorced woman is especially difficult in other ways. She has to remake her social life at the same time she is coping with the work-a-day world. Women friends and relatives who rallied around her at first soon go back to their former concerns or they may see a possible rival in her. They may resent the younger boomer woman acting like an adolescent and the woman herself might in turn find it difficult to act as an eligible woman, at the same time looking after her children. The problem of children enters the picture, also— what do you tell them about a new man in your life. They might resent him and create problems for his visits to the home. A second marriage is not uncommon even if a woman has been marred twenty or thirty years. Children may act to control their mothers' plans for future matrimony particularly if they are determined and older.

The following study by William Goode, Sociologist and famous author of the heralded work *World Revolution and Family Patterns*, doesn't report whether the divorced women he studied had children or not but he found as a result of questioning 425 divorced women in Detroit that 37 percent had not suffered seriously after separation. Only 30 percent felt they had been discriminated against as divorcees, more than half reported that they had been able to keep their old friends, and most of the others said that they had been successful in making new friends.

For most women loneliness is their lot, at least for some months despite Goode's survey the results of which suggest that many women would put a brave face on the events in public or in an interview which possibly belie the actual private circumstance. Women undergoing hormonal changes, many the cessation of the menses, etc., have compounded financial, stress problems and may therefore seek solace in eating and drinking, becoming for the first time overweight or even obese. This further militates against their self image. Their children frequently are put upon by a lonely mother who makes outrageous emotional demands, particularly on small children.

The needs of a woman can be overwhelming and for that reason it is easy to understand the emotional support they feel they need to elicit from their children. Most women divorcees have several months of frequent crying sessions where the young daughter and sons get involved in the crying spells. This has an ulterior effect on the children. Divorced women need companionship, that is, adult friends, and some need a sexual partner. Modern research indicates that sexual urges do not ordinarily slacken off to zero, whatever the age of the divorced person. Many divorced women and particularly widows, according to William Masters, former Director of the Masters & Johnson Institute in St. Louis, Missouri, "have this incredible need to be with men, and they do something about it." In many instances the man they select is married. Women who would not consider cheating in their marriage, once that marriage is terminated, don't feel so strongly about that any more. Paul Gebbard of the Indiana Institute for Sex reports that most widows who find new sexual partners do so in the first year of widowhood, and he adds, "there is no lack of men willing to give solace to a new widow." Divorced women find men also but not with the same ease or as often as does the younger widow. Much of this has been tempered by the advent of herpes and particularly AIDS. As for opportunity to remarry, divorced women, and for that matter men also, have greater chances to marry than those never married. Religious views of many and the views of the church, although altered somewhat in the past decade, pose a problem to many who divorce or are facing it; the early Christian church forbade divorce on any grounds. Monsignor Stephen J. Kelleher, a former Judge of the Marriage Tribunal of the Archdiocese of New York, published a book called *Divorce and Remarriage for Catholics?* In this work he maintains that conflict among marriage partners prevents human growth and suggests that not everyone should be expected to live up to doctrinal principles of the indissolution of marriage. Though the Catholic Church is generally firm on the issue, certain segments (Italian women have the right to divorce and keep their own names even if married) of the church do not inveigh against it. We must remember that no matter how much we might have wished that things would have turned out differently for us, we could not control all the factors and conditions working to cause a marital breakdown.

We must finally realize that it is our lives and precious few people will care whether we succeed or fail. Success or failure will be largely due to our efforts; we are the catalysts. There are things women can keep in mind to help them during the transition from divorce to afterwards. The author has observed many marriage breakups and recommends the following as a strategy to start to live a more fulfilling life.

1. One must not accept the view that this is the end of the world. Sure one party is over! But another can be planned and enjoyed. Today is the beginning day of my second life.

2. One needs help from a variety of sources—our families, friends, a professional counselor perhaps, and usually our physician. The latter can understand our need to control our emotional lives, therefore can prescribe what we need and give advice about our health matters. One should not increase the number of tranquilizers, i.e., Valium, Xanax, Librium, Donatal, Meprobamate, etc. on her own ideas. Diet needs should be looked after also.

3. Get involved in a regular routine which allows little time for moping around or being by yourself. This will help you from becoming engrossed in self pity and ego crucifixion. If you don't have a routine, get one which provides time daily for self-improvement; that is, some reading, rest, taking care of your personal matters, dress and bathe each day—put on lipstick; don't overdo this and make up when you go out for this telegraphs your problem or advertises you in a way you really don't want. Make yourself eat breakfast and if you do not exercise, start this as a set thing. Walk or run or work in the yard, but if possible make it vigorous exercise. Eat out often, if it can only be McDonald's or the corner Drug Store. Take in movies, plays, and enroll in a course at a college or university. They have non-credit and credit courses on everything. The idea is to keep yourself occupied constructively. Go to the beauty shop and get a new hairstyle. You'll get compliments and attention.

4. Force yourself to reconstruct your life and thereby improve your mental health. This will give you self-respect. There is something to be learned from divorce. If you haven't worked outside of the home, get a job, go back to school if necessary to train yourself. If children keep you tied closely in this enterprise, be certain of that—now, chin up, chest out, full speed ahead!

GETTING A DIVORCE

There are a number of things we should be aware of in a divorce case. At the outset one should get competent advice. Remember many lawyers provide initial consultation with no charges. Such a lawyer is more difficult to find than it seems. If there is any chance of reconciliation, do not go to a lawyer for your initial help unless he is trained in mediation and reconciliation. Many lawyers take the adversary position and are intent upon legally separating you from your spouse with the least amount of effort and for the maximum amount of money and they are often slow to get the divorce finalized. Go to a marriage counselor first; the answer may still be divorce but he or she will not set about to untie you. One such bit of knowledge is that there are states in which you can arrange for your own divorce. Guides for doing this are constantly being revised, so check in your state for a guide. Some states for whom guides have been made are: California, Illinois, Maine, Maryland, Massachusetts, Virginia, and the District of Columbia.

FINDING A LAWYER

Many men seek a lawyer only after their wives have filed for divorce. One man, thinking that he would talk it over with his wife's lawyer hoping that reconciliation was in the offing, admitted to the lawyer that he had been a poor husband in many regards but that he loved his wife and wished to remain married. Unfortunately he said too much and what he said he later found written in the bill of particulars against him. Men should be wary of lawyers who say they practice family law for they are viewed by many as only a grade above the accident-indemnity lawyer. This is probably unfair and many men may expect too much from the lawyer; nonetheless, to be cautious is important. Check for a lawyer that specializes in divorce. The Martindale-Hubbell Law Directory is a start and can be found in most libraries. It will enable you to find the specialization you want, and some names of lawyers. The local bar association usually has referral service. Some men's and women's groups have referral service as a part of their membership fee. Once you have several names of former clients, (NOW, YWCA) it would be worth it to interview several of them and get their opinions. Bar associations who refer legal counsel to you are lawyers who generally expect to get $100-$500 an hour for their services once they take your case. The initial consultation should be free. The attorney you select should be one you're comfortable with and proactive, for you are responsible for his actions, in forwarding your interests. Don't be shy—you're paying and you're looking for the best possible results.

Information Needed to Pursue a Divorce

According to Socrates Editors of *Divorce* (2006) you should gather the following material in an approach to an interview with an attorney. Information bearing on the problem would include: your case, family facts, your financial situation and be prepared to state your objectives. If, for example, you refuse to pay alimony (there may be no way around it) or must have the better of two cars because of your work, tell the prospective lawyer. Where you will compromise is also important, like trading a share of the home for the wife's share of the business. If you are a woman and have little knowledge of your husband's financial circumstances, investments, holdings, it becomes important to find out if possible, or at least alert the lawyer to the possibilities. Here are some things you should discuss with the prospective lawyer: (1) personal information (including your assets) but do not give details of sexual activities for those are beyond what is necessary; (2) support needed particularly for the woman, what monies do both make, what prospects considering age for the future; (3) custody of children and visitation rights (who pays what for travel expenses involved in visitation), this is important for women too as men today are receiving custody of children; (4) child's support and education; (5) medical and dental costs; (6) life insurance, property, stocks and bonds; (7) tax matters, wills, trusts, debts and obligations;

and (8) fees for lawyers, expenses, (9) camps, piano lessons etc. You suggest this is too much for just deciding on a lawyer, perhaps, but this usually is a onetime thing and in preparing for this will make you conversant with the ramifications of divorce; in addition the interview itself will clarify things for you and provide some information that is important.

Now, beyond this, inquire as to the experience of the lawyer, his record of handling such matters. Obtain neutral opinions on him and if possible the names of two people who have used his or her services. Will he be available at a time of emergency and is he trustworthy? The author knows a friend who engaged a "name lawyer" who compromised him with the wife's lawyer by agreeing to let the wife go into the home which she had deserted, while he was out of town and get the pick of the furniture although an agreement (This is malpractice.) had been reached that both parties would be present and the disposition of the furniture following the previously made accord. A good bet for both men and women may be a woman lawyer, and don't overlook a minority one (only a few are available outside urban centers) for frequently these people will work harder for justice and have reasonable fees. At best, unfortunately, it is a hazardous undertaking and unfortunately at a time when you are most vulnerable to any kind of help offered. But be assured this process of selecting from several lawyers will save you money and satisfaction in the end.

Remember in all of this, when you do choose a lawyer, level with him no matter how hurtful it is and draw up an agreement simply stating what he has agreed to as to payment of fees, time to be given (some lawyers usually provide their services in terms of half or whole hours—typically $200-$500 an hour or more!). Then, if you have the money, send him a retainer—usually $500-$1000 will suffice. If, having secured a lawyer, you feel he has done nothing for you, or he refused to move the case along or has cheated you, fire him and get some other legal counsel. If the lawyer has abused you, report it to the Bar Association's Ethics Committee in your area. The author knows a man whose ex-wife's lawyer called him at odd hours (midnight and early morning) effecting a change in his voice to threaten him in order to scare him from making such a grievance petition. He reported this to his own lawyer for advice and was surprised that it was passed off as "just bizarre behavior." If you're on the receiving end of this, it's more than bizarre, but lawyers frequently, like other professionals, stick together. However, this kind of behavior should be reported to the ethics committee of the local Bar Association.

No-Fault Divorce

No-fault divorce is designed to minimize blame and the adversarial incentive that exists in a divorce case. This type of divorce is now the most common. California instituted the first law (1970) abolishing any requirement of fault as a basis for marriage dissolvement. No-fault divorce laws, though they vary in the different states, is found in all fifty states. California law, perhaps the most liberal, began as a conservative attempt to reduce the number of divorces, stipulates the following:

1. No grounds are needed to obtain a divorce.
2. Proof of fault or guilt is unnecessary to obtain a decree.
3. One spouse can decide to get a divorce without the consent or agreement of the other.
4. New standards for alimony and property awards seek to treat men and women equally annulling former sex based traditions.
5. Financial awards are no longer linked to fault, rather they are based upon current financial needs and resources available to meet those needs.
6. The new protocol is designed to create a social and psychological climate which will foster amiable divorce rather than adversarial procedures.

New York has not adopted strict no-fault laws. Laws in Arkansas and Arizona give couples an option before marriage, covenant marriage or no-fault. The covenant agree to pre-marital counseling and to limit the grounds and options should they decide to divorce.

No-fault has affected property division, alimony, child support, and custody decisions in and out of the courts. The court's main legal guidelines are based on what is fair and equitable between the parties. Courts are devising child support and spousal tables to make their rulings more consistent. Actuarial tables are developed according to income and local cost of living and should be available at most courthouses in counties and cities, also in public libraries. No-fault is a breakthrough toward creating more humane and effective divorce procedures. Many states have simplified divorce laws allowing couples to do their own divorce. Divorce manuals abound for couples, these usually outline, step by step, the procedures. *How to do Your Own Divorce in California* published by the Nolo Press has sold over a million copies. One work is *How to File Your Own Divorce* (Fifth Edition) by Edward Haman is used by many. Many other manuals exist representing specific states individual requirements and may be found in bookstores and stationary shops. The practical result of "no-fault" divorce for older women, who have been principally the homemaker, has been to drastically reduced settlements they have received. Adjustment maintenance increasingly adds a plus to this situation for women.

Negotiated Settlements

This divorce is a resolution of the issues between the couple out-of-court. The better divorce lawyers handle most of their cases in this fashion. When the parties are not after revenue or airing their grievances this method allows them to cooperate and satisfy each other's needs. Little time is wasted nor is money thrown away on legal warfare. Cooperation between the couple can provide:

1. Child-care scheduling thereby reducing expenses for this service.
2. When business is involved this provides a negotiation or a mediation opportunity allowing the business to prosper whereas the contentious might destroy the business.
3. Tax savings approach can be effected by cooperative tax planning, allowing both to have more cash. For instance, if a parent in a low income bracket is receiving both alimony and child support while the payee parent is in a high tax category both can have more money if they call the payment family support which combines alimony and child support. This is fully deductible.

Mediated (Cooperative Divorce) Settlement

This is a method whereby couples can have a third party mediate their differences relative to property divisions, child custody, payments of support and the like without the damaging adversarial approach allowing for a more humane way to end a marital relationship. The third party may be a mental health professional or a counselor and some are lawyers who have committed themselves to this philosophy. Joan Blades, an authority on Marriage Dissolution through Mediation, authored *Mediate Your Divorce* by Prentice Hall, suggest the following benefits from mediation:

1. Parents develop richer and more rewarding relationships with their children after divorce particularly fathers who spend more time with their children after a divorce than before.
2. Individual spouses recover old skills and strengths that were dormant and discover new ones. Traditional gender roles are expanded upon by learning new skills of the other sex—car repair, bookkeeping, carpentry for the woman, for the man—cooking, child care and shopping, etc.
3. Divorce is a catalyst for reassessment of one's life resulting in possible change of work, going back to school, moving, or gaining a new perspective on life.
4. Damaging and nonfunctional communication patterns that existed between the partners are terminated and if noticed in future relationships are then corrected.

There are typically five steps in mediation; (1) introduction and commitment stage, (2) the definition stage, (3) negotiation stage, (4) the agreement stage and (5) the contracting stage. The process allows time to become comfortable with the process, reduce emotional agitation and perhaps resistance to the mediation itself. The focus of mediation is an attempt to get the couple to forecast their lives after the final separation. The mediators have access to the necessary legal or attorney's information and forms to conclude the settlement or brochures. The final settlement is reviewed by a judge. Mediation is required in contested divorces certainly where children are involved.

Generally the cost of mediation is less than traditional divorces and studies such as sociologist Stephen Bahr's indicate children adjust better following this method than in the adversarial one. Also, there is more likelihood that the agreement will be honored and that more cooperation will exist after the divorce. Spouses will have greater self-determination and self respect after mediation. Less money is spent by the couple and the state and, on the whole, mediating couples tend to be more satisfied with the outcome of the divorce. They are both better able to begin building their new lives emotionally and better able to cope with possible child custody disputes before any court appearance. In 1981, California was the first state to require mediation. Some typical forms relating to the mediation process are shown below.

CONTRACT & CONFIDENTIAL QUESTIONNAIRE

CONTRACT TO PARTICIPATE IN MEDIATION

We, _____ agree to abide by the Rules

(clients)

of the Southern Mediation Service which we have received and read. We agree

to pay the sum of $_____ per hour for the services of the mediators when

the services of the mediators when the services are performed, and a $25.00 set

up fee. This will be paid by:

1) the clients in equal shares: (2) all by _____; (3) the

clients in these proportions: _____

We, _____, agree to abide by the Rules of the

(mediators)

Southern Mediation Service and to use our utmost effort in helping the clients

reach a mutual agreement on the issues before them.

Franklin Ross Jones

DATED: _____

_____   _____
           Client   Mediator

_____   _____
           Client   Mediator

CONFIDENTIAL

QUESTIONNAIRE FOR CLIENTS

CONTEMPLATING MARITAL TERMINATION

This questionnaire has been designed to aid our legal staff in advising you of your legal rights and obligations with respect to a marital termination. All information is covered by attorney-client privilege

and will, therefore, be kept in strictest confidence.

Please do your best in filling this form out based upon your knowledge at this time.

Name of Person Filling in Questionnaire _____

_____

Name of Client if Different _____

_____

Date of Completion _____

_____

Note that unless otherwise agreed at the commencement of the consultation, your initial

consultation will be charged at the attorney's normal hourly rate and payment must be

made at the end of the consultation.

        A.   INFORMATION ABOUT YOU

    1.   Name: _____

_____

2.   (a) Telephone: Home – ( ) _____

                  Work – ( ) _____   May we call

                  you at work? _____

                  Mobile – ( ) _____

        (b) In what county do you reside? _____
How long? _____

        (c) Mailing address: _____

_____

        (d) Residence address (if different from above) : _____

_____

3.   Birth date: _____

4.   (a) Former name(s): _____

_____

        (b) Do you wish your former name restored? _____

        (c) If yes, which name? _____

5.   Social Security Number: _____

6.   (a) Employer: _____

_____

        (b) Location address: _____

_____

        (c) Days/Hours at work: _____

_____

        (d) Pay: Approximate monthly net from employment:

_____

        (e) Other monthly net income: _____

_____

(Note: There are 4 1/3 weeks per month; to determine "net pay" deduct only SDI, Soc Sec, withholding

tax, mandatory retirement contributions. Do not deduct credit union payments, stock or savings plan,

etc. Other net income includes that after taxes from investments, rentals, savings, or business.)

        (e) Do you have medical and/or dental coverage through your employer? _____

        (f) At what cost to you? _____

        (g) How long have you worked at this place of employment?

7. Do you have any health problems for which special attention is required? _____
   If so, describe briefly: _____

8. What is the cost of childcare enabling you to work? _____

9. Are you contemplating remarriage at present? _____

10. If you are currently residing with anyone (other than your spouse or children) state: Name:
    _____ Age: _____
Relationship to you: _____

11. Also, please describe the monetary arrangements between you and the above person, if any:
    _____

B. GENERAL INFORMATION ABOUT YOUR PRESENT MARRIAGE

1. Your name: _____

2. Your spouse's name: _____

1. Date of marriage: _____

4. Place of marriage: (City) _____
   _____ (State) _____

1. How long have you lived in _____(fill in)_____ County
   Your spouse: _____

6. If you have been served with divorce-related papers, date
served: _____

1. Which of the parties wishes the dissolution? _____

2. Do you desire reconciliation? _____ If so, are you interested in marital counseling?

_____ Has there been marital counseling in the past?

With whom? _____

3. Describe any violence which has recently occurred between you and your spouse or which your
spouse might allege has occurred. _____

_____

_____

B. SUPPORT ARRANGEMENTS BETWEEN YOU AND SPOUSE

1. If you have already separated or discussed separating, detail the financial arrangements you have
made:

(a) Periodic payments (how much, how often, etc.)

_____

_____

(b) Direct payment of living expenses (monthly and other) such as mortgages (list items, amounts,

and how often paid):

_____

_____

(c) Other: _____

_____

2. Is there an agreement in writing covering support arrangements?

____

3. What support arrangement do you believe would be fair? _____

_____

_____

The "No Divorce" Approach

A number of sociologists have reported a phenomena that is occurring and growing among young adults and the young boomers 45 to 55 that should be observed. This is the situation which has existed for some time, namely that of not getting a divorce—just separating. This situation is hazardous to property rights of the parties in years to come. This approach was mainly one utilized by the lower and lower middle class persons in yesteryear. Today thousands of couples leave each other by moving out and/or in cohabitation with a new partner without any inclination to affirm a divorce by legal means. How much this will grow or be problematic is unknown but where remarriage and children are involved most couples will legally divorce and I believe they should! For the poor many certainly couldn't pay for it.

Grounds for Divorce

In the past, grounds for divorce in the United States have been very restrictive; as evidenced by the fact that several decades ago when adultery was virtually the only basis for divorce. Now, no-fault divorce laws make grounds for divorce a moot point since any variety of reasons are allowed. Mutual agreement is all that is required. New York is the only remaining state that only permits the termination of a marriage for valid reasons. It is not enough that the middle aged couple have grown tired of each other, for many middlescent people have fantasies about divorce, envisioning unbridled freedom and bliss through divorce (many find once done they really didn't need or want it). In Virginia living apart and separate with or without cohabitation of one year before filing is sufficient grounds for divorce. Grounds for divorce in New York occur by petition to the courts under the following grievances:

1. Cruel and Inhuman Treatment: This involves the regular abuse and attack on the partner's emotional well-being and physical body.
2. Desertion: One year continuous duration.
3. Adultery
4. Imprisonment: For more than three years.

5. Conversion of a separation judgment
6. Conversion of a written and acknowledged separation agreement after living separate and apart for more than one year

In the past, other grounds for divorce were:

Chronic Drunkenness or Narcotic Drug Abuse—some states spell out the time; New Hampshire said two years, others longer. Testimony of several witnesses who know the subjects is usually sufficient.

Insanity—provisions are made for divorce under this circumstance in at least half of the states. Most states require three to five years of incurable insanity which means that in most cases this will be judged by their being institutionalized.

Lack of support—the chronic gambler, the reckless spender and drunk provides a prospect for relief to those using this approach. These elements usually accompany the grievance; just being unemployed is generally not enough evidence as they can get welfare assistance

Getting a Lawyer

In finding a lawyer you must get one you can trust, one that knows the stress most clients are under and therefore be the most helpful. Pick a lawyer with a good record by asking local judges, or look for those listed in professional journals, or seek a referral from a friend or acquaintance. The following statement will give you a good idea of the what to expect from any lawyer you might select.

STATEMENT OF CLIENT'S RIGHTS

Your Attorney is providing you with this document to inform you of what you, as a client, are entitled to by law or by custom. To help prevent any misunderstanding between you and your attorney please read this document carefully.

If you ever have any questions about these rights, or about the way your case is being handled, do not hesitate to ask your attorney. He or she should be readily available to represent your best interests and keep you informed about your case.

An attorney may not refuse to represent you on the basis of race, creed, color, sex, sexual orientation, age, national origin or disability.

You are entitled to an attorney who will be capable of handling your case; show you courtesy and consideration at all times; represent you zealously; and preserve your confidences and secrets that are revealed in the course of the relationship.

You are entitled to a written retainer agreement which must set forth, in plain language, the nature of the relationship and the details of the fee arrangement. At your request, and before you sign the agreement, you are entitled to have your attorney clarify in writing any of its terms, or include additional provisions.

You are entitled to fully understand the proposed rates and retainer fee before you sign a retainer agreement, as in any other contract.

You may refuse to enter into any fee arrangement that you find unsatisfactory.

Your attorney may not request a fee that is contingent on the securing of a divorce or on the amount of money or property that may be obtained.

Your attorney may not request a retainer fee that is nonrefundable. That is, should you discharge your attorney, or should your attorney withdraw from the case, before the retainer is used up, he or she is entitled to be paid commensurate with the work performed on your case and any expenses, but must return the balance of the retainer to you. However, your attorney may enter into a minimum fee arrangement with you that provides for the payment of a specific amount below which the fee will not fall based upon the handling of the case to its conclusion.

You are entitled to know the approximate number of attorneys and other legal staff members who will be working your case at any given time and what you will be charged for the services of each.

You are entitled to know in advance how you will be asked to pay legal fees and expenses, and how the retainer, if any, will be spent.

At your request, and after your attorney has had a reasonable opportunity to investigate your case, you are entitled to be given an estimate of approximate future costs of your case, which estimate shall be made in good faith but may be subject to change due to facts and circumstances affecting the case.

You are entitled to receive a written, itemized bill on a regular basis, at least every 60 days.

You are expected to review the itemized bills sent by counsel, and to raise any objections of errors in a timely manner. Time spent in discussion or explanation of bills will not be charged to you.

You are expected to be truthful in all discussions with your attorney, and to provide all relevant information and documentation to enable him or her to competently prepare your case.

You are entitled to be kept informed of the status of your case, and to be provided with copies of correspondence and documents prepared on your behalf or received from the court or your adversary.

You have the right to be present in court at the time that conferences are held.

You are entitled to make the ultimate decision on the objectives to be pursued in your case, and to make the final decision regarding the settlement of your case.

Your attorney's written retainer agreement must specify under what circumstances he or she might seek to withdraw as your attorney for non-payment of legal fees. If an action or proceeding is pending, the court may give your attorney a "charging lien," which entitles your attorney to payment for services already rendered at the end of the case out of the proceeds of the final order or judgment.

You are under no legal obligation to sign a confession of judgment or promissory note, or to agree to a lien or mortgage on your home to cover legal fees. Your attorney's written retainer agreement must specify whether, and under what circumstances, such security may be requested. In no event may such security interest be obtained by your attorney without prior court approval and notice to your adversary. An attorney's security interest in the marital residence cannot be foreclosed against you.

<u>You are entitled to have your attorney's best efforts exerted on your behalf, but no particular results can be guaranteed.</u>

If you entrust money with an attorney for an escrow deposit in your case, the attorney must safeguard the escrow in a special bank account. You are entitled to a written escrow agreement, a written receipt, and a complete record concerning the escrow. When the terms of the escrow agreement have been performed, the attorney must promptly make payment of the escrow to all persons who are entitled to it.

In the event of a fee dispute, you may have the right to seek arbitration. Your attorney will provide you with the necessary information regarding arbitration in the event of a fee dispute, or upon your request.

Date: _____

Receipt Acknowledged:

By: _____

Signature Line—Attorney

By: _____

Signature Line—Client

Source: Adapted from New York State Unified Court System

STATEMENT OF CLIENT'S

RESPONSIBILITIES

Reciprocal trust, courtesy and respect are the hallmarks of the attorney-client relationship. Within that relationship, the client looks to the attorney for expertise, education, sound judgment, protection, advocacy and representation. These expectations can be achieved only if the client fulfills the following responsibilities.

1. The client is expected to treat the lawyer and the lawyer's staff with courtesy and consideration.

2. The client's relationship with the lawyer must be one of complete candor and the lawyer must be apprised of all facts or circumstances of the matter being handled by the lawyer even if the client believes that those facts may be detrimental to the client's cause.

3. The client must honor the fee arrangement as agreed to with the lawyer, in accordance with law.

4. All bills for services rendered which are tendered to the client pursuant to the agreed upon fee arrangement should be paid promptly.

5. The client may withdraw from the attorney-client relationship, subject to financial commitments under the agreed to fee arrangement, and, in certain cases need court approval.

6. Although the client should expect that his or her correspondence, telephone calls and other communications will be answered within a reasonable time frame, the client should recognize that the lawyer has other clients equally demanding of the lawyer's time and attention.

7. The client should maintain contact with the lawyer, promptly notify the lawyer of any change in telephone number of address and respond promptly to a request by the lawyer for information and cooperation.

RESIDENCY REQUIREMENTS FOR FILING FOR DIVORCE

No residency time, only bona fide Residency	State Requirements	No residency time, only bona fide residency	State Requirements
Alabama	6 months	Nevada	6 weeks
Alaska	30 days	New Hampshire	1 year[1]
Arizona	90 days	New Jersey	1 year
Arkansas	60 days[1]	New Mexico	6 months
California	6 months	New York	1 year
Colorado	90 days	North Carolina	6 months
Connecticut	1 year	North Dakota	6 months
Delaware	6 months	Ohio	6 months
Florida	6 months	Oklahoma	6 months
Georgia	6 months	Oregon	6 months[4]
Hawaii	6 months	Pennsylvania	6 months
Idaho	6 weeks	Rhode Island	1 year
Illinois	90 days	South Carolina	1 year[5]
Indiana	6 months	South Dakota	None
Iowa	1 year	Tennessee	6 months
Kansas	60 days	Texas	6 months
Kentucky	180 days	Utah	90 days
Louisiana	12 months	Vermont	6 months
Maine	6 months	Virginia	6 months
Maryland	1 year	Washington	1 year
Massachusetts	1 year[2]	West Virginia	1 year
Michigan	1 year[2]	Wisconsin	6 months
Minnesota	180 days	Wyoming	60 days
Mississippi	6 months	Washington, DC	6 months
Missouri	90 days	Puerto Rico	1 year
Montana	90 days	Virgin Islands	6 weeks
Nebraska	1 year		

[1]Sixty days prior to filing and three months prior to final decree.

[2]One year, if cause arose outside of state.

[3]Cause must have arose in state.

[4]Unless married in Oregon, and one party is a resident of or domiciled in Oregon at the start of the

 action.

[5]Three months, if both parties are residing in South Carolina.

Source: Adapted from *American Bar Association, Family Law Section*

Annulments are usually granted for causes occurring before the marriage. Many grievances listed earlier fall in this category. Pregnancy before marriage or even lack of it, where the woman claims a man made her pregnant and coerced into a marriage; if the woman defrauded the man by falsely claiming pregnancy to induce marriage. In fact, fraud is a major ground for annulment, e.g., lack of intent to live as man and wife. Exaggeration of one's financial status is also used as a basis for annulments, as is under age for legal marriage. There are few annulments in most states. Increasingly states allow divorce under the rubric of incompatibility or irretrievable breakdown in the marriage. Constructive desertion is allowed also; this is where a spouse leaves the home under threats, bad treatment, etc. Some courts have a waiting period, and some lecture to the participants. The duration of residency requirements follows. The U.S. Supreme Court has ruled that divorce granted in one state is valid in another state providing that: (1) both parties are aware of the proceedings; (2) at least one party has established residence in the state granting the decree, and (3) either both principals are present at the hearing or the absent one is represented by an attorney. The usual divorce takes three to nine months if things go normally. But this is not the case when arguments over property, money, insurance, home equity, etc. and involved—the trial may take two years, the system involving lawyers, courts, etc., take their own sweet time. A divorce can be gotten in Las Vegas in six weeks. One member of a couple must be a resident of the state giving the decree. The residence requirement varies from six weeks in Nevada to five years in Massachusetts. Even less time for divorce is required in places like Mexico but one wants to be sure this is accepted by the state he or she lives in some cases it will not be.

Legal Steps To A Divorce

The first step to divorce is to file a petition for divorce. This is usually done with the help of a lawyer. This petition tells the court the facts of your marriage, it describes the grounds for the divorce and asks the court to grant the divorce with certain considerations. If you are a woman filing, you will be the plaintiff and your husband the defendant. The following shows the legal grounds for divorce which uniformly show no fault to be the basic approach to divorce. Even so many states have facilitated, the restrictions and the protocol involved. Judicial separation is attached the no fault in most instances. In some states living apart and having a separation for a certain length of time is sufficient like New Jersey, New York, Arkansas, Connecticut, District of Columbia, Hawaii, Illinois, Maryland, Minnesota, Missouri, Nevada, New Hampshire, Oregon, Pennsylvania, Rhode Island, South Carolina, Tennessee, Texas, Utah, Vermont, Virginia and West Virginia. Changes occur often so one should check the requirement in their state to be sure they meet the legal responsibility required.

Legal Grounds for Divorce

Jurisdiction	LEGAL GROUNDS
Alabama	No-fault; traditional; incompatibility; living separate and apart for 2 years; judicial separation
Alaska	No-fault; traditional; incompatibility; judicial separation
Arizona	No-fault; traditional; judicial separation
Arkansas	No-fault; traditional; living separate and apart for 18 months; judicial separation
California	No-fault; judicial separation
Colorado	No-fault; judicial separation
Connecticut	No-fault; traditional; living separate and apart for 18 months; judicial separation
Delaware	No-fault; living separate and apart for 6 months

District of Columbia	No-fault; living separate and apart for 1 year; judicial separation
Florida	No-fault
Georgia	No-fault; traditional
Hawaii	No-fault; living separate and apart for 2 years; judicial separation
Idaho	No-fault; traditional; judicial separation
Illinois	No-fault; traditional; living separate and apart for 2 years; judicial separation
Indiana	No-fault; traditional; judicial separation
Iowa	No-fault; judicial separation
Kansas	No-fault; traditional; incompatibility; judicial separation
Kentucky	No-fault; living separate and apart for 60 days; judicial separation
Louisiana	No-fault; traditional; living separate and apart for 6 months; judicial separation
Maine	No-fault; traditional; judicial separation
Maryland	No-fault; traditional; living separate and apart for 2 years
Massachusetts	No-fault; traditional; judicial separation
Michigan	No-fault; judicial separation
Minnesota	No-fault; living separate and apart for 60 days; judicial separation
Mississippi	No-fault; traditional
Missouri	No-fault; traditional; living separate and apart for 1 year; judicial separation
Montana	No-fault; incompatibility; living separate and apart for 180 days; judicial separation
Nebraska	No-fault; judicial separation
Nevada	Incompatibility; living separate and apart for 1 year; judicial separation
New Hampshire	No-fault; traditional living separate and apart for 2 years

New Jersey	No-fault; traditional; living separate and apart for 18 months
New Mexico	No-fault; traditional; incompatibility; judicial separation
New York	Traditional; living separate and apart for 1 year; judicial separation
North Carolina	No-fault, living separate and apart for 1 year; judicial separation
North Dakota	No-fault; traditional; judicial separation
Ohio	No-fault; traditional; incompatibility; living separate and apart for 1 year
Oklahoma	Incompatibility; judicial separation
Oregon	No-fault; judicial separation
Pennsylvania	No-fault; traditional; living separate and apart for 2 years
Rhode Island	No-fault; traditional; living separate and apart for 3 years; judicial separation
South Carolina	no-fault; traditional; living separate and apart for 1 year; judicial separation
South Dakota	No-fault; traditional; judicial separation
Tennessee	No-fault; traditional; living separate and apart for 2 years; judicial separation
Texas	No-fault; traditional; living separate and apart for 3 years
Utah	No-fault; traditional; living separate and apart for 3 years; judicial separation
Vermont	No-fault; traditional; living separate and apart for 6 months
Virginia	No-fault; traditional; living separate and apart for 1 year, 6 months if no children; judicial separation
Washington	No-fault
West Virginia	No-fault; traditional; living separate and apart for 1 year; judicial separation
Wisconsin	No-fault; judicial separation

331

Wyoming	No-fault; traditional; incompatibility; judicial separation[1]

---

[1]Source: Adapted from American Bar Association, Family Law Section

---

An example of a fictitious petition to the court follows, which includes basic data and an appeal to get relief of a number of issues, support, custody and protection.

IN THE CIRCUIT COURT OF _____ COUNTY

COUNTY DEPARTMENT, DIVORCE DIVISION

SUSAN BROWN,

    Plaintiff

ROBERT BROWN,   No. _____

    Defendant

COMPLAINT FOR DIVORCE

          What follows in the complaint are the charges connected with the divorce and

    plea for relief. Given here is the data relative to place of residence, children, residency time, marriage date, request for custody of children, support and to keep the domicile; finally the bill of particulars which argue for the severing of the marriage ties.

                  it concludes the document....

WHEREFORE plaintiff Susan Brown, prays as follows:

For a Judgment of Divorce; for temporary and permanent care, custody, control, and education of the children; for such relief as in equity may be just.

_____

Susan Brown, Plaintiff

STATE OF _____

COUNTY OF _____ S.S.

    Susan Brown, being first duly sworn on oath, deposes and states that the contents of the foregoing complaint are true (except to matters alleged to be on information and belief and those she believes to be true).

_____

Susan Brown

Subscribed and Sworn to Before Me

this _____ day of _____, 200

_____

Notary Public

    The law demands that you make a reasonable effort to notify the other party that you have filed for divorce. This is done through a summons; a legal notice that the other party is suing for divorce. The summons can be gotten by appearing with the spouse at the Clerk of Court's Office or having it delivered by a third party or the Sheriff's Department to the residence. The summons and petition for divorce are published in a legal periodical; for most this means a local and/or country newspaper. A typical summons follows:

Franklin Ross Jones

IN THE NAME OF THE PEOPLE OF THE STATE OF
_____

IN THE CIRCUIT COURT OF _____ COUNTY _____

SUSAN BROWN,

Plaintiff

ROBERT BROWN,   No. _____

Defendant

SUMMONS

To each defendant:

YOU ARE SUMMONED and required to file an answer in this case, or otherwise file your appearance, in the office of the clerk of this court within ____ days after notice of this summons, not counting the day of service. IF YOU FAIL TO DO SO, A JUDGMENT BY DEFAULT MAY BE TAKEN AGAINST YOU FOR THE RELIEF ASKED IN THE COMPLAINT.

To the officer:

This summons must be returned by the officer or other persons to whom it was given for service, with endorsement of service and fees, if any, immediately after service. If service cannot be made, this summons shall be returned so endorsed.

This summons may not be served later than 30 days after this date.

WITNESS _____, 201____

Signature

_____

Clerk of Court

It is usually important to ask the courts for a temporary order when you file the divorce petition. In this you ask the judge to grant certain rights until the divorce becomes final, like custody of the children, financial consideration, right to the home, and attorney's fees. In most cases the request for an order is done by the wife. In the case where one of the partners does not respond to the summons of the plaintiff, two things can happen: first, the judge can hold a hearing on the basis of a temporary order and grant everything asked or secondly, you (the plaintiff) may get the divorce granted by default. If the defendant isn't present, the divorce is granted. Sometimes this is pre-arranged; this is done to facilitate the decision making. Judges will, upon discovering collusion, fail to grant the divorce under these circumstances. In the case where the party does not default, the defendant will have (usually) a lawyer draw up the legal papers for a defense of the charges and may counter-charge (file a cross-complaint). The judge will then issue a temporary order determining what disposition in the interim is to be made of money, domiciling and custody of children, etc. If reconciliation occurs, the proceedings may be stopped.

Usually before the trial for divorce goes into court an attempt at negotiation is made. Issues are resolved hopefully on property, custody, support, etc. This is the time to gather facts—most states require extensive financial revelations to be made of debts, income, etc. Here is a typical Financial Disclosure (some are shorter) used in New York.

Franklin Ross Jones

FINANCIAL DISCLOSURE AFFIDAVIT

F.C.A. 413-1, 424-A: Art. 5-b   Form 4-17

D.R.L. 236-B, 2240   (Financial Disclosure Affidavit)

                                                  9/99

FAMILY COURT OF THE STATE OF NEW YORK

COUNTY OF

....

In the Matter of a Proceeding for Support   Docket No.

(Commissioner of Social Services, Assignor,

on behalf of   , Assignee)

                                                           FINANCIAL

                            Petitioner
DISCLOSURE

S.S.# (Assignor)   AFFIDAVIT

       -against-

                            Respondent.

S.S.#

....

NOTICE: YOU ARE REQUIRED TO ATTACH TO THIS FORM A CURRENT
AND REPRESENTATIVE PAYCHECK STUB AND A COPY OF YOUR MOST
RECENTLY FILED STATE AND FEDERAL INCOME TAX RETURNS, INCLUDING
A COPY OF THE W-2 WAGE AND TAX STATEMENT(S) SUBMITTED WITH THE
RETURNS. YOU MAY ALSO BE REQUIRED TO PRODUCE OTHER PAYCHECK
STUBS, EMPLOYMENT OR BUSINESS RECORDS AND PROOF OF CLAIMED
EXPENSES. IN ADDITION, YOU ARE REQUIRED TO PROVIDE INFORMATION
RELATING TO ALL GROUP HEALTH PLANS AVAILABLE TO YOU FOR THE
PROVISION OF CARE OR OTHER MEDICAL BENEFITS FOR THE CHILDREN)
FOR WHOM SUPPORT IS SOUGHT.

STATE OF NEW YORK   )

                           ):SS.:

COUNTY OF   )

336

_____, the (Petitioner)(Respondent) here in, residing at _____ _____, being duly sworn, deposes and says that the following is an accurate statement of my income from all sources, my liabilities, my assets and my net worth, from whatever sources, and whatever kind and nature, and wherever situated:

I.   INCOME FROM ALL SOURCES: The correct amount of the child support obligation is

presumed to be a percentage of income as defined by law. The percentages are set forth in Addendum A. Other pertinent information is set forth in Addenda B and C. List your income from all sources as follows:

a.   Wages and Salaries (as reportable on Federal and State income tax returns):

b.   Self-Employment Income (Describe and list self-employment income; attach to this form the most recently filed Federal and State income tax returns, including all schedules):

c.   Income/Dividend Income:

d.   Other income:

e.   Income from other sources: (List here and explain any other income including but not limited to: non-income producing assets; employment 'perks' and reimbursed expenses; fringe benefits as a result of employment; periodic income, personal injury settlements; non-reported income; and money, goods and services provided by relatives and friends)

II.   ASSETS: The Court can consider the assets of the custodial parent and/or the non-custodial parent in its award of child support. List your assets as follows:

III. DEDUCTIONS FROM INCOME: The Court allows certain deductions from income prior to applying the child support percentages. List the deductions that apply to you as follows.

IV. HEALTH INSURANCE, UNREIMBURSED HEALTH-RELATED EXPENSES, CHILD CARE EXPENSES AND EDUCATIONAL EXPENSES: As part of the child support obligation, parents shall be directed to provide health insurance, pay a pro-rated share of unreimbursed health-related expenses, pay a pro-rated share of child care expenses and in the Court's discretion pay educational expenses. List your information as follows and cross out or delete inapplicable provisions.

V.   VARIANCE FROM THE PERCENTAGES: The Family Court Act allows the Court to order support different from the percentages if the Court finds that the support based upon the percentages would be unjust or inappropriate due to certain factors. The factors are set forth in Addendum D. The following is/are the factor(s) that the Court should consider in this case.

VI.   EXPENSES: In ordering support by the percentages the Court is not obligated to consider expenses. However, if the Court varies from the percentages, expenses may be considered. List:

337

Franklin Ross Jones

VII.

VIII. <u>LIABILITIES, LOANS AND DEBTS:</u> In ordering support by the percentages the Court is not obligated to consider liabilities, loans, and debts. However, if the Court varies from the percentages, they may be considered. List your liabilities, loans and debts as follows:

VIII. <u>LIFE AND ACCIDENT INSURANCE:</u> The Court may direct you to purchase and maintain life and/or accident insurance benefits or assign benefits on existing policies for the benefit of your children. List your insurance policy or policies as follows:

_____

(Petitioner)(Respondent)

_____

Print or Type Name

_____

Signature of Attorney, if any

_____

Attorney's Name (Print or Type)

_____

Attorney's Address and
Telephone Number

I have carefully read the foregoing statement and attest to its truth and accuracy.

Sworn to before me this _____

day of _____, _____.

_____

(Deputy) Clerk of the Court

Notary Public

Adapted from the New York State Court System

ADDENDUM A

CHILD SUPPORT PERCENTAGES

The child support percentages that shall be applied by the Court unless the Court makes a finding that the non-custodial parent's share is unjust or inappropriate are as follows: 17% for one child; 25% for two children; 29% for three children; 31% for five children; and no less than 35% for five or more children.

ADDENDUM B

COMBINED PARENTAL INCOME OVER $80,000.00

Where combined parental income exceeds $80,000.00, the Court shall determine the amount of child support for the amount of the combined parental income in excess of such dollar amount through consideration of the factors set forth in Addendum D and or the support percentage set forth in Addendum A.

ADDENDUM C

SELF-SUPPORT RESERVE

Where the annual amount of the basic child support obligation would reduce the non-custodial parent's income below the poverty income guidelines amount for a single person as reported by the federal Department of Health and Human Services, the basic child support obligation shall be twenty-five dollars per month unless the interests of justice dictate otherwise. Where the annual amount of the basic child support obligation would reduce the non-custodial parent's income below the self-support reserve but not below, the poverty income guidelines amount of a single person as reported by the federal Department of Health and Human Services, the basic child support obligation shall be fifty dollars per month or the difference between the non-custodial parent's income and the self-support reserve, whichever is greater.

ADDENDUM D

VARIANCE FROM THE PERCENTAGES

The Court has the discretion to vary from the percentages if it finds that the non-custodial parent's pro-rata share of the basic child support obligation is unjust or inappropriate. This finding shall be based upon consideration of the following factors:

339

1. The financial resources of the custodial and non-custodial parent, and those of the child.
2. The physical and emotional health of the child and his/her special needs and aptitudes.
3. The standard of living the child would have enjoyed had the marriage or household not
   been dissolved.
4. The tax consequences to the parties
5. The non-monetary contributions that the parents will make toward the care and well-being of the child.
6. The educational needs of either parent.
7. A determination that the gross income of one parent is substantially less than the other parent's' gross income.
8. The needs of the children of the non-custodial parent for whom the non-custodial parent is providing support who are not subject to the instant action and who support has not been deducted from income, and the financial resource of any person obligated to support such children, provided, however, that this factor may apply only if the resources available to support such children are less than the resources available to support the children who are subject to the instant action.
9. Provided that the child is not on public assistance (i) extraordinary expenses incurred by the non-custodial parent in exercising visitation, or (ii) expenses incurred by the non-custodial parent in extended visitation provided that the custodial parent's expenses are   substantially reduced as a result thereof.

    1. Any other factors the Court determines are relevant in each case.

NOTE: The language in the above Addenda is paraphrased from that in the statute for the purposes of simplification. For statutory language, see Family Court Act Sections 413(1) and 424-a and Domestic Relations Law Sections 236-B and 240. Adapted . American Bar Association, Chicago, IL

If a partner is concealing something, as a wealthy woman hiding her true worth, then a court order or a subpoena ordering her bank to produce a statement and also an injunction can be issued forbidding any money to be taken from the account until the matter is settled in court. You may also directly question your spouse through court permission and have a court stenographer take it down. Her lawyer can be present. You will pay the bill. During the period before the divorce trial, you may want to get witnesses to support your claim as to your business, if one claims unjustly to be involved with it, or on custody where proper parenting is an issue. Getting information by wire tapping is legal under certain situations such as on your own phone if you do the installation, but in most cases—nine of ten—are settled out of court and most states provide leeway in their statutes so this is not needed. In some states there may be other matters required in similar cases.

Uncontested Divorces

The hearing in an uncontested divorce case is routine with your lawyer asking questions from the material stated in the petition to divorce such as:

In the course of your marriage, were you a true and faithful affectionate woman?

Yes (Plaintiff)

Has your husband severely mistreated you over the last three years and harassed you, calling you vile names in public?

Yes (Plaintiff)

Finally the lawyer (Plaintiff). If the judge should grant this divorce, do you request the terms of settlement be approved by this court and be made a part of this divorce decree?

Yes (Plaintiff)

If the divorce is contested, then it will be more complicated and drawn out. The evidence will have to be specific and verified. There will be cross-examination of the statements, the presented documents, and possibly witnesses of both parties by their respective lawyers. The judge may take a hand in the procedures questioning, clarifying, etc. When this is over and the judge signs the decree, in most states you are free and considered single. In some states, however, there is a required waiting period of a few days to several months (call the interlocutory period); during this period one is still married, then the person is free to remarry. A final decree then is given awarding the divorce and stating the manner in which the finances, custody, property, etc., are to be handled.

Handling Your Own Divorce

Deciding to do your own divorce can be a saver of money but is only recommended where the couple has been married only a few years, have no children and little money, property or assets to worry about. It is essential that both husband and wife agree on everything. If there is disagreement, then a court fight will probably ensue. In using the do-it-yourself divorce, you should use the kits or related books written for this purpose; the public library will have information on the state laws where you live. Also seek the advice of women's rights and men's rights groups. The forms for filing a petition and the summons form that are necessary can be bought at many stationery stores for about $30 (a kit). Books such as *How to File Your Own Divorce* (Edward Haman) provides information on how to file and the necessary forms. You can then fill in the blanks. Be sure to use forms accepted in your own state. They can be purchased at the Clerk of the Court's office. Remember, too, that on file in the courthouse are copies of documents filed by other couples, so ask the clerk of the court to direct you to them and the forms their venue requires. You will need most of these forms (1) divorce complaint, (2) answer and affidavit in support of judgment, (3) final decree or divorce judgment, (4) certificate of corroborating witness, (5) certificate of divorce or marriage dissolution, (6) marital settlement agreement, (7) financial settlement disclosure. Read a few as illustrations, then guided by the wording, do your own. Ask the clerk for help if you need it; at the least he or she can tell you whether or not you have filled it out satisfactorily. Another thing you can do is to visit the court to observe what happens in other divorces; knowing this aid in reducing your anxiety. In the court in the do-it-yourself kind, you take the part of the lawyer as outlined earlier, making your statements as clear and brief as possible. When it is over, that is, when you have finished making your presentation, your final question to the judge will be: "Your Honor, may I prepare the final decree?" If the judge says "Yes," you've won your divorce! You must then prepare the final decree using the forms supplied by the clerk in the manner agreed to by the court.

A Word of Caution

The Editors of Socrates say that if any of the following conditions exist in your marriage you should not file yourself at pro se (the legal term—without counsel):

1. One or the other has a tax problem,
2. You or your spouse has a pension plan,

3. You or your spouse has cosigned a debt for the other,
4. One or the other spouse has hired a lawyer,
5. You or your spouse has started proceedings,
6. You or your spouse are in the military,
7. You and your mate do not agree on child support, custody or spousal support.

Be certain money matters, property settlement, etc., are included, for it becomes the document of record. Usually several hundred dollars or more will pay for this kind of divorce. It will take time to do this, attention to detail, but it isn't too difficult and you check the final decree for accuracy for changes are sometimes made by the judge that may not find their way into the final document of divorce. A lawyer I know has this to say about "do-it-yourself" divorce. "This is like saying that a layman can lance a boil, by consulting a medical guide." But, there are subtle points that, if missed, can result in infection and gangrene, in the medical example. I'd rather go to a doctor! In divorces, beware of such issues as jurisdiction, venue, elements of proof, wording of petition and decrees, etc. You can find a lawyer who will handle an uncontested divorce for these amounts and then it's his responsibility. You're trying to avoid those high costs so purchase a kit and save.

Uncontested Divorce Issues	Cost Range
No children, few possessions	$200 - $5,000
No children, many possessions	$500 - $7,000
Children, many possessions	$1,000 - $10,000

If one can control their emotions and maintain a calm, objective demeanor, then surely there is an advantage to the do-your-own divorce. Advantages are: (1) You save the cost of a lawyer. (2) Judges often feel more sympathetic toward a person without an attorney and give a certain amount of leeway. (3) This procedure would normally speed up the divorce also cut down frustration in trying to reach your lawyer and get movement toward concluding the divorce. (4)

Selecting an attorney is not easy—many mistakes are made here. Getting a good attorney is a problem you don't need.

Children in Separation and Custody

Two out of every three divorces involve children. Up until recently in only about one in ten divorce cases was there a contest over custody; however, increasingly courts are awarding children, even young ones, to their fathers. It may not mean there will be more fights over custody, though there may be. Many experts in human development believe that young children (below 6 or 7) typically should remain with their mother. (There are exceptions depending upon the quality of the parenting.) Some boys after 6 or 7 could go with the fathers and other persons (aunt, grandparents); some girls after 8 or 9 wish to live with fathers. We find generally the middlescent (those between the early forties and upper sixties) father of forty or so is more nurturing oriented than one in his twenties or thirties and has been found in many cases to understanding parenting. Custody, nonetheless whatever disposition that is made, it is the most sensitive issue in the divorce settlement. Where parents agree on custody, the court usually concurs. If it is thought by the court that the parents are not capable of handling the situation, the custody of children is given to a foster family or grandparents. Of course, older children may be asked with whom they wish to live and occasionally agencies are asked to decide with specialists like psychologists, family specialists, social workers, etc., called upon to determine the best situation for the child. Many judges are not trained in the behavior sciences sufficiently nor have the time to investigate in order to make the decision alone and they need to seek some help in these matters. Most judges in the past have assumed that men should not (judging by the fact that in about 90% of the divorces women get custody) have the children.

Costs of a Custody Contest (Varies depending on your location)

Lawyers' fees	$200 - $500 per hour
Child evaluator or Child Representative fees	$75 - $350 per hour
Expert witness to test your children and report to the court	$100 - $400 per hour
Legal fee for service cost (copies, telephone calls, mailings, legal research, secretarial)	$50 - $350 per hour
Court costs	$200 - $500

Divorce by Socates Editors

Most states have joint custody laws based on the "best interests of the child" as sex neutral standard that allows the court to consider whatever it deems relevant. This does not mean joint physical custody, which usually amounts to liberal visitation rights. The joint legal custody awards give both parents the right to make decisions such as authorizing medical treatment of the child but not necessarily a split in living time between two parents.

Many men attempting to get custody often refuse to pay alimony often manage to prevail because their wives cannot afford to litigate the issue. Conversely women wanting custody sometimes give up alimony, some child support and/or property to get to keep the children. The men argue with their wives and sometimes get an agreement to have custody of the children by harassment—daily calls, threats of prolonging legal fights, discussions about the unfit nature of the mother, her future inability to maintain a decent life in a decent situation for the children are accustomed. These attempts usually fail, particularly in court adjudicated custody but in negotiated settlement they do somewhat better. Many men who struggle hard to get custody are attempting to punish their spouse, feeling this would affect them more than anything else.

In California (and some other states), the law makes mediation mandatory whenever custody is contested. Mediation in these cases is required before the judge hears the case. California has a joint custody preference and under their laws a judge can award custody to both when only one parent wants it or when neither parent wants it. The law puts the burden on the judge who does not order joint custody to justify in writing why he has not done so. The effect of this is to weaken or do away with the maternal presumption.

Dr. May Howell, a pediatrician and researcher at Harvard University, says that in her pediatric practice she cared for more than 3,000 children from about 1,000 families and there is a small but significant number of families in which the father was the effective primary caretaker. She goes on to say that from a study done with eighteen-month-old children, about equal proportions of toddlers are attached to their fathers only, as are attached to their mothers only, and that about two-thirds of them are attracted to both fathers and mothers. This probably is not typical and the number of subjects in the sample small. Of the two biological differences, breast feeding is of minor importance, and the rough and tumble style of the latter is usually modified to be more gentle. Consistent affection and acceptance of children is important, as is protection from hazards both physical and psychological. Clearly men can be good parents, like most women, if they give their energy and devotion to it. Most men however recognize that women should be the principal source of mothering for very young children (1-3) and they probably would be overwhelmed if suddenly given sole responsibility.

Sometimes custody changes in situations where the couple have other responsibilities which have to be considered in caring for children, such as new jobs requiring a change in location or the death of a parent or their sickness which demands consideration. Where the wife has received custody of the children but finds she has to help aging or sick parents, it frequently means giving up a child or children to the husband, and a former husband who is transferred across the country which may necessitate his former spouse keeping the child temporarily. Many cases where this is "temporary" it turns out to be permanent. The issue of custody is the most complex and difficult of all divorce cases requiring considerable time, effort and intelligence to reach a fair judgment and protect the client. Due to this the fees are high where children in families of considerable possessions. The cost can start at $10,000 and go as high as $30,000 or more. The cost depends on the state and county where the child caretaker lives.

Forcing the Issue of Custody

Some parents have used "child taking" as a method of getting custody. Sometimes cases, which are decided in two states, custody in one instance, will be given to the man and in another to the woman. All states have adopted the Uniform Child Custody Jurisdiction Act. The state whose courts have the most pertinent information have jurisdiction and will honor a decree initiated in another state but it will violate state law in these places if the child is taken.

The hiring of parents of a "Mean Gene" to get their child is nearly over. Mean Gene may have referenced Eugene Austin from Coley, Missouri, who had been employed by parents in over 500 cases where they have legal custody order or the custody matter is in dispute in the courts. Austin required that the parent accompany him in his theft, otherwise he would not do the kidnapping. About one-third of his clients were women. Others are in this business in nearly every state. Being taken (kidnapped), however, must be a traumatic experience for the child, particularly if the child has lived with the parent for any length of time. In some instances he would probably wish to live with the parent who arranged for him to be stolen. Any parent—man or woman—needs to consider seriously the effect upon the child before he takes him or her from the home of the other parent. One can conceive of an instance where it might be the wisest thing to do but I don't believe there will be many such situations. In any case The Parental Kidnapping Prevention Act of 1980 (P.L. 96-611) was passed designed to deter child snatching. when it occurs authorities can use the Federal Parent Locater to find those on child support. The Fugitive Felon Act will apply allowing a search for kidnapping parents. Suffice it to say today because of the Uniform Child Custody Act a parent cannot begin a custody determination de nova (all over again). They must return the case to and defer to the state of original jurisdiction. Many states also provide actual and punitive damages to be assessed against a parent who tries to circumvent a custody decree.

Alimony

The problem of money and alimony commonly called maintenance or spousal support is the second most important concern to custody with divorcing couples. A North Carolina man said all he was left with was some old clothes and the dogs. Alimony is a bad word for men—it still exists in some states but since no-fault divorce, alimony is being replaced by the term maintenance support for the spouse during and following dissolution proceedings. Increasingly women are paying maintenance to men because of greater earning ability, etc. However where alimony is awarded (twenty-eight states) the law states marital fault (as in adultery) is relevant. Desertion, abandonment of children, taking up with another man or woman, etc., will annul alimony in many cases. In the past several years alimony has been granted in only about 1 of 7 cases (15%). The longer the duration of the marriage the more certain you can be that the court will award support to the spouse that needs it. Maintenance or support is provided to the woman or man on the basis of custodial support, Transitional support (adjust to new life situation—work, housing, etc.) and the state of one's earning capacity. An additional element is new that is demanding attention as a financial consideration—sharing partnership assets. Helping the husband get through law school, supporting his career, etc. are the type of things to be considered. Most states have legislation requiring consideration of spousal contribution in professional degrees. In short, pardon the pun, marriages less than five years are infrequently awarded alimony.

Permanent alimony is given in only a small percent of the divorce cases. Where the wife is in her early years (35-45) or Boomer years (45-55), support money is awarded to help care for children which may continue until they are eighteen unless otherwise agreed upon, but that given to the wife if marriage was between 5 to 10 years but will usually be adjusted downward until she is able to get back into the work market. If she is already working, she may get no support for herself. Increasingly, when alimony is given to men, cash settlements are made to take care of joint ownership of property that went with the marriage, and because the woman made more than the man did in his job. Up until recently (it still exists in many states) alimony was given typically for a total of half the years of a marriage, so that a man who was married for twenty years gave alimony for ten years. Alimony in cases of marriages of twenty years and over is usually made permanent, especially when the spouse did not work outside the home and had become accustomed to a given lifestyle. Newer alimony approaches, like the one adopted in Florida, gives temporary support to the woman for the purpose of adjusting herself to work and possibly a new home setting. Alimony is usually based upon the money one makes and style of living one is accustomed to. If you make $80,000 a year the court will make provision for your wife and set support payments for children in accordance with your capacity to pay. A wife may waive the alimony if the thought of receiving it from him is abhorrent to her. If this is the case, brother you should get this into the separation agreement. If he gives her anything, however small, it opens the door to ask at a later time for more. Some states will not allow alimony if the husband gets a divorce on the basis of his wife's adultery. If there are other sources of income, as in dividing the marital property with the wife getting part of the property, a percent of the business profits, stocks and bonds, etc., she may then not get any support money for children or herself. Frequently the amount of money given as temporary, that is, until the court makes its final decision, becomes the permanent amount. The argument usually taken by the wife's attorney is, why not continue as permanent the money already given for the living conditions have not changed? Some men have fallen for this and their lawyers allowed it to go unquestioned, only to find shortly thereafter the wife goes to work, lives with her parents and needs no money excepting where there are children, may not even then.

The matter of alimony should not be taken lightly but examined carefully; for neither man nor woman should be the fall guy or gal. Support can change over the years. If the wife marries, she relinquishes the alimony and typically when children reach eighteen, support is no longer a legal obligation. But if the man remarries, it does not affect the money he has to pay unless his former spouse agrees to it. If the economic circumstances change, alimony and support payments are curtailed (when the court agrees to this upon the petition of one of the parties) entirely or in proportion to the reduced salary situation. Faced with installment payments for alimony, it would be well to consider a lump sum cash settlement (although many wives will not agree to this), for at least you know with a fixed sum what you will have to pay; the other could go on for years. If you agree to a lump sum settlement and your wife dies the day of the decree, you have to pay the estate. I do not subscribe to many of the ideas it presents but I read the book of Lawyer Maurice R. Franks entitled *How to Avoid Alimony* in which he says alimony is a form of slavery and violates the equal protection clause and due process clause of the Constitution. In essence his advice to men and supposedly to women also who are required to pay alimony is to file a petition with the federal, not state, courts claiming antidiscrimination clauses of the various civil rights acts as the basis for not complying. He used this approach in his second divorce, and though the Supreme Court has refused to hear the case, it is alleged he has paid no alimony. Many men cheat on their payments (now laws give the federal authorities the right to find the delinquent party); if oppressed, man or the woman should seek changes through the court. It occurs to me that a man whose wife has done a good job of caring for his children and has been a good wife for most of their life together, it certainly would not be right to just turn her out to pasture. We should not divorce our children just because custody is given to the wife, nor expect the housewife without having a job for a long period of time to make it quickly on her own. This is difficult to handle for most, but where fathers are involved I believe over the years children will certainly honor such a parent for helping the former wife and mother. Go to www.divorce. net for a reasoned source of information on alimony, visitation, child support state by state. Or, call the Help Line at 1-800-359-7004.

Child Support

The question of child support differs from alimony in that it is absolutely obligatory while alimony is not. The burden relative to small children falls on both parents though the man usually pays most of the bills, certainly if he is in his middlescent years. It is true that among the newly married or among those married for just a brief time, most of these current young people divorces are resolved on the basis of no-fault. Sometimes when mothers work they often receive more pay than their spouse, mothers therefore often have to provide child support. The responsibility rests fundamentally with each parent. Some men feel put upon because they are ordered to pay support and yet have difficulty in getting access to their children. I have known women under court order who do not let the father see the child or have visitation, even when it has been spelled out in the decree. I suppose they are fearful of the child leaving or being taken away. How do they avoid it, you ask, by using bonefied or otherwise excuses—the child has prior visitation with a grandparent or aunt or school trip or they are sick; to buttress this they will get collusion with a physician who will write that the child is upset or has the flu pre-empting visiting. Of course, this isn't fair, but this is war—total war!!

In the final analysis, the amount of support is based upon:

1. The needs of the child
2. The financial status & needs
3. The standard of living the child would have enjoyed had the marriage continued
4. The physical & emotional conditions of the child and his or her education needs
5. The financial resources and needs of the non-custodial parent.

In some states like Virginia the code sets out specifically how much each parent must contribute considering the income of both parties to child support, the older the children the greater the amount usually demanded. Though support allotment varies, in Illinois and some other places many judges use a rule of thumb that goes like this: For one child around 30% of the father's take-home pay, for two children 40%, for three 45%, and for four 50%. This is dependent on the economic status of the father. A man's salary of $20,000 is relieved of a higher percent than a man with an $80,000 salary. This does not include alimony. Fault is not supposed to enter into support allotments but in some cases does. Fathers are obligated to pay for a variety of "extras" but they are only legally obligated to pay for whatever is spelled out—like $400-800 per month and hospitalization are usually always included. Other things may be written in the legal obligation like summer camp, insurance, piano lessons, private schooling and/ or college education, dentist bills and braces, etc. When, however, the child becomes emancipated—marries, takes a full-time job or enters the Armed Forces, reaches his or her majority, or in the case of death, the support ceases. A few states—like Virginia require a court order stating the obligation is ended to discontinue the support. You should note that support, if you marry a person with a child, is included in a subsequent divorce settlement regardless of kinship. Though not in all states in a common law marriage—living together constitutes—a binding of interest occurs and sharing of property is sometimes judged mandatory when brought to the attention of the court. The term palimony developed out of a living together suit brought against Lee Marvin and since then many others. Taking care of children growing out of this long-term relationship is also the responsibility of both parties. Not all states recognize a common law marriage.

Court Ordered Support

All states have statutes that permit the court to order the payer of child support to assign wages or income from other sources to be made payable to a court official or directly to the person who has physical custody of the child or children.

Lenore Weitzman, an expert on divorce says in her book *The Divorce Revolution,* "no matter what his income level a divorced man is rarely ordered to part with more than one-third of his net income." This is not true today. She says that some judges set the ultimate limit of one-half of the net income. In practice usually less is given. Some judges emphasize that you shouldn't touch the goose that lays the golden egg, meaning you need to protect the father's motivation to earn. If he is overwhelmed by the burden of payment some men will quit and/or flee. Most men (80% according to a Michigan and Canadian study) when fully complying with a court ordered support will still live comfortably. More recent research indicates many less than 80% live comfortably. In recent days—several years ago—93% of the women if they lived on the support in California (probably true for most states) allotted to them by the court would be below the poverty level. This has changed due to studies like those done in Maryland in Montgomery County which revealed most women two years after divorce (no fault) were less well off than before. If a man makes or woman makes as much as $80,00 per year then most judges will award 35% of the total for five children ($28,000), for three about 25% and one less. Usually most married couples do not have enough income to live separate or apart.

A related problem to child support is inflation that has eroded the value of the dollar. The court rarely considers a built-in cost of living adjustment. Non-compliance is another issue. The U.S. Census Bureau in a study conducted several years ago found less than half received the support ordered by the court, one-third received partial payments and the other third received nothing. Compliance with alimony awards is said to be improving according to Weitzman, probably, she says because alimony tends to be awarded only in higher-income families but also tracking systems are catching the non-compliance offenders. As of 1985 thirty states gave judges the discretionary power to have child support payments made directly to the court. Most states allow 60 to 90 days grace before attaching the salaries of men or women in the arrears with support payments. Some men send the payments just before the deadline as a harassment tactic. Many women get discouraged or are caught in a Catch 22 situation by the problems of bringing charges because they do not have the funds to pursue the man failing to pay. They often make only one or two attempts to force payment before they quit trying. Others fail to file a complaint at all. A college librarian was an example of this. Her husband worked in the same college. Her first attempt was thwarted in bringing results. She was embarrassed by it and upset over the cost and never attempted to get the money due her even though she and her former husband worked on the same campus.

Property Division and Money Matters

As we have discussed earlier, payment for child allotment and alimony are considered support payments. Property allocation relates to the distribution of everything a wife and husband owns. This matter is settled after one has filed for divorce or separation and before either has been decided by the court. The period between filing and the final settlement is a difficult one, for in anger one or both parties can use the personal possessions of the other or jointly held items, credit, destroy gifts, misuse equipment, take important papers and treasured items. One can suffer severe loss of credit rating in a brief time during this period. It is wise for a person to get an injunction (through your lawyer), if there is uncertainty as to what the spouse will attempt to do, from the court forbidding withdrawal from checking accounts, savings and loan, etc. All joint credit cards should be collected and one should write to the companies involved requesting issuance of new individual cards—that is, one for you. If a couple can trust each other, they could go down to the bank, draw out the savings and checking account funds and divide them on the spot.

Property comes in two categories—real and personal. Land and buildings are real property; everything else is personal property—furnishings, cars, money, sporting goods, jewelry, etc. Most of the problems over property come from decisions about the home, the car, furniture, and monies. Not all persons concerned have homes and real estate, and this reduces the friction between the parties making a settlement. The individual usually keeps the property brought into a marriage, other things are divided; if you are in a "community property" state (Arizona, California, Idaho, Louisiana, Nevada, New Mexico, Texas, Washington and Wisconsin) the things you both accrued together are community property except gifts or inheritance. The other forty-two states have equitable distribution of marital property provisions.

No-Fault Law Revisited

The law in California instructs the court to divide the community assets and liabilities equally. This action has influenced other states. Equitable division does not mean 50-50 in these states. Lack of certainty in property division makes for more litigation and unfortunately also results in the court order for homes to be sold. Mothers with children or men with children are displaced often with traumatic results. Settlements in California under no-fault (1977) and fault (1978) find men getting higher awards in the division of assets as follows: the single family car, family business, and community property debts. Women receive the majority of assets that deal with family having household furnishings and money, stocks, and bonds. Most of the states have laws decreeing that the distribution of real property be as the "courts deem just and reasonable." However, in a community property state that recognizes fault, the supposition of equitable distribution bends to often favor the "innocent" party. In a number of states, property is considered as alimony. If the wife, for instance, suffers due to this, the court might award larger amounts of alimony to compensate for this loss. There are a few states that give only a third of the real property to the wife and considering the circumstances (if they are at fault) less than his or none. Dower's rights (that portion or interest in the real estate of a deceased husband which the law gives for life to his widow) are barred by divorce in many states, though the property of each is not affected. State laws change so check in your state for the latest.

Many authorities suggest in divorcing that you stay in your home if you can. It looks better for the person who maintains the house. Most judges thinking the home is most valuable to the women therefore tend to award it to them. If one gets the home, then this should usually be offset by concessions on the other side. In one case, a San Francisco woman agreed to allow her husband to sell the home as part of the settlement. He sold the home to a friend and gave the wife her share of the equity. He then bought the home back at the same price which, in effect, amounted to a swindle, for the home was worth much more. Do not use this approach, and it should be mentioned that wives have used this one also. This is usually avoided because of the great suspicion that one partner has of the other, a lawyer's advice and the determination supported by the advice of friends and relatives "don't get burned" and "stick it to them." Usually an agreement is made on an appraiser or one is assigned by a judge to place a value on the home, it is then advertised and sold with the money divided; but if the home is not sold, whoever keeps the home usually gives half of the equity to the former spouse or some consideration.

It may be cheaper for a man to let his wife live in the home if there are a large number of children and a small mortgage payment, then to pay the extra support needed to give them another place to live. A man also might give the house to his wife until she remarries and in some cases agreement may be reached on mortgage payments and the upkeep. This condition exists where the man can control the home disposition.

Nearly half of the states require conversion of a few insurance policies upon divorce and it would have relevance in most of the other states if presented with the argument over property (assets). Insurance is considered by most people as a career asset and refers to benefits a worker receives in the form of health, accident, and life insurance. This is sometimes called "new property and realistically should be considered for division upon divorce. It is overlooked or put aside obviously when many women according to the Older Women's League has called women without health insurance the "no-woman's land between menopause and Medicare." There were four million women in this category several years ago. There may be more now.

Some men think that wives should have everything in view of the fact that they stayed at home, raised the children, and provided for their comfort. They deserve consideration but should not have everything. Some men also think they can hide their worth by putting the family business or their savings in another person's name. Most women often have a fair idea of what their husbands are worth and the reverse is also true. Anyway this usually comes out and it's not worthwhile to lie and risk the charge of perjury; although this advice will fall on some deaf ears, it is still good advice.

Unfortunately when a couple with children divorce, it is probably that the man will become single but the woman will become a single parent. Poverty for many women begins with single parenthood. More than half of the poor families in the United States are headed by a single mother after divorce (NY Times World Almanac 2010). Men go on in their occupations with their careers expanding and their salaries growing. The courts have generally treated men via the "golden egg syndrome" benignly. Some changes are being effected via insurance divisions, share in building a career or business, spousal contributions to professional degrees, pensions, but much more needs to be done for the newly poor.

Debts are often an area of controversy, particularly among younger middlescents for they have obligations many times beyond the divorcing middle age couple of 50 and upward, for these usually have unpaid mortgages, car payments, the second home, a boat and trailer, college education, operations, dental work and even clothing—furs, etc. A man in most cases is not required to assume the entire responsibility in absolving the debt both incurred. If a man pays the debts, the woman should expect less from the equity in property—real and personal—like automobiles. If a woman pays the lion's share of the debt, she should be accorded reciprocity. An agreement among the parties concerning the property is usually more satisfactory than having the court do it for you. The things you each wish should be written down as memorandum, reviewed by the attorneys, agreed upon and carried out fairly. I know of a man who continued to have his daughter go into his former wife's home to purloin certain items, even though an extensive list of items was drawn up in advance and an agreement made. The battle for property, changes in alimony and support go on after the divorce is final, hence discretion is constantly advised. Albert Teich, Attorney Law Consultant, 2008, Norfolk, VA.

DIVORCE STATUTES—SPOUSAL SUPPORT FACTORS

JURISDICTION	FACTORS CONSIDERED
Alabama	Standard of living; marital fault relevant
Alaska	Statutory list; standard of living; marital fault not considered
Arizona	Statutory list; standard of living; status as custodial parent; marital fault not considered
Arkansas	Marital fault not considered

357

California	Statutory list; standard of living; marital fault not considered
Colorado	Statutory list; standard of living; status as custodial parent; marital fault not considered
Connecticut	Statutory list; standard of living; status as custodial parent; marital fault relevant
Delaware	Statutory list; standard of living; status as custodial parent; marital fault not considered
District of Columbia	Standard of living; marital fault relevant
Florida	Statutory list; standard of living; length of marriage
Georgia	Statutory list; standard of living; marital fault relevant
Hawaii	Statutory list; standard of living; status as custodial parent; marital fault not considered
Idaho	Statutory list; marital fault relevant
Illinois	Statutory list; standard of living; status as custodial parent; marital fault not considered
Indiana	Statutory list; standard of living; status as custodial parent; marital fault not considered
Iowa	Statutory list; standard of living; status as custodial parent; marital fault not considered
Kansas	Marital fault not considered
Kentucky	Statutory list; standard of living; marital fault relevant
Louisiana	Statutory list; status as custodial parent; marital fault relevant
Maine	Statutory list; marital fault not considered
Maryland	Statutory list; standard of living; marital fault relevant
Massachusetts	Statutory list; standard of living; marital fault relevant
Michigan	Standard of living; marital fault relevant
Minnesota	Statutory list; standard of living; status as custodial parent; marital fault not considered
Mississippi	Marital fault relevant

Missouri	Statutory list; standard of living; status as custodial parent; marital fault relevant
Montana	Statutory list; standard of living; status as custodial parent; marital fault not considered
Nebraska	Statutory list; standard of living; status as custodial parent; marital fault not considered
Nevada	Standard of living; status as custodial parent; marital fault relevant
New Hampshire	Statutory list; standard of living; status as custodial parent; marital fault relevant
New Jersey	Marital Property
New Mexico	Statutory list; standard of living; marital fault not considered
New York	Statutory list; standard of living; marital fault not considered
North Carolina	Statutory list; standard of living; marital fault relevant
North Dakota	Standard of living; marital fault relevant
Ohio	Statutory list; marital fault not considered
Oklahoma	Standard of living; status as custodial parent; marital fault not considered
Oregon	Statutory list; standard of living; status as custodial parent; marital fault not considered
Pennsylvania	Statutory list; standard of living; marital fault relevant
Rhode Island	Statutory list; standard of living; status as custodial parent; marital fault relevant
South Carolina	Statutory list; standard of living; status as custodial parent; marital fault relevant
South Dakota	Standard of living; marital fault relevant
Tennessee	Statutory list; standard of living; status as custodial parent; marital fault relevant
Texas	Statutory list; standard of living; status as custodial parent; marital fault relevant
Utah	Statutory list; standard of living; marital fault relevant

Vermont	Statutory list; standard of living; status as custodial parent; marital fault not considered
Virginia	Statutory list; standard of living; marital fault relevant
Washington	Statutory list; standard of living; marital fault not considered
West Virginia	Statutory list; status as custodial parent; marital fault relevant
Wisconsin	Statutory list; standard of living; status as custodial parent

NOTE: State laws are subject to change. Check with your local authorities for the latest updates. Adapted from the American Bar Association Family Law section.

Tax Planning in Divorce and Separation

A good start with the issue of tax in divorce is to secure and read the IRS Publication 504 (2010) Information for Divorced or Separated Individuals free at any IRS Office. Community property defined is found in Publication 555. A variety of teletax tapes on Divorce are available by calling 800-829-4477; punch 701 for information on Alimony. The principal questions as it relates to divorce and tax are alimony, custody and exemptions and the cost of getting a divorce. Alimony payments are tax deductible, the persons receiving alimony must list it as income. The person giving the alimony has to supply the recipient's Social Security number on their tax return.

A payment to a spouse under a separate or divorce instrument is alimony only if the spouse does not file a joint return. In addition, according to IRS Publication 504 (2009) the following requirements must be met.

- The payment is paid in cash (money order, cashier's check, check, etc.).
- The instrument does not designate the payment as not alimony.
- The spouses are not members of the same household at the time the payments are made. The requirement applies only if the spouses are legally separated under a decree of divorce or separate maintenance.

- This is no liability to make any payment (in cash or property) after the death of the recipient spouse.
- The payment is not treated as child support.

Under the Tax Reform Act of 1986, the parties to dissolution of marriage filing separate should file alike, that is both itemize or take the standard deductions. A caution here, filing separately may not only cause you to lose several tax benefits but may potentially demand more tax payments than if you had filed together. Some examples of the limitations placed are listed below.

    a. If one spouse itemizes then the other spouse must do so as well.

    b. You cannot claim either the earned income credit or the credit for child and dependent care expenses.

    c. No deduction is permitted for interest paid on qualified education loans.

    d. Only $1500 of excess capital losses can be claimed.

Also, you may have to include one half of any social security benefits. As for children support, the support of children is allowed if over half of the total year's expenses are paid by you.

Typically, exemptions are allowed to one parent with custody or if both parents are given care responsibilities a trade-off is arranged. This arrangement should either be part of the final judgment or settlement agreement incorporated into the final judgment by reference. If considerable alimony is given often, the payer is given the exemption whether or not he or she has custody. Exemptions to one part or the other is only allowable to legally separated or divorced persons.

Large alimony payments (Front-loaded Payments) have been limited as deductions; for instance it worked like this if a first post-separation year payment of $25,000 is made and the 2nd and 3rd years is of $4,000 each an average of these years is $4,000. This is subtracted from the $25,000 which was paid the first year leaving $21,000. The recapture rule requires subtractions of $15,000 from this $21,000 leaving $6,000. This is to be added to the payees' tax the third year. This amount can be deducted by the receiver of the alimony via the recapture rule stated above. Under the recapture rule, payments made in the second post-separation year (defined below) will be recaptured if the payments made in their post-separation year by more than $15,000. Payments regularly made in the first post-separation year will be recaptured if those payments exceed the average of the alimony or separate maintenance payments made in the second post-separation year (not including the payments recaptured as described above) and the post-separation year by more than $15,000. The excess amounts for both the first and second post-separation years will be recaptured only in the third post-separation year.

Special rules apply to post 1986 agreements concerning front-loading. As a deterrent against property settlement being disguised as alimony, special rules apply to payments in the first or second year exceeding $15,000. Any payments that are received in excess of $15,000 (the statutory limits), then an alimony recapture results to the extent of the excess alimony payments. In the third year, the payer must include in his or her gross income the excess alimony payments made in the first and second year. The recapture formula is presented below and is a guide for a taxpayer to ascertain any potential alimony recapture.

$$R = D + E$$

$$D = B - (C + \$15,000)$$

$$E = A - ((B - D + C/2) + \$15,000)$$

R = Amount recaptured in Year 3 tax return

D = Recapture from year 2

E = Recapture from year 1

A, B, C = Payments in the first (A), second (B), and third (C) calendar years of the agreement or decree, where $D \geq 0$, $E \geq 0$

You cannot deduct legal fees and court costs for getting a divorce however, you may be able to deduct legal fees paid for tax advice in connection with a divorce and legal fees to get alimony. Such fees incurred for tax advice that may be deductible include the following; Federal, state and local taxes of all types, including income, estate, gift, inheritance, and property tax. In addition, you may also be able to deduct fees that were paid to appraisers, actuaries, and accountants for services in ascertaining your correct tax or in helping the taxpayer pursue alimony. Ray Friedman, Tax Consultant, Tampa, FL (2008).

If you itemize the allowable deductions mentioned beforehand then you can claim them on Schedule A (Form 1040) as a miscellaneous deduction which is subject to the 2% of adjusted Gross Income. It should be noted that the spouse who receives custody over the children following the divorce can claim as head of household. In doing so, the tax liability for tax payers in this scenario falls between the joint and single return tax rate schedule.

For the taxpayer to qualify as head of household they must meet the following requirements:

- The taxpayer must pay more than half the cost of maintaining a household as his or her home.
- The household must also be the principal home of the dependent.
- A dependent must satisfy either the qualifying child or the qualifying relative criteria. (Willis, Hoffman, Malloney & Raabe, West Federal Taxation, 2008)

Along with head of household tax benefits, the custodial parent with custody of the children may claim a child tax credit. According to IRS Publication 972 (2009), a taxpayer can qualify for the tax credit if their child or children are; under age 17, a U.S. citizen, did not provide over half of his or her own support, lived with you for more than half of the year, and is claimed as a dependent or dependents on the taxpayer's return. Presently, for taxpayers that qualify, the maximum credit available for each child is up to $1000. This available credit is phased out for higher income taxpayers beginning with an adjusted gross income of $55,000 for married taxpayers who file separately and $75,000 for single taxpayers. The credit is eventually phased out by $50 for each $1000 of Adjusted Gross income above and beyond the threshold amounts.

What we have been trying to point out is that despite the anguish and difficulty because of the divorce (some have lost or never had the emotional aspect), you must try to effect some judgment. By way of summary, realize that in most divorces something is different, therefore you must be diligent to check everything you can under the following lists. Write them out even if you have a lawyer; he is often in a hurry and will forget items that later become important.

1. List Your Personal Information and all your assets along with information of the marriage—length, problems in, date of, location of, and children.
2. Items under your support, expectations for support, how to be given, does it include automatic increases for cost of living raise, benefits at spouse's death, etc.
3. Real and Personal Property—what do I have and want, make an inventory list, what debts exist on the house, the car(s), for education? What property is deeded to me, what are my belongings, how will a division be made, discover every obligation and write it down. Are there liens on anything, your house and/or business?
4. Life Insurance and Medical Policies—what provisions for medical care for children or yourself. What disposition is to be made of policies, who can borrow on them, who pays the premiums, etc.
5. Child Support, Custody and Visitation—who will have custody of the children, who makes the decisions about education of the children, what about visitation, who arbitrates in case of a dispute, is notice to be provided when a child is sick or hospitalized: How much contribution is to be made for each child by each parent? Who pays for special things: Camps, music lessons, band instruments, etc., and insurance to cover in the event of the father's or mother's death, college attendance or professional training. Those that give child support cannot claim it or those receiving it.
6. Obligations, Taxes and Debts—how much does each party owe, how is the indebtedness to be treated? Is there any litigation involved with a business, etc.? What monies

can be saved through special features like giving money for alimony rather than specifically for child support? Do you file jointly for any year before the divorce is finalized or the year of the final decree: Are there other considerations?

7. Wills, Fees and Other Matters—does a will require modification, probably in most cases, is each part waiving their claims on the other's estate? What obligations for the husband to leave children and/or wife certain sums of money or property? In joint enterprises who acts for the children? Who pays for the attorney's fees, what about title searches, audits, appraisals, how can the billing aid in payment of taxes? How to arbitrate when agreements can't be reached: Is the separation agreement to be made part of the decree or independent of the decree? Where protection is desired, do you draw up a memorandum of separation permitted in some states listing obligations and settlement of property. Filing separately keeps this from being universal knowledge.

The matter of a divorce as indicated is complex and cannot be done without some trouble and attention to detail. We have not covered all the contingencies here; one should secure help and read some of the references we mentioned earlier. We should have mentioned cost of attorneys and fees. This is a recognized hazard due to inflation, which, for the years after this, add 10% for advancing cost. These figures ranging from low (usually in small towns and rural settings) to higher (usually found in large cities) and are typical divorce costs. Remember you cannot deduct legal fees and court costs legal fees on your taxes.

Filing Fees—$100-$300 paid when the petition is submitted.

Summons Fee—Around $15 but in some locations double this amount, plus mileage for serving the papers by a deputy in a Sheriff's office. Fee is $5 by some Sheriff's offices.

Court Reporter—$100-$125 (half or day hearing) per hour of court time, or $10 to $15 per page. Court may pay for the reporter.

Depositions—$300-$800 plus expenses if your lawyer has to go out of town for these "proofs," or $25 to $50 per page per deposition in some states.

Copy of the Final Decree--$100-$260; none for self-filing divorcing procedures.

If you appeal to an appellate court, the transcriptions of your case could cost four to five hundred dollars plus other costs incidental to an appeal. The cost of an attorney will vary widely, for those new in the profession much less will be charged, in the typical small town or city, $250 to $300 for uncontested divorces. Older and more experienced lawyers will charge $3,000 to $5,000 for the non-contested cases. The fee in contested circumstances involving custody fights and money issues could go as high as $25,000, and for the very rich, much more, though even these kinds in the typical city and town under 100,000 population range from $2,000 to $5,000. On an hourly basis some lawyers will agree to $50-$70 an hour in a rural area to $500-$1,000 for a high class New York lawyer. The usual cost will be something in the order of $50 to $100 an hour. Whether you get an attorney by the hour or the case, be sure you get the arrangement in written form and an understanding what constitutes time. Remember most lawyers are willing to work out arrangements for payment over a period of time if needed. This also is an avenue for some but one should know the lawyer or have good recommendations that he or she has integrity and is competent.

Our life will suffer because of divorce in most cases. Where people are removing shackles—they are now free to go to a possible new love, they have been mismatched or terribly treated, then divorce is a jubilee time! For most of us who felt unsure, guilty, inadequate and a pervasive sense of loss, it is a tragedy! Recognized, noted and absorbed, but it is not the end of life. If we learn lessons from divorce, it provides "open sesame" to a new life, a time for personal growth and increased self-awareness. Although the upheaval is great and for many traumatic.

If you cannot afford legal advice, you can go to the Legal Aid Society in your locality, which can be found in the telephone book. You will have to submit a detailed report on your financial status. If you qualify you will be assigned a lawyer; usually a neophyte who may not do as well as a lawyer having practiced a number of years. If you have questions but no office number to contact, call the county or state bar association and they will direct you to a source or provide information themselves. Take our advice if you get to the point of marrying again and have a pre-nuptial agreement. It provides trust for both partners. If living together a co-habitation agreement should be made to protect your rights and your money.

Norman Levy, noted New York Psychiatrist says, "those who have grown through their personal experience, tragedies, and pain find it gives them a new dimension as well as appreciation and understanding." We learn from our shortcomings. We learn what the needs of others are and to more effectively meet them. And we may learn the fragile nature of being human where the give and take in relationships is required to make them work out.

Take time to look back to the chapter on Love, Sex and Marriage, for if you marry again, many second marriages are better than the first; we find more complementary mates and have the maturity to make it succeed. Happy hunting!

CHAPTER NINE

THE GOOD LIFE

"The best is yet to come"

"Youth is a silly vapid state:
Old Age with fears and ills is rife.
The simple boon I beg of fate-
A thousand years of middle life."-

-Carolyn Wells

This expresses what some people know about middle age. The word "middle age" may have bad connotations—fatigue, discontent and boredom. But as Hervey Allen in *Anthony Adverse* says, "Grow up as soon as you can." It pays. The only time you really live is from 30 to 60. The young are slaves of dreams; the old, servants of regrets. Only the middle-aged have all their five senses in the keeping of their wits. This is a distortion of the other ages in life but it bespeaks a fundamental truth. The Boomer is not troubled by the impetuosity of youth, which pulls it madly into life-traps; they are stronger than the old and wiser than the young. The boomer usually has enough perspective to keep from being led astray by the shallow and glamorous and to search for the true and most valuable. He or she has time to assess his errors of the past, to adjust his sights and to fulfill the opportunities, which lie ahead.

There is a special synthesis in the Boomer found nowhere else in the stages of man's life. This period is one of maturity—neither green nor overripe. Here the experiences of life are welded together in sensible understandable patterns, from which meaning is drawn from life. In the earlier part of adult life, the preoccupation with immediate pleasure and demands has been tempered and the Boomer evaluates life in terms of what is worthy rather than what is worth. If middle age were reckless as the twenties or early thirties, we would change panaceas for solving social and economic ills so frequently we would bring chaos to our lives. On the other hand, if the Boomer years were caught in the framework of regression to memory like many of our old, society wouldn't move at all. Aside from these broad platitudes, what constitutes the "good life"? There are some assumptions that this is based upon. What are they? They are; that one possess reasonably good health, both physical and mental, have enough financial resources to sustain one's life with a modicum of adequacy. Without these, the freedom to be one's self and to be creative is clearly limited. Without money enough to survive and/ or to be physically ill, a person may have a positive outlook, but still it would be stretching the definition of "good life" to say they were the same.

To talk about the "Good Life" may seem to be unlikely in the nation's life today. The possibility of tranquility and normality that allows people to go about their lives as usual at the present time and the near future is gone. The terrorist attacks have changed our ways of living by disrupting transportation, our work lives, our mental health as we develop paranoid postures, ever watchful for impending doom and cues that puts fear that some plague is upon us or is impending like Damocles Sword hanging tentatively above our heads. On the other hand in a way greater than ever before the freedom we have, the open horizon for growth and opportunity to make our place in our land is now more precious, less taken for granted and it gives us courage to overcome whatever circumstances we find ourselves confronted, be it disease, sacrifice of luxury, greatly reduced standards of living with a poorer standard of living and disruption of our society. Increasingly the aspects of the good life that I speak of will be more important than ever—the common enemy will make us feel closer to our neighbors and each other, force us to recognize the importance of work, to burgeon out all we can make of ourselves, the commitment to a cause far beyond the mundane world that is our usual purview and the need love plays in our lives. Love which expressed itself from our earlier national days—first for freedom, then equality, then to provide for the poor, and the blind—allowing the kind of environment that guarantees in our great country the right to express love as individuals and as a group to defy the enemies of our motherland.

Sure there are problems in the in-between years—the "change of life," but many have denied the myths surrounding it by projecting increased confidence in their sexuality and maintaining their appearance, in looking their best and at the same time being mature. Increasingly the boomer looks after his body, keeping trim, exercising, proscribing the overindulgence in smoking, drinking and use of drugs, all of this denial helps to give a vitality to enjoy life. It is true that many middle-aged persons are afflicted with some chronic health problem, but they have found a way to stabilize it. The problem of diabetes or a heart problem can be a blessing in disguise in that one is saved from the brink and having done this can reconstruct their lives in more healthy productive ways. Having been able to manage one's life and have good health means that the anxieties, depressions and emotional upsets of the middle years will finally be rewarded with tranquility and equanimity. The notion that we are failures with our partners, our children and careers takes on new perspectives. When we have muddled through, we arrive at a maturity level we might have thought impossible. Though we are divorced, our children have left the nest or are getting ready to leave and we are shakily beginning a new career and/or marriage; we are hopeful and not without resources. Father Time does not have us in a bind, for now we are free from the "nattering nabobs of negativism"—that there is no time. At 35, 45, even 55, we can do something worthwhile in our lives—plan an adequate retirement, remarry, have a new career and change our life styles. The frantic drive for success no longer plagues us; we know we have time to do our own thing! And though we mourn the loss of our past selves—as the best looking woman in the room, the club Tennis Champion, when we were slim and trim and had fewer aches and pains we understand the illusion of our childhood, the destructive form of our urgency (Id.). We are at peace now more than ever. The good life beckons. Duke University Longitudinal Studies shown life satisfaction to be the best in middle age peaking at 55. Though it drops somewhat from then until 65 it rises from then into the seventies according to their sample.

There are those like F. Scott Fitzgerald who declared: "There are no second acts in American lives." Maybe he was right, in a sense that we can't recreate our lives—be young again, have energy to spare, look like we did twenty years ago and attract men or women physically like we did at an earlier time. If we have been sensationally successful like Fitzgerald was following the publication of the novel *Tender Is the Night* perhaps we have no second act. But he was wrong too, in a sense, for millions of Americans or Europeans are beginning second acts in the middle years with verve and purpose. The good life begins and finds its basis in the first act and what happens in the second act depends on the first. The same with the third act. Dr. Taylor Morgan in his book of yesteryear, *Welcome to the Middle Years*, suggests that those who have had good first acts in their lives can expect to have some special gifts which come by being favored by the gods in their middle years. These are the things we get as payoff for our past investments in giving effort and by persevering. Morgan lists:

1. Seasoned maturity. It comes from having succeeded in one's job, you've gained an expertise on the job so now you can enjoy it.
2. Personal Respect. This goes hand in hand with maturity; you are recognized for knowing your field, or it is said of her, "she's tops in her field," others seek your counsel.
3. Tranquility at Home. All our wives bad habits have been corrected along with ours; we have learned to live together. The period of adjustment is over, we can relax and be at peace with our spouses and others.
4. Financial Security. The saving and hard work we've done begins to pay off. The fruit of our labor bears a good harvest. We can burn the mortgage at some time

during this period and have additional money to invest for
retirement or to spend on ourselves.

5. Creature Comforts. With the children gone and home
    ownership finalized an additional room—club or
    den—can be added; we can take a trip—California,
    Hawaii or Europe, or add some luxury item you want.

6. Personal Freedom. As boomers we are no longer troubled
    with feverish search for a career as the young adult is; in
    many cases our time is our own as we can adjust it to suit
    our needs. We have time to follow what beckons in new
    horizons.

You say this is not hardly the expectation of the younger boomer?
True, and it is more likely to be reserved to those in their late fifties
and sixties, which is precisely those Morgan is writing about. But
they do apply, even to the person in their late forties. The thing that
is important here is that it is possible to construct a better life and to
have the "good life" even before all the ultimate rewards are obtained
like those from earlier investments and when the children are grown
up allowing for more time and less responsibility.

The "good life" has many definitions or synonyms, depending
upon whom you ask about it. For many one word—money or leisure
or fame, health, love, power or sex—characterizes the "good life."
The "good life" is much broader than those isolated aspects of life
and it is greater in its impact than a single-handed one could ever
be. Adults in our time are driven to be "self actualized"—that is, to
reach their ultimate potential. They seek kinetic happiness constantly
agitating for change to achieve it. Increasingly, men and women are
recognizing that adult life is not a stagnation or a plodding passage
across an endless plateau but a matter of negotiation with ourselves,
with our families, our work, spouses and friends. We also know that
life consists of many ups and downs and the changing of direction.
In most cases there is a consensus that adult development embraces,
in the young adult period, the getting of a job and marrying. About
thirty, for men, maybe earlier for women, a period of discontent and
self-analysis begins which sometimes heralds divorce or a first time
marriage and change of careers. Following this comes a period of
"settling down." This phase usually ends by the time one is forty

(man) or earlier for women with a stage in which they become one's "own man." During the forties and fifties changes occur which lead to greater fulfillment in the lives of many; for some, women for instance, will enter the labor market for the first time, divorce and find new men. Many men will marry for the second time and some will begin a new work life. Both men and women will usually enter after 65, into a period of transition—the young-old 65-75 (Bernice Neugarten's category) later adulthood after 75. If you look at a number of people in the middle years (39-69), you will find a variety of differences. They are different in looks and health, the state of their mind, the family life, their work life and expectantly their views about life, certainly of what is "good" and important in life. So you undoubtedly find different emphasis on what constitutes the "good life."

THE GOOD LIFE

I believe the "good life" consists of an amalgam of work, play, love, and a commitment to a cause or worship. Although adults with varying backgrounds will give these different weights, for it seems obvious that our value systems were built from those of our parents and though they are modified, still remain much the same and reflect their views about the ideal life. That the "good life" consists of a balance between work, play, love and a cause seems deceptively simple. They do not of themselves bring happiness. I think happiness is a by-product of leading effective and ordered lives that are infused with the liking for work—the need to do it; to enjoy play—to be creative in it; to love—someone and others as much as we love ourselves; and to dedicate ourselves to a cause—commitment to something higher and beyond ourselves. You do not aim directly at being happy for it grows out of a number of things but not the satisfaction of something specific such as having money. You think that will solve all your problems. Errant nonsense, it might well be the beginning of them! On the other hand, even the presence of work, play, love and a cause cannot insure we will reach the Elysian Field where the sirens will provide a soothing of our problems and a fulfillment of all our wishes. There is a structure upon which this mix is based. This, we should note, resolves upon our parents—their (our) value systems, life styles and commitment to work, play, love and a cause, all of which have to some degree we internalized from them. All of our prospects for the "good life" come from them initially. Even the negative helps us to see a better life.

WORK

In the case of work, which is the first necessary ingredient of the good life, there are two aspects: (1) the method in which we handle our obligations (work) to family and children, and (2) the attention and effectiveness we give to our jobs, our professions and occupations. On the first point, you may object to my calling family obligation work (it may not be for many men and some women) but it is not just a matter of love, or loving to do it—keeping house, washing clothes, disciplining, waiting and worrying—it's routine and sheer hard, sacrificing work and devotion to duty.

As parents the important responsibility most of us will ever undertake is the rearing of our children. Fathers and mothers have to be dedicated to the task of homemakers. A successful home is the early schooling for love. Children need to be loved from infancy through their growing years, for how else can they learn to love others and become happy adults. But love is not enough, for children need discipline if they are to develop as competent adults. Discipline is love in action! Those parents who do not persevere in rearing their children are leaving them free to develop on their own, letting other children and youth shape their views and habits or the media, principally television and the movies, do the job of rearing your children.

Requirements of a work or chore routine for children is appropriate in teaching that value is that which is worth saving for, working for, sacrificing for. It brings enjoyment in exactly the terms of energy expended. Even the development of security depends in children on guidelines laid down by parents—that limits are set on their activities in which they receive commendation and out of which they receive censure.

The work involved in family obligation is not simply dealing with the routine responsibilities of children and housework but dealing with the principals of the home—mother and father. In this one doesn't have to be routine, for that smacks of work in the most derogatory way, but consistent attention should be given to the other, in recognition of special events, their particular needs, and their value. A pleasurable kind of work, enjoyed but constant and effective. The same sort of thing should be given to our larger families and kin, for they too are a part of our lives usually in increasing proportions. Maintaining good relations with our friends and neighbors is also of great importance. When we work at this task at the lowest level, we will find we touch everything higher up in our regard.

The jobs we hold and the service we give through them are of signal importance because they serve our economic needs in purchasing the necessities of life. Beyond this, the satisfactory work life is the hub virtually of our entire lives. The most successful people obviously are busy people, the most happy appear to be busy people—in short people who are busy, work and usually they work very hard. John Gardner says the best kept secret in America today is that people would rather work hard for something they believe in than enjoy a pampered idleness. Other satisfactions relate to and certainly the good life hinges upon the work life! For without the work world, there could be no effective play. Play is the offset from the routine, it gives relief from the tiring physical exertion and debilitating mental strain which often accompanies our work, it also allows us to unwind, it reduces the ennui that has set in and prepares us to enjoy recreation and leisure. This may be worked at as much as our occupations and professions, but it renews the spirits, settles the nerves and gives us strength to continue our work. Our work when it is done well has predictable fall-out allowing a plus to living and improving our lives contravening the old cliché "when poverty comes in the door love flies out the window." It provides the feeling of security, relaxation and worthiness through giving a plus to 'just getting by.'

According to William Shannon writing in *New York Times* magazine, "Work in the best sense is an expression of a person's intellectual powers, artistic sensibility or physical strength or personality. If one's work does not provide any kind of distinctive outlet, though Voltaire said it saves us from three great evils: boredom, vice and need, it may still provide the psychic rewards of being a member of a group with its own élan and cohesiveness." Those organizations that implement these outlets and rewards like family, schools, communities, recreation programs and churches are allies in building the "good life" for the future.

PLAY

In the chapter on "Leisure and Recreation" I devoted a section on how to get started with play. It sounds foolish to suggest that adults do not know how to play. But one should not confuse "playing around," "doing nothing," "goofing off," as play. It can be play without organizing it, but it can be organized; requiring as much energy as work and as demanding in skill. Whatever the nature of play, as Boomers we should have it and enjoy the kind we have. A number of activities are categorized under play—travel, social life, entertainment, hobbies, and sports. Play in the sense of activity which is contrived on the spur of the moment is also valuable. All serve to be refreshing. Recreation refers to any activity that is both creative and re-creative, giving emotional satisfaction to the person involved. Of the categories of play listed above, travel is one of the most desired by the Boomer. Many have never been able to play or travel as they wished because of the obligations of the work and home life, which interfered. Now since our children are older we have this opportunity. We can arrange more time for vacation, therefore travel. We know also that the slower you travel the more you can see. Travel represents a field of civilized human activity in which maturity has real and tangible advantages over youth. It provides a sense of leisure that comes with maturity, leisure to travel slowly and to savor the mood, the flavor, and the atmosphere of the places you visit as you go.

Social life is another promising aspect of play. For many, this is the only outlet which allows persons to relax, to let off steam and enjoy other people. Most people would rather socialize than nearly anything else. The number of clubs, ladies aid societies, social organizations attest to this. The only drawback here is the fact that we often under exercise and overeat on these occasions. Nothing, in fact, is better than eating and drinking when we are in our middle years—we have learned to like many things, varieties we could not stomach in our earlier years—now we have this spice of life, we become gourmets. Card games for some, dancing for others, cocktail parties, camping and traveling together or just visiting friends or relatives satisfies others. Social life can be arranged with little effort and hardly any cost. For many of you who have never had a party at your home or apartment, you ought to try it. It will cost something, to be sure, but it's worth it. You can do it as a single or a married person, with little or no formality—it's a gesture of generosity and reveals you a person of sociability.

Entertainment for leisure and enjoyment is frequently invigorating—the theater, the movie, television, athletic events, concerts, art exhibits can all be great. I have found that a steady diet of television viewing gets stale in a hurry, even though I watch often while I read, sports, news, movies, special events, etc. I like a variety of programs found on the Public Broadcasting Television Stations—commentaries, debates, concerts, educational and travel presentations. The television programs provide considerable entertainment and relaxation; it even has some other attributes—my daughter, when she was very young, a few years ago told me the television was a comforter. For many it serves as complete relaxation—sleep—as the controlled noise is like rain on a tin roof. We should offset viewing the television with in-person attendance at concerts, football and basketball games, and the festivals our towns and cities organized around themes—October Fest, Harbor Fests, Smoky Mountain Blue Grass Sing, Gasparilla Week, Mardi Gras, Centennials, etc. Some of them leave you gagging perhaps, but we should support them and argue for their improvement. Participation is the thing, not just passive listening or viewing. Increasingly we have paid entertainment and this provides us opportunity many times to be titillated when otherwise we could not be. We should not, however, depend upon this entirely, forgetting what we can do to enliven our lives and others with our own locally arranged fun.

Hobbies can be the most fun and joy many people can have. It can be exclusively ours beyond public inspection. True it takes us from people, but for those who work constantly with people, this provides a good counteracting activity. It tends to slow the stimuli we constantly receive and allows a slower ingestion of it. Hobbies range from sewing, modeling, to reading. Hobbies can be an excellent avocation—many begun for fun become the fun way to make a living. More importantly hobbies provide a release of emotion from in us, they allow the aesthetic to be explored and experienced. Age is no drawback for those interested in painting, music, stamp collecting, embroidery, craft work and the like. A hobby is something we can become engrossed in, allowing us to shut out the mundane things giving us something to look forward to hope and delight, whether it's gardening or fixing old furniture or toys. If you don't have a hobby, you need one!

Athletic and sports activity is a marvelous source of play for many. I like it—that is, swimming, tennis (played since 8 years of age), running, pick-up games, formerly touch football and softball. You don't have to be twenty years old to enjoy and play these games. What I like about sports and exercising games is that the benefit is great for keeping your weight down, the sugar and cholesterol in check, and there are also social accruals. The body's muscle tone is much better when exercise is regular, allowing greater enjoyment for anything else you wish to do. The chance to work off tensions, reconstruct your feeling by reducing the charge up animus of the viscera, and finally to have a comfortable relaxed tingling sensation after you have exercised. Hopefully we can make our exercise play and fun. I try this but don't always succeed. Some days I can't swim, play tennis or dance, so I have to jog—it's tough on hard earth and impossible on the street for it jolts my legs and joints after a couple of sessions. Nevertheless I get with it—it's better than stationary running or floor exercises, for me anyway. It's work, sometimes, and not play like at the beach for when you run there you can enjoy the scenery! Find some exercise that is fun—bicycle rides, take walks, hikes, but don't overlook the possibility of play even here.

LOVE

The songster said, "love makes the world go round." This is inexorably true! It gives meaning to our work, it enables play to be enjoyable, it ennobles our compassion for others and humane causes. Love is something we learn beginning in childhood; we are loved and in turn we love others besides mother and father, our first teacher, perhaps our first playmate. We come to understand that occasionally we lose people we love—through moving, through death and just because it can't always be permanent. The fact is when we get to be adults we sometimes wonder about whether there is any permanence or not. That we need to love and be loved we usually do not doubt. The truth is that no two people reach adulthood with the same capacity to give and receive love. If we have been loved in our early years, we usually feel secure with giving love to others. Our success in love, marriage, parenthood and to an extent in our work, our job or professional, depend on understanding these kinds of variations between people. Freud suggested that our earlier loves influence the way we love presently. The boy who suffers an unrequited love affair will bring to the next love a certain distrust or caution. The child who is the product of a family where all their affectionate energy is utilized to sooth bruised egos may, upon reaching adulthood, have little love to give or demands too much for himself. The quality of early love—enjoyed or suffered—affects later love. Eric Fromme, the psychologist, says we usually think of love as attachment to someone. Broadening this definition we suggest that love is any kind of attachment to a person, an idea, a place, an object, activity or even to oneself. It embraces the stories of each one that Sternberg, the love theorist, suggests brings to bear on our love to another. This provides a more profitable way, I believe, of looking at love. It suggests that the way we relate ourselves each day to people, places and events is an integral part of our life. Our capacity to love is gauged and is affected by our relationships, not alone by the romantic one we set apart as sufficient to call love. Love is a concept that applies to many things, friendship, patriotism, kinship, romance, brotherhood, parental and aesthetic appreciation. Many experts say that love is the main characteristic of normalcy and health—most agree that the ability to love is intimately tied to maturity. The "good life" requires maturity. Abraham Maslow, Psychiatrist, suggests maturity means the following:

- Comfortable relations with reality.
- Acceptance of self, others, nature and spontaneity.
- Problem centering—detachment, has need for privacy, friendship and attachments to family which are not of the possessive variety.

- Independence of culture and environment—continued freshness of appreciation and limitless horizons.
- Social feeling—deep by selective social relationships; democratic character structure (respect for humans as humans), ethical certainty, unhostile sense of humor and creativeness.

This is a large order, I'm afraid. There are not too many of us who fulfill all the requirements for being mature. Certainly the "good life" requires that we measure up or approach this ideal. Hugh Downs, a television host, in addressing the "Congress on the Quality of Life" a few years back said that "if we look closely at the characteristics of maturity (as in the above list), they fit into two broad categories: work and love."

What he is saying is that our work should not be thought of as drudgery, that we should find pleasure in it, be committed to it. Work is fundamental and doing nothing but lying under the breadfruit tree absorbing nourishment from what drops into your mouth is not happiness. Maybe Mr. Downs has had the kind of stimulation, adulation and constant ego stroking which allows work to be play that we love and to which we are committed. Sometimes the last thing I need is to have an appointment with one more student about a thesis (the culminating aspect of their degree work). Their egos are intimately tied to completing their research, their goal and development. My work in suggesting, correcting, guiding, encouraging is frequently fraught with difficulty and sensitivity, it is accompanied with energy debilitation and ennui. This has to be balanced by recreation and leisure. Rituals are also important.

The ritual nature of play, religion or work enables most of us to function regularly and gives a feeling of being a part of the wider world. Our aspirations are listed in the solemn routine of church going, alms giving and confession of sins. The routine, the ritual makes us feel comfortable and safe, it relieves anxiety. I believe that ritual in the psychological sense is fundamental to living securely and well. The ritual has its place for it reduces fear, desensitized our irritabilities through habituation and serves to organize a pattern to our lives. The ritual of reflection, our fantasies and daydreams release tensions unrealizable in motor activity and life's events; it also conjures up the good from the past through memories and prospect for the future through our imagination. In worship the bowed head, the prayer book, the communion cup, the litany, all serve to impart a stimulus for the promise of a better and good life.

Love is respect not just consideration for others but for ourselves, it is not self-denial per se. In a little volume I discovered several years ago—"How to Be Your Own Best Friend" by two psychoanalysts, Newman and Berkowitz, the authors contend that adults are an admixture of the child and the mature person. Some selfishness remains with us, and within limits should, for as the authors of the above they suggest to me, doing what makes you feel good yourself is the opposite of self-indulgence. The Bible says, "Love they neighbor as thyself," not better than thyself! Self-denial in and of itself is not love; it may be duty or habit, but not love. Self-denial is one of the worst kinds of self-indulgence. It is the feeding of the part of you that feels worthless. This doesn't mean you can't decide to give up things or sacrifice for children or others, but that is a choice you make—it is done out of self-regard not self-hatred. It is existential. Charity begins at home, as Polonius suggested in Hamlet, a line quoted before but which I think indicates the sort of balance that is needed, when he said to his son, "to thine own self be true, and it must follow as the night the day, thou canst not then be false to any man." Self-love and egocentricity are not the same things nor are they mutually exclusive. Learning to savor your own success is important.

A CAUSE -or- A COMMITMENT

We can have causes or be committed to something or someone, but it may be mostly self-love—we support someone, some charity, some church, some organization, some foundation for it is tied closely to our egos or allows us to shine in some reflected glory. These are not causes but ego trips. A worthy cause is one where we are required to give of ourselves through sacrifice, through direct energy application, the commitment of time and reflection to a project. I know that much good comes from the guilt with which we find ourselves strapped. Perhaps Freud was right when he suggested that progress in civilization and humanism (founding of hospitals, orphanages, etc.) came from the sickening feeling of sin brought about by religion. Religion which sensitizes our conscience. We need not make light of the matter that is sin, however it produces good results. But we must recognize that the "good life" comes from sorting out our motives; what we join as a cause should take us out of ourselves. Institutionalized giving and busy work should take us a step beyond the superficial do-gooding—"it makes us feel good if I've given my fair share." We should have a cause, which we want to have for ourselves depending upon a mature choice and our existential concern.

Causes grow out of our recognition of need—to be involved in helping others—of course to help ourselves. A good cause is one that demands our best—our best intelligence, our best ethics and our best ability in making a contribution. This is not unlike our jobs and work life, which should be characterized by the same devotion. Certainly our contribution can be quiet and unassuming. In fact I am struck by the numbers of persons working very hard for charities, etc., yet not wishing or allowing any publicity. It is not all due to fear of discovery and attempts to forego multiple requests for help for many of these have little money. We are essentially only what we give—our time, resources, our ideas, and hopes. Charity is a good, mature defense mechanism used by some, you do not need a million to be a volunteer, a contributor, a giver at least only time and energy. The anxiety ridden Boomer striving but never making it to a part of success often finds charity as an antidote and humor as a companion when surveying the valuable in their life.

Causes (what is worth most?) should involve us in the reflection of our life—"the unexamined life is not worth living." In the in-between years we have matured enough, seen enough of life—experienced its tragedies and the thrill of victory—to seek that part of us that connects us with the greater universe of purpose and peace. Many find their ultimate feeling of purpose to be rooted in the religious and the organized church. They worship paying tribute to the immutable, acknowledging man's and God's place in the scheme of things. Through faith they bind themselves to the cause of God or its idea—give to educational institutions, missionary work, homes for children and the elderly. As a consequence, communities, large and small, are better places to live because of them. Worship relates to wonderment, not of people but ideas about eternity and the essential nature of life. For most of us who "live lives of quiet desperation" as Thoreau wrote, the reverie, the philosophical is a boon! It is the renewal of curiosity seen in the children who ask "What makes it go?" It is a revival of that lost art, curiosity which makes us ask, what makes it go? Meditation helps bring order to our frantic lives.

Causes are not just religious or for charitable purposes. Causes also relate to organizations seeking to insure better life for others. The drive to create new parks and to protect lands is a worthy cause, to get passage of legislative programs, increased consideration for the elderly is another, as is also the caring for kin who are incapacitated—crippled, have chronic and/or terminal illness. These causes can be short termed so we may be involved in many such as these. We all need to be committed to something bigger than ourselves.

The final cause that we all must concern ourselves with is morality, mainly our own. Whether this is related to the morality of the church or to some other code of ethics, morality serves as the cement of our lives. We are counterfeit if we are not honest—it's hard to be for we have so many roles to play and masters to serve. A self-analysis sorting out the truth of our lives and the nature of ourselves is in order. The man who owes no allegiance to anyone or thing or has no faith or hope for improvement has forfeited the prospect of the good life—he has nothing left for which to live.

In our day of moral relativism, I suppose we would change the fact of right and wrong if we could. We certainly seem to act on this premise. For we know all too well that right and wrong varies in different cultures and times, situational ethics provides a rationalization, but nothing has validated the slow-learned wisdom that mankind has accumulated from ancient times. To kill, to steal, to lie, or to covet another person's possessions still leads to varying degrees of misery. As we must learn to eat the right things to sustain our physical health, we must learn to do the right thing to sustain moral health, for in the Twenty-First Century we have found no way to repeal the Ten Commandments. Materialism has affected our civilization's ability to enjoy life. A material object which should be cherished at age 16 because it has been earned by odd jobs on

Saturdays is nowadays a broken castoff when a child is half that age.

The good life of the mature years comes from arriving there with a healthy body (or with limited disabilities) respect for others, recognition that work is good, making leisure time and play desirable, and that the love that binds comes from commitment to some cause and to others. The "good life" for the in-between years is a compound of work, play, love and worship. Simple, cornball, illusory you say, certainly for Americans who regard frustration as ranking higher than cholera on the scale of human afflictions! There is more to life than work you say! You should work to live and not live to work. The Western World is racked by the insatiable demand for less work, more pay. Work is seen as something that wears you down, that produces stress, and stress is known to take a heavy toll. Dr. Hans Selye, expert on stress, says "it is true that biologic stress is involved in many common diseases such as ulcers, high blood pressure, etc. But does this mean that we should avoid stress whenever possible?" Certainly not. Stress is the spice of life!! It is associated with all types of activity and we could avoid it by never doing anything. No one would enjoy a life of "no runs, no hits, no errors"! To function normally, man needs work as he needs air, food, sleep, social contacts and sex. Our aim should be not to avoid work but to find the kind that suits us best. Work wears you out mainly through the frustration of failure. Each period of stress, especially if it results from unsuccessful struggles leaves scars.

As Americans we need to pull together and support each other and create a bond of united effort against those seeking to do us harm. Successful activity, no matter how intense, leaves virtually no scars. Instead, it provides you with the exhilarating feeling of youthful strength, even at very advanced age. Short hours are a boon only for those underprivileged who are not good at anything, have no particular taste for anything, and no hunger for achievement. These are the true paupers of mankind! George Bernard Shaw suggested that the great elixir of life is to be thoroughly worn out before being discarded—"a force of nature, instead of a feverish, selfish, clod of ailments and grievances."

As important as work is, play—leisure and avocational pursuits are equally crucial to enjoyment in life. It is the antidote for emotional and routine aspects of life. Americans feel guilty about having nothing to do, so those who can just "do nothing" should develop a hobby, learn new sports or games. Nothing renews life as well as just good play. The need to slow down and change the rhythm of life is a constant one. With work and play there must be love and commitment to a cause. It suffuses all of life, for without love, life is hollow. We must give and receive it. When we come to our middle years with health and strong values, then work, play and love can make the good life. Eric Fromme proclaimed that "happiness is proof of partial or total success in the art of living." With some luck and careful planning, you can enjoy the good life! Every Boomer should try. Good luck!